Advance Praise for
JIHADIST PSYCHOPATH

"Hard as it is to believe, many in the West simply will not take the time and trouble to understand the threat posed by radical Islamicist terrorism. James Burnham once wrote of a similar problem with international Communism in his masterful *Suicide of the West*. Now, Jamie Glazov has written this century's counterpart to Burnham's classic work and will doubtless upset those determined not to analyze for themselves the nature of the underlying phenomenon."

—JOHN BOLTON, President Donald Trump's National Security Adviser

"I have long argued that the usual likening of evil to darkness may not be nearly as accurate as likening it to bright light. The reason? People can look into the dark, but they cannot look into very bright light. The natural instinct is to look away. The denial of evil is therefore the most dangerous of all the denials in which human beings engage. We saw it during Communism, the most genocidal ideology in history, and we are seeing it today with violent Muslims. What Jamie Glazov does is explain this phenomenon, thereby making Jihadist Psychopath *one of the most important books of the present time.*"

—DENNIS PRAGER, nationally syndicated radio talk show host
and *NY Times* bestselling author

"Jamie Glazov's Jihadist Psychopath *is one of those truly rare books that is so brilliant and deeply original in its holistic analysis of the emergence of the modern jihadist that it will emerge as one of those books that will change your life forever. This work is steeped in the richness of history, psychology, military conflict, and religion—and exposes the pathological Stockholm syndrome that the West has developed in the hands of our enemy.* Jihadist Psychopath *is destined for permanent greatness for all classes and sectors of society, from the masses of readers of all books to the highest levels of academia to law enforcement to your own family. It will captivate and mesmerize any reader. Failure to read it is not an option.*"

—STEVEN EMERSON, executive director of the Investigative Project on Terrorism and author of American Jihad: The Terrorists Living Among Us

"Dr. Jamie Glazov is one of the most courageous and perceptive journalists of the free world. In this book, he explains why so many of our leaders in academia, media, and politics behave like ostriches when confronted with the dangerous threat of Islamic jihadism. His book not only analyzes Islam and how it inspires jihadist psychopaths, but it also describes the equally pathological unwillingness of our elites to deal with the danger. Dr. Glazov deserves the highest praise. He not only helps us to see the threat more clearly, but he also encourages all the defenders of freedom and dignity to persevere against the biggest threat humanity is facing today. I hope that Jihadist Pyschopath finds as many readers as possible."

—GEERT WILDERS, MP, leader of the Party for Freedom (PVV)
in the Netherlands

"The peculiar dynamic of our times, of Islamic jihadis killing people followed by Western authorities defending Islam and increasing measures to grant more concessions to Muslim groups cannot be fully explained by any counterterror strategy or geopolitical consideration. In this enlightening and groundbreaking book, Jamie Glazov reaches into the realms of psychopathology to clarify this odd phenomenon and succeeds in shedding light on it where numerous conventional thinkers have failed. This thought-provoking book should be on the desk or nightstand of everyone who wants to change the prevailing dynamic and counter the global jihad effectively."

—ROBERT SPENCER, bestselling author of The Complete Infidel's Guide
to the Koran and Confessions of an Islamophobe

"A fascinating and eye-opening political thriller. Glazov's ferocious takedown of the Jihadist Psychopath and his leftist minions reveals, in frightening detail, the menacing monstrosity we are up against. This book is an indispensable masterpiece of the utmost importance in our perilous times."

—LIEUTENANT GENERAL THOMAS MCINERNEY, USAF (Ret.)

"Most people are terrified of the elephant in the room, but Jamie Glazov courageously charges in after the beast. With his latest book, the author of United in Hate once again explores and explains the psychology and philosophy behind the current events of our struggle with Islamic terror. Jihadist Psychopath is an invaluable lens for understanding not only the enemy, but his appeasers on our own side."

—DANIEL GREENFIELD, Shillman Journalism Fellow,
author of The Great Betrayal

"A crushing blow to a deadly psychopathic mass cult. In Jihadist Psychopath, Jamie Glazov packs a masterful right hook to a modern embodiment of the Black Death. This absolute must-read is the result of solid politological research and highly professional journalism. Its most important and unprecedented contribution: exposing the deep and chilling link between Islam, leftist ideology, and crowd psychopathology, all in one vial. A tour de force."

—IGOR MEL'ČUK, Scientist, ex-Soviet ex-dissident,
Professor Emeritus of Linguistics at the University of Montreal,
and member of the Royal Society of Canada

"In Jihadist Psychopath, Jamie Glazov unveils a very real and menacing psychological phenomenon, a task to which he brings deep wisdom and broad learning. While drawing extensively on other writers' insights into such topics as white guilt, self-delusion, transference, Stockholm syndrome, con artists and their dupes, and (especially) the psychopathic mind, he has produced a remarkably original work—a book that makes an illuminating and highly valuable contribution to the contemporary literature of Islam and the West."

—BRUCE BAWER, author of *While Europe Slept and Surrender*

"Dr. Jamie Glazov's Jihadist Psychopath unveils the self-destructive relationship we blindly submit to with our Islamic enemies in the hope that it will stop their advances. As this book masterfully elucidates, such submission only further cements our ultimate downfall. Only by understanding the dynamics (the techniques of our enemy and our psychological tendencies in response) so skillfully described in this work can we find a pathway to reverse course. This is a brilliant must-read—as one will be unable to blind him or herself to the reality of this relationship ever again. Bravo Jamie Glazov!"

—BILL SIEGEL, author of *The Control Factor: Our Struggle to See the True Threat*

"According to the famous military strategist Sun Tzu, if you know the enemy and you know yourself, you will not be imperiled in hundreds of battles. Read Jamie Glazov's illuminating, well-documented Jihadist Psychopath and you'll learn how our beloved country arrived at this low point in its history, and how we can make it the light of the world again."

—LIEUTENANT GENERAL ION MIHAI PACEPA,
the highest-ranking official to have defected from the Soviet bloc

"*Jamie Glazov's* Jihadist Psychopath *profoundly captures the essence of the seductive but deadly nature of the Jihadist Character. With fascinating and original insight, this classic exposes how the pathological nature of the Jihadist's mind, molded by his Allah, has given him no restrictions over his relentless pursuit to control others rather than control oneself. A remarkable achievement.*"

—NONIE DARWISH, author of *Wholly Different:*
Why I Chose Biblical Values Over Islamic Values

"*Jamie Glazov's moral and intellectual incisiveness vis-à-vis the threats posed by totalitarian ideologies and by the invariably accommodating responses of many of their would-be victims in the West was forged early in life in the crucible of his family's confrontations with Soviet Communism. He brings that incisiveness to bear in this important, unflinching examination of today's onslaught against the West by Islamist forces. He addresses the psychological components of the attack and the psychopathology of the attackers, as well as the political and psychological dynamics behind the unilateral disarming of so many in the West, the acquiescence to and accommodation of the Islamist assault. Only by absorbing the messages of the book can the West hope to mount, finally, an effective response to the threats now confronting it.*"

—KENNETH LEVIN, psychiatrist, historian, and author of
The Oslo Syndrome: Delusions of a People under Siege

"*If you are a thinking person who values facts and desires a better understanding of terrorism, then this is the book for you. Refreshing new insights clearly laid out with exhaustive investigation, unambiguous evidence, and rational conclusions. All of this wrapped up in a book that is hard to put down and just plain enjoyable to read.*"

—BRAD JOHNSON, retired CIA operations officer and
president of Americans for Intelligence Reform

"*This fascinating book needs to be applauded mightily. Jamie Glazov reveals how the Islamic supremacists who seek to conquer our society employ the methodology of the psychopath. They play the pity card, they use charm and deceit, and once they have their victim in their grips, they move in for the kill. Their leftist allies, meanwhile, utilize Jihad Denial and moral equivalency to help the rat-infested plague ship to draw near. Read* Jihadist Psychopath *to learn how to identify the banners of this dire threat—and arise to join the fight for our civilization."*

—KENNETH R. TIMMERMAN, author of *Shadow Warriors: The Untold Story of Traitors, Saboteurs, and the Party of Surrender*

*"*Jihadist Psychopath *casts a critical eye on Islamic radicals' beguiling dance of death, which is luring so many victims into willing submission. This timely book shines a light on the mass psychology of those coming under the sway of jihadist intimidation. Moses-like, Dr. Glazov invites individuals, communities, and nations to renounce beguiling lies, which can only lead to death, and instead to 'choose life': 'This day I call the heavens and the earth as witnesses against you that I have set before you life and death, blessings and curses. Now choose life...' (Deuteronomy 30:19)."*

—MARK DURIE, author of *The Third Choice: Islam, Dhimmitude and Freedom*

"Phenomenal. Jamie Glazov provides keen insight into the jihadi mindset with Jihadist Psychopath. *Much of the global Islamic movement's strategy for jihad hinges on the ignorance of the West regarding their doctrine and modus operandi.* Jihadist Psychopath *is the antidote for that ignorance the Islamic movement so desperately needs for victory. To say that this is recommended reading would be an understatement;* Jihadist Psychopath *is crucial reading if freedom is to survive."*

—CHRIS GAUBATZ, coauthor of *Muslim Mafia: Inside the Secret Underworld That's Conspiring to Islamize America*

"Jamie Glazov's Jihadist Psychopath *should be required reading for every American and Westerner interested in saving our civilization. This book gives a dire warning about what is coming and contains monumental revelations that will shock and disturb you.* Jihadist Psychopath *should be studied carefully by all law-enforcement and government officials of the West—as well as by everyone who values freedom."*

—BRIGITTE GABRIEL, renowned terrorism expert, *New York Times* bestselling author, and founder of Actforamerica.org

JIHADIST PSYCHOPATH

HOW HE IS CHARMING, SEDUCING, AND DEVOURING US

JAMIE GLAZOV

Post Hill
PRESS

A POST HILL PRESS BOOK

Jihadist Psychopath:
How He Is Charming, Seducing, and Devouring Us
© 2018 by Jamie Glazov
All Rights Reserved

ISBN: 978-1-64293-007-8
ISBN (eBook): 978-1-64293-008-5

Cover design by Cody Corcoran

Post Hill Press
New York • Nashville
posthillpress.com

Published in the United States of America

To Papochka

TABLE OF CONTENTS

FOREWORD

This is a fascinating and important book, in which Jamie Glazov explains how *jihadists*—radical Muslims totally dedicated to the destruction of Western civilization and its replacement with their reading of Islamic (Shariah) law—have managed to convince their intended victims that the religious/political war is the fault of the West, and that our best strategy is surrender. Jamie Glazov explains this tour de force by examining the ways in which radical Muslims' tactics resemble those of psychopaths. And along the way, he reminds us that, just as "everyday" psychopaths convince their targets that their actual relationship is a fantasy, while the fantasy is the real relationship, so the jihadists have managed to convince the Western world that they, the jihadists, are the innocent victims of an "Islamophobic" campaign against all Muslims.

As Daniel Patrick Moynihan observed decades ago, if we cannot distinguish our friends from our enemies, we end by adopting our enemies' view of the world. We have done this with the radical Muslims, at all levels of our societies. Our schools and universities have made it taboo to criticize Islam, Hollywood avoids filming true accounts of Muslim history, political leaders, from President Obama on down, credit Islam for epic cultural achievements that never took place. You will find all this well documented, along with the amazing story of how the United States Government hired radical Muslims to work at the State Department, the CIA and DIA, the national security council and within the ranks of

White House staff. Those who found these practices alarming were either fired or silenced.

This is no mean accomplishment. Anyone who looks at the differences between the Islamic world and the West will easily see that the Muslim world is a failure, while the West abounds in significant achievements. Whether we measure success by wealth creation or the quantity of Nobel Prizes, the Islamic countries are swamped by the Western world. Nor do the Muslims show any real signs of trying to catch up. A couple of years ago, more books were translated into Spanish in a single year than into Arabic in a thousand years. And a recent study by the Atlantic Council found

> The Arab world is now publishing only between 15,000 and 18,000 books annually, as many as Penguin Random House produces on its own. Egypt was once the largest producer of books with an output between 7,000 and 9,000 per year. Although its output was previously on the rise, it dropped by a whopping 70 percent after the 2011 revolution, and as of 2016 was only 'showing signs of recovery'. Greece translates five times as many books into Greek as all 22 Arab nations combined.

The ruling Muslim elites are well aware of their backwardness, and that is why their own sons are sent to Western universities. Most of them return to their native countries. Yet the jihadist psychopaths and their allies nonetheless insist that Western "racism" is responsible for the miserable condition of most of the world's Muslims. This was one of the mainstays of left-wing doctrine for a long time; they invariably blamed the backwardness of the Third World on Western imperialism. That helps explain the otherwise baffling unity between leftists and radical Muslims, an anti-Western alliance between a fanatically religious movement and lifelong "materialists" who have typically treated people of faith with utter contempt. Both have insisted that Western Imperialist racists are the primary sinners against innocent Muslims, totally ignoring the actual content of radical Islamic doctrine. We, like all victims of skilled psychotics, have fallen for it.

This seduction of their targeted enemies is one of the great successes of radical Islamists, whether it goes under the name of "Stockholm syndrome" or the more recent label, the "Oslo Syndrome." Whatever we call it, it's a political error that puts us at great risk. During the Clinton presidency, just before the Rabin-Arafat handshake on the White House lawn, his aides asked the great Middle East scholar Bernard Lewis for a Qur'anic quotation lauding peace and peacemakers. He gave them one. "No," they said to Lewis, "we've already used that one. We need another one." Lewis sadly replied that, so far as he knew, that was the only one.

The claim that Islam is the "religion of peace" isn't supported by Muslim holy writ. So on what grounds have Westerners accepted the false charge that they are the cause of conflict? It's a psychological mystery that is carefully explored and analyzed in this excellent scholarly work, abundantly documented, well argued, and, I believe, effectively treated. I find it both convincing and elegant.

What, then, are we to do? This book points the way. The first step is to demolish the mythological claims about radical Islam. Glazov knows, and stresses, that the war against the West is not a feature of Islam as such, but only a part of it. That part must be exposed as nonsense, and its wicked intentions must be made clear. As this is done, we must be sure that our policy makers have not been seduced by the jihadi psychopaths. We don't want foot soldiers of the Muslim Brotherhood advising our top leaders, as they have since the Clinton years.

Second, the United States needs to support non-radical Muslim leaders in the Islamic world. Leaders of countries like Egypt and Saudi Arabia are challenging the radicals, and are worthy of our support, as are Muslim officials in Indonesia (the world's biggest Islamic country), as well as Tunisia and Jordan. We need to embrace their struggle against the radicals in their own countries, as we fight the same struggle in the United States.

Finally, we need to decisively challenge the monotonous psychotic refrain that Islam is all about peace, when in fact many Muslims are at war with us. We have to win that war, and we can, if and only if we define it accurately and expose its strategy.

—MICHAEL LEDEEN, Freedom Scholar at the Foundation for Defense of Democracies and co-author of *Field of Fight: How to Win the War Against Radical Islam.*

WARNING

Before we begin our journey, it is necessary to issue a warning: As will be made transparently clear in the pages that follow, the thesis of this work is *not* that all Muslims are psychopaths. Rather, this book's focus is on *the Jihadist Psychopath*, on those Muslims who follow him and the violent commands of Islam, and on those inside our own camp who are aiding and abetting the enemy.

This book operates out of a love of *all people*, which includes Muslim people; its warning is about a pernicious *ideology* and the pathological psychology that inevitably results in a surrender to it.

Despite this warning, and no matter how many times this work will make plainly evident that its thesis is *not* about *all* Muslims, the Jihadist Psychopath and his minions will nevertheless reflexively smear this book with precisely this pernicious and false accusation.

This type of slander is entirely predictable, of course, since, as this work will reveal, it is a significant weapon in the Jihadist Psychopath's arsenal, which plays a major role in destroying us—and in bringing about our surrender.

PREFACE

*"What I like better than anything else is when people feel sorry
for me. The thing I really want more than anything out of life is
people's pity."*

These were the earnest words spoken by a very typical psychopath in an interview with Martha Stout, the author of one of
the most authoritative books on the psychology of psychopaths.[1]

The psychopath speaking with Stout was candidly relating
one of the core tricks of his malicious trade: playing the pity card
to get people to give him what he wants, which, primarily, means
getting them to give him complete power over their lives. Through
his words, this psychopath revealed that he shrewdly understood
that when you get good people to pity you, and to feel responsible
for your plight, they become defenseless—especially against those
who have no conscience. And this is where the psychopath's masterful reign of terror begins.

The psychopath is an expert at detecting his potential victims.
In his view, a big shining light hovers over their heads; he knows
exactly who they are. And once he finds his target, he zeroes in
with merciless, laser-like precision. His assault almost always
begins with the *charm offensive*, by which the psychopath seduces
and deceives his prey—a prey that all too often is desperate to be
seduced and deceived. And then, within the blink of an eye, the
prey is under the psychopath's hypnotic spell. As the roots of this

spell deepen and grow, it becomes increasingly difficult for the prey to break free.

Once the psychopath has a tight grip on his victim, he knows exactly how and when to deploy the numerous potent and ruthless weapons in his arsenal. These weapons include his seemingly heartfelt and passionate testimonials of how he and his victim "are a lot alike," how they both really want the same things, and how, most importantly, *he is operating in the victim's own best interests*. The victim becomes convinced that the road the psychopath leads him down is good for him. The dark reality, of course, is that the road will end in the victim's enslavement and ultimate destruction.

Psychopaths have learned their trade exceptionally well from their chief mentor, because they possess his spiritual genes. His mark is firmly embedded in their DNA. He is the Serpent in the Garden of Eden, whose intentions for mankind are toxically malignant and saturated with malice and ferocious hate. But the Serpent deviously camouflages his true intentions with the pretense of good will and, most importantly, with his purported desire to bestow upon his prey perfect knowledge, perfect freedom, and the power of self-redemption.

It was through an alluring promise to Eve, in which the Serpent postured as though he were "looking out" for the woman's best interests, that the Serpent destroyed Eve and thereby cursed all of humanity. With this sinister tactic, the Serpent carved into man's heart a crevice through which he could torment and pollute man and increase the possibility of dragging him into his (the Serpent's) own pit of agony and hell.

The psychopath has his master to emulate. He is an expert in the con game of charming and seducing his prey. Once he succeeds in lodging his hooks into his target's body, he inflicts the key wound, convincing him that he (the victim) is the actual offender and guilty party, and that the psychopath is the actual victim.

To be sure, the psychopath deals the pity card with a keen sense of purpose: *he is the victim* and no matter what pain his prey is enduring, it *never* matters and is *never* relevant, because *the psychopath's suffering is always the issue at hand*, and it is always worse than everyone else's.

The hooks that entrap the victim are so deeply dug into him that an *unhooking* would result in numerous agonizing injuries and potential minefields. It is easier, therefore, in the short term for the victim to just leave the hooks in place. Yes, he could survive his own unlinking, and in so doing could free himself, but the inevitable agony of the break fills him with too much dread.

Thus, the prey finds himself in a state of imprisonment, of which he is often not even fully conscious. Desperately seeking an easier and more painless path, he rationalizes that the safest road lies in remaining locked in the chains that bind him—and that he simultaneously convinces himself are not there. In so doing, he deludes himself with myriad denials, which are generously fed him by the psychopath himself.

The psychopath utilizes numerous other crucial weapons to tighten his grasp. He makes sure, while posing as the real victim, that he *never* takes responsibility for any of his actions and, most importantly, that he *never* says he is sorry. He perpetually poses as the unappreciated martyr and displays unending moral indignation about where he was wronged—a charge that comes accompanied by his eternal (and groundless) accusations against his victim. The psychopath makes sure to justify this disposition by making references to the many details of his past—a past that is soaked in myths and fairy tales. *It is a fake past.* And it is with this icing on the cake that the psychopath ascribes to himself *a grand sense of entitlement.* It is *he*, and *he alone*, who is owed something.

The final blow comes when, at the moment that he is confident enough, the psychopath opens the curtains for the rest of the world to see, and he deviously shapes its view of the relationship between him and his prey. Make no mistake: psychopaths are diabolically consumed with, and are experts at, *shaping the perception of others*. They understand the propaganda war perfectly. Normal people, meanwhile, do not. And when encountering a psychopath, they are most often not even aware that a propaganda war is in play. As a result, average people are at a severe disadvantage when they get stuck in the psychopath's web. And without a tough resistance, they begin to crumble, since they typically *very much care about what others think of them*.

Terrified of the negative judgments of others, the victim of the psychopath is paralyzed at the thought of crossing any party line set by his master. He is filled with dread at the very notion of defending or freeing himself. The master is, after all, the righteous party in the relationship, and it is he who is owed respect and deference. It is a crime, therefore, to resist him. The victim would have to be *a very bad human being* to even think of putting up any resistance, let alone try to escape. Much of the world, meanwhile, brainwashed by the psychopath, watches in judgment—siding with him as he points an accusatory finger of moral indignation at his prey.

The misery of the victim's enslavement is amplified by the devastating fear he has of his captor. And this is no surprise, for the psychopath is a violent and dangerous individual who exists on, and succeeds through, domination, threat, and intimidation. While the victim is paralyzed by fear, he simultaneously denies his fear—and what causes it. Admitting the truth would destroy the entire narrative in which he is so desperately invested.

There is a crucial element in this narrative: the victim develops a deep hatred of, and disdain for, *the resistance*—those individuals who resist the psychopath and tell the truth about him. The resistance embarrasses the victim and exposes his sorry and pathetic state. The resisters threaten the victim's identity, his self-image, and the imaginary world in which he has built his delusions and false hopes. The victim dares not identify his abuser *by his real name*, nor admit it to himself, for this would reveal who the abuser really is and what he is up to, and would cast the victim into what he sees as a hopeless situation. The victim therefore ascribes a different character to his abuser and tries to whitewash the abuser's real motives; consequently, he *hates and slanders* those who try not only to expose the abuser and resist him, but also to liberate his slaves.

And now we turn to our terror war—and to the obvious replica of the psychopath-victim dynamic that is the emblem of our current surrender to a vicious totalitarian enemy. Those who are consciously attuned to Islamic supremacism's relentless onslaught against the West, and to the manner in which it is winning its battles, will detect something eerily familiar in the paradigm described above. This is because Islamic supremacism's gains in the terror war are a carbon copy of the manner in which the psychopath captures and defeats his prey. To be sure, in *every* element of the formula by which the psychopath subjugates his victims, we see a reflection of how Islamic supremacism is subjugating the West today. This should be no surprise, since *Islamic supremacism is psychopathic* and the West has now become its helpless prey. Indeed, we are being devoured by the Jihadist Psychopath.

Without a doubt, the way America and the West are today allowing themselves to be exploited and manipulated by Islamic supremacists and are deluding themselves on the road to their own destruction, is exactly the way the prey of the psychopath behaves. The manner in which America and the West are today denying who the enemy is, and the way their leaders, culture, and media are demonizing those individuals who dare to fight Islamic supremacism and to call it by its name, mirrors exactly the way that victims of the psychopath behave.

This book, like no other, unveils this catastrophe. It reveals, step by step, how a psychopath thinks and operates, and how his targeted prey attracts him and is complicit in its own capture and subjugation. In illuminating this dynamic, this work demonstrates how Islamic supremacism's current conquest of the West is transpiring in a manner that precisely mirrors the psychopath's conquest of his individual victims. And in so doing, this book shows how and why the West is itself engaging, with willful complicity, in its own surrender.

As we watch the West's voluntary suicide transpiring today before our eyes, the profound observations of author Alexander Maistrovoy come to mind. In his book, *Agony of Hercules or a Farewell to Democracy (Notes of a Stranger)*, Maistrovoy notes how this act of civilizational suicide will likely confound future historians:

> Probably, the phenomenon of the modern Western civilization will be a mystery to researchers in [the] future. In fact, the economically powerful, politically mature system, within only several decades (not centuries—as with the Roman Empire, but decades!), voluntarily, with some inexplicable enthusiasm rushed to a thin ice, sweeping away all obstacles in the way.... We don't know a single case where shoals of fish commit a mass suicide voluntarily, but there are many examples where highly intelligent animals, such as whales and dolphins, throw themselves on the shore and die in painful and vain sufferings.[2]

The objective of this book is to make our painful and vain sufferings much better understood. That sad and tragic tale—the tale of America's and the West's surrender to the Jihadist Psychopath— is laid bare in the following pages.

INTRODUCTION

At approximately 3:05 p.m. on Halloween afternoon, October 31, 2017, twenty-nine-year-old Sayfullo Saipov drove a rented truck onto a Manhattan bike path and slammed into nearly two dozen cyclists and pedestrians. He then crashed into a school bus and emerged from the vehicle wielding a paintball gun and a pellet gun. He screamed "Allahu Akbar" throughout the whole ordeal and succeeded in murdering eight people and wounding fifteen—until an NYPD officer shot and wounded him, dropping him to the ground.[1]

Saipov was a married Muslim father of three who had come to the United States from Uzbekistan seven years earlier on a "diversity visa lottery" program, a system that allows foreigners into the country, not through their merit, but through random games of chance.[2]

The evidence was overwhelmingly clear that this Uzbekistani immigrant was engaging in Islamic jihad during his massacre on that Halloween afternoon in Manhattan. Indeed, he was already known to law enforcement "for his direct ties to other terrorism suspects under investigation," and the FBI quickly tracked down a second Muslim in connection with his attack.[3] Saipov had also left a note behind in the truck, stating that the Islamic State "would endure forever" and that "There is no god but Allah, and Muhammad is his prophet."[4] His cell phones contained thousands of Islamic State–related images, including about ninety videos depicting Islamic State fighters killing prisoners by running them over with a tank, beheading them, and shooting them in the face.[5]

When he was recovering in the hospital, Saipov requested that the Islamic State's flag be displayed in his room. He waived his Miranda rights and gloated about what he had done, acknowledging that he had acted in response to the Islamic State's online calls to Muslims to attack non-Muslims. He also boasted that he chose to carry out his rampage on Halloween, so as to maximize the body count.[6]

Saipov was a resident of Paterson, New Jersey, an area known to the locals as "Paterstine" for its sizable Islamic community, where the PLO terror flag flies over city hall, and where Islamic terrorist sympathizers celebrated after their compatriots murdered thousands on 9/11.[7] Saipov's twenty-three-year-old wife, Nozima Odilova, wore a niqab, a Muslim garment that reveals only the eyes. The Muslim couple had two girls (ages six and four) and a six-month-old baby boy. A neighbor observed that "the girls didn't have friends. There were no parties."[8] Notwithstanding all of the empirical evidence pointing to the Islamic nature of Saipov's Halloween massacre, the establishment media, New York's leaders, and America's higher culture just couldn't seem to a find a motive in it all. Saipov's shouts of "Allahu Akbar" throughout his terror attack, for instance, were quickly explained away by Zainab Chaudry, a member of the Hamas-linked Council on American-Islamic Relations (CAIR), who informed the *New York Daily News* that the Arabic term simply meant "God is greatest" and that Muslims use that term in a variety of contexts, and not only while they are murdering infidels.

The *New York Times* was also most happy to assure Americans that Saipov's "Allahu Akbar" pronouncements had absolutely no connection to his crime. The paper tweeted that although the phrase had "somehow become inextricably intertwined with terrorism...its real meaning is far more innocent."[9] CNN's Jake Tapper jumped forward to explain all of that innocence, noting that "Allahu Akbar" meant that "God is great" and that it was "sometimes said under the most beautiful of circumstances."[10]

During these curious developments, the leaders and authorities in New York joined the peculiar chorus. The governor of New York, Andrew Cuomo (D), stepped forward to assure everyone that Saipov was just a "lone actor," that there was "no evidence to suggest a wider plot or wider scheme," and that there was, therefore, no "ongoing threat or any additional threat."[11] The mayor of New York City, Bill de Blasio, was of a similar mind, announcing that what had happened in Manhattan was *very* un-Islamic. "The last thing we should do," he pleaded with his constituents, "is start casting dispersions on whole races of people or whole religions or whole nations. That only makes the situation worse."[12]

New York Deputy Police Commissioner John Miller was also on the same page, announcing that what Saipov had perpetrated "isn't about Islam" and "isn't about the mosque he attends."[13] Even H. R. McMaster, President Donald Trump's then-national security adviser, got into the mix, affirming that Saipov should be classified as a "mass murderer," a statement that clearly implied that the jihadist was not motivated to carry out his crime by a religious conviction.[14]

In this bizarre atmosphere of denial, Muslims were depicted as the victims of it all. And the establishment media went the extra yard to drive that particular theme home. The *Press Herald* led the way, titling its main article on the terror attack: "In aftermath of bike path killings, mosques near NYC face hostility again."[15] The story featured Dr. Mohammad Qatanani, an imam at a mosque in Paterson, New Jersey, voicing his concern that, after Saipov's murder spree, Muslims in the area would now feel "blamed as a religion and as a people." The article also highlighted the views of a Muslim interviewee named Abu Mohammed, who blamed Saipov's massacre on the policies of the United States.[16]

The *New Yorker* made sure to help out with the whole narrative, running a piece that focused on how Muslims and Islam were the real victims of Saipov's act. The story featured Annie Thoms, an English teacher at Stuyvesant High School in Lower Manhattan, who was very worried about Islam being maligned and about the feelings of her Muslim students. "Especially after 9/11," she said in the article,

> every time I see that something is a terrorist incident, and someone has said "Allahu Akhbar," I feel a pit in my stomach, because terrorism is the evil opposite of what Islam is. So many of our kids here at Stuyvesant are Muslim, and they fear being tarred with this kind of thing.[7]

It was probably Isaac Stone Fish, a former *Newsweek* correspondent who was on sabbatical from the magazine *Foreign Policy*, who best encapsulated the establishment media's view of the Manhattan massacre. Seemingly unable to grasp what all the fuss was about, he tweeted, "The most Trumpian thing most people do is overreact to a small terrorist attack."[18]

Even the U.S. court system couldn't seem to find a speck of Islam in Saipov's Islamic act. When a federal grand jury returned a twenty-two-count indictment against the jihadist, it treated him as though he were a Mafia member, charging him with murder "in aid of racketeering"—a charge that federal prosecutors typically use in organized crime cases. The message rang out loud and clear: Saipov had nothing to do with a religion or with an ideological movement.[19]

Despite all of this denial about Saipov and his terrorist act, the truth nonetheless stared everyone in the face: Saipov was a devout Muslim and was clearly devoted to ISIS and to his prophet Muhammad. The fairy tale of "Allahu Akbar" that Zainab

Chaudry, the *New York Times*, and Jake Tapper tried to foist on Americans couldn't erase one undeniable fact: that the Arabic phrase is a declaration of Islamic superiority and supremacism. Those who understand Arabic are well aware that the phrase does not mean "God is great" but "Allah is greater"—because Allah is greater *than the other gods of other religions* and that is why Islam's followers, like Sayfullo Saipov, are commanded to subjugate and/or kill them.[20]

What Chaudry, the *New York Times*, and Tapper also failed to tell their audiences was that the actual origin of "Allahu Akbar" lies with the Prophet Muhammad himself, who shouted the phrase upon destroying the Jews of Khaybar in the year 628.[21] When jihadists shout those words, therefore, they are emulating their prophet and declaring Allah's superiority by killing non-Muslims.[22] This is why the last words heard on the flight recorder of United Airlines Flight 93, the domestic passenger flight that was hijacked and driven into the ground by four al-Qaeda terrorists on 9/11, were "Allahu Akbar."[23] It is also why Mohamed Atta, ringmaster of the 9/11 plot, advised his fellow hijackers to shout that phrase, since, as he explained, "this strikes fear in the hearts of the unbelievers."[24]

Thus, when the *New York Times* tweeted its confusion about why "Allahu Akbar" had somehow become "inextricably intertwined with terrorism," the paper revealed its breathtaking ignorance regarding the millions of Muslims who have screamed that phrase over the centuries in the process of murdering millions of unbelievers.[25]

When Tapper stated that "Allahu Akbar" is "sometimes said under the most beautiful of circumstances," he was partially right, but he failed to explain the context, which, as Cheryl K. Chumley of the *Washington Times* has accurately noted, is that "Heil Hitler" was also said in circumstances that many Nazis perceived as "beautiful."[26]

The statements of New York's leaders also left much to be desired. In terms of New York governor Cuomo's assurance that Saipov was just a "lone actor" and that there was no "wider plot," one couldn't help but wonder: upon what evidence had Cuomo based his assessment? How did his assurance square, exactly, with the fact that law enforcement knew of Saipov's *direct ties* to other terrorism suspects under investigation, and that the FBI had tracked down a second Muslim in connection with Saipov's attack? How was Cuomo's assurance consistent with all of Saipov's other ISIS connections and with his personal declarations? How did it fit with the fact that in June 2017, the Islamic State published a poster depicting an SUV driving over a heap of skulls and bearing the legend "Run Over Them Without Mercy"? How could Saipov have possibly been a "lone actor" if he was a foot soldier for ISIS, and ISIS had issued a directive to Muslims to engage in vehicular jihad?[27] And how could there have been no "wider plot" if Saipov's vehicular jihad mirrored many other terror attacks, from the vehicular jihadist attacks in Barcelona to France to the UK?[28]

No one asked Cuomo these questions directly, so he did not have to answer them. Nor was Mayor de Blasio taken to account on his warning against "casting dispersions" [sic] on whole religions. Neither was New York Deputy Police Commissioner John Miller called out personally on his contention that Saipov's attack wasn't about Islam or about Saipov's mosque. But de Blasio and Miller had left one very pertinent question unanswered: What if Saipov's religion and his mosque's teachings *actually had* inspired him to wage terror against unbelievers?

In terms of the court that treated Saipov as though he were in the Mafia, one matter remained extremely disturbing: Saipov was not, in fact, in the Mafia. He was a soldier of Islam and of the Islamic State. As leading scholar of Islam, Robert Spencer, noted on this issue:

The Islamic State is not a mafia family, and jihad mass murder is not racketeering. This is a war, and the New York City truck jihad massacre was one battle in that war. Yet authorities continue to prosecute these jihadis as if they were a series of criminals committing separate and discrete criminal acts that are unrelated to one another.[29]

In the end, one of the most troubling aspects about Saipov's Halloween massacre was that it could have easily been prevented. But it wasn't prevented precisely because of the attitudes exhibited by the Chaudrys, de Blasios, Tappers and all of their other ideological comrades. Indeed, evidence surfaced that the NYPD had actually suspected Saipov's mosque of terror ties over a decade *before* the massacre, and that it had kept the mosque under surveillance for a number of years. But all of that stopped because an individual by the name of Linda Sarsour, the notorious Palestinian-American political "activist" who was one of the organizers of the 2017 Women's March, considered the NYPD's surveillance of the mosque to be discriminatory. With the help of the ACLU and other pro-terror groups, she waged a campaign to stop this surveillance, and Mayor de Blasio complied, terminating the NYPD's capacity for investigating all mosques and Islamic radicalization.[30] This dire development resulted in eight dead in Manhattan.

What had inspired de Blasio to make his decision about the NYPD was, of course, very clear, just as it was very clear what Sarsour and the *New York Times* were expecting him to say about Saipov. And that is exactly why they so approvingly embraced his announcement. It was the message that has been sanctioned by our society's elites; the message that is now the only one allowed to be spoken or heard. And that message is that Islamic terrorism has absolutely nothing to do with Islam. What Saipov had done on that Halloween afternoon in Manhattan, therefore, also had nothing to do with the Religion of Peace—even if Saipov himself thought it did.

De Blasio's, Cuomo's, and Miller's message was just the latest in a long and consistent narrative of messages that had been emanating from American leadership, media, and popular culture long before Saipov plowed a truck into innocent civilians on a Manhattan bike path. Its hackneyed theme had been heard after every single Islamic terror attack on American soil, from Fort Hood in 2010 to the Boston Marathon Massacre in 2014, and from San Bernardino in 2015 to Orlando in 2016. And that theme was that no matter how proudly and unambiguously jihadists point to Islam to justify and explain the mayhem and violence that they perpetrate, their pronouncements are never to be taken seriously. Rather, it is *other factors*, the ones connected to racism, unemployment, and climate change, that, we are told, are actually the main causes of the terrorists' actions.

As we stand back and examine this picture, it becomes painfully evident that something very wrong is transpiring right before our eyes in the terror war. Some kind of "pressure" is in the air—a pressure that ensures that after every jihadist attack, we call the attack everything but what it actually is. We are to ascribe many different motives to the perpetrators, except the very motives that they themselves have candidly identified. Indeed, we have been given a template of mantras to repeat each time, with just a few blanks to be filled in for each new attack, so that the different set of names, times, and places fit accordingly.

Accompanying the "pressure in the air" are several articles of faith that we are expected to dutifully embrace. The *party line* is unmistakable: first, when jihad strikes, we have to accept that *the guilty party is us*. We are expected to believe that *it is America and the West that are responsible*. That's right: *the devil made them do it*. Second, and perhaps most importantly, we have to embrace the sacred rule that *it is Muslims who are the real victims*. Any deviation from this perspective is now considered tantamount to a hatred of all Muslims in general. In other words, *you are an awful and bad person* if you fail to embrace every single tenet that the "pressure in the air" instructs you to believe about terrorism.

What we have here is a situation in which any desire to protect the West from the terrorist enemy is now categorized as *a hatred of an entire group of people*. It is also labeled "racist"—even though jihad is not a race and its Muslim practitioners come in all shapes, colors, and ethnicities. And no matter how illogical and erroneous this line of thinking may be, it now prevails as the only permitted narrative in our cultural and official discourse.

Consequently, we have a disaster facing us. And that disaster, in a nutshell, is this: a totalitarian and expansionist ideology called Islamic supremacism is waging a deadly war on the West. It is a war that Islamic supremacists have openly proclaimed and shouted from the rooftops. They have made it abundantly clear as to why they are waging this war, why they hate us so much, and why they are so determined to destroy our way of life. But standing up to this ideology and protecting ourselves from those who heed its call is now, as noted above, considered hateful, racist, and, of course, "Islamophobic." And since most people's most dreaded fear in our leftist and politically correct culture is to be called a racist, our civilization's will and ability to defend itself has been severely disabled. What we have, in essence, is our surrender to Islamic supremacism.

The "pressure in the air" can take credit for this surrender. And it has done its job extremely well. This "pressure" has been created, of course, by a pernicious and treacherous entity: the *Unholy Alliance*, that sinister pact between Islamic supremacism and the Left that seeks to destroy the democratic-capitalist West and every liberty that comes with it. As empirical reality reveals, and as author David Horowitz has meticulously documented in his book *Unholy Alliance* and on his website DiscovertheNetworks.org, leftist and Islamic supremacist totalitarians are working feverishly together to destroy America and the West.[31]

It is transparently clear who our enemies are today, and there is no mystery about the agendas they are pursuing. But tragically, the Unholy Alliance controls our culture, which is why it has succeeded in creating the "pressure in the air" that is now so effectively sealing so many eyes and lips and, in turn, allowing the enemy to encroach with so much ease.

This book is dedicated to unveiling the causes and elements of this tragic catastrophe. It will reveal Islamic supremacism's assault on our society and the Left's complicity in that assault. In so doing, it will expose the Left's inner nature, its method of regulating our thoughts and language, and the treacherous manner in which it empowers our deadly foes. The work will also crystallize how Jihad Denial, which manifested itself so blatantly and disturbingly in the Saipov Halloween massacre, plays a key role in the Left's agenda— and in our own suicide.

Our story will be told in a completely original and unprecedented context, unambiguously laying bare the fact that Islamic supremacy is rooted in psychopathy. To make this case, we will document how a psychopath behaves and then demonstrate how Islamic supremacism's behavior is classically psychopathic. As a result, this work will make manifestly clear that our psychopathic enemy is doing what a psychopath does best: *charm, seduce, and devour his prey*—all while playing the role of the victim. We will be able to see that Islamic supremacism is subjugating the West in exactly the same way that psychopaths subjugate their victims. In turn, we will also see that the manner in which we are surrendering is exactly the manner in which victims surrender to psychopaths.

INTRODUCTION

And thus, the Jihadist Psychopath will be unveiled for the first time for all to see.

In demonstrating this thesis, this book will reveal the powerful temptation in human nature to accept a pernicious lie like Jihad Denial, showing how and why humans desperately cling to its subliminal and comforting assurances that a safe and ordered world is possible, if only we will turn a blind eye to the very forces that seek to annihilate us. In illuminating this human need to delude oneself in the face of a dire threat, this work will make clear what the psychopath's conquering of his prey is really all about.

The pages ahead will focus primarily on the battle taking place in America, which is reflective of what is happening in the rest of the world, especially in Western Europe, where the battle is now almost totally lost. There are, of course, still many brave people left in Europe who want to save their freedoms and are valiantly rising up and fighting back, but they face a colossal uphill battle.

This book maintains that the election of President Donald Trump in America has brought great hope that we may be able to prevail in our own struggle with the Jihadist Psychopath—a struggle that seemed irretrievably lost during the Obama era. Trump's victory revealed that there are still many Americans who want to preserve their country and who are ready to do what is necessary to halt Islamic supremacism in it tracks. Thankfully, the new president has shown many signs that he intends to take on the Jihadist Psychopath and his minions. And admirably, he has demonstrated a willingness to name the enemy and to take the fight to him.

The significant problem, of course, is that even with President Trump in office, the Unholy Alliance remains robust and retains its power on many levels, enjoying a vast army of leftists who have penetrated the U.S. government itself. The manner in which the State Department and the courts have frustrated Trump's attempt to impose a travel ban on individuals from terrorism-infested countries reveals the vast leftist resistance that remains against Trump.[32] Indeed, legions of Unholy Alliance devotees remain heavily entrenched, not only in all realms of U.S. government, but also within the Trump administration itself.[33] Trump has, of course, made extremely positive strides in replacing some of the worst of these devotees with strong individuals who seek to confront Islamic supremacism.[34]

To compound the resistance against Trump, the Left, as always, continues its suffocating monopoly over the media, academia, public schools, Hollywood, popular culture, and, consequently, the boundaries of permitted discourse. Progressive ideas are so deeply ingrained in our society that confronting them, let alone reversing their dominance, represents a Herculean challenge. The battle is on.

And so, this book sets out to tell the story of this battle. And it will do so through the scope of psychopathy and the psychology of the psychopath's victims. There is no more effective way to do so. The first chapter explains how our surrender was nurtured and institutionalized by the Obama administration. To fully appreciate the influence of the Jihadist Psychopath, we must first show how deeply Islamic supremacists entrenched themselves in our government with Obama's help. Our journey therefore has to begin with seeing this treachery for what it really is—and with witnessing how much power the Unholy Alliance has actually acquired, all the evil it has spun with that power, and all the dark things it still plans to do with it.

And so we embark on dissecting and crystallizing the threat of the Jihadist Psychopath and the process by which, with the willing aid of his leftist minions, he is charming, seducing, and devouring us. It is a harrowing tale that, this author prays, lovers of freedom will heed with gravity, taking every lesson and warning to heart.

For there is not much time.

PART 1

The Seduction

CHAPTER 1

THE CASE

On May 13, 2010, Attorney General Eric Holder had an incredulous and perplexed expression on his face as he sat before the House Judiciary Committee. He just couldn't understand what Representative Lamar Smith, the ranking Republican on the committee, was asking him, over and over again. Specifically, Smith wanted to know if Holder thought that "radical Islam" had any connection to jihadist attacks perpetrated against the United States. Representative Smith had to ask the same question, repeated in different ways, *six times* while Holder looked confused and uttered short rejoinders about how Smith's questions weren't making sense to him. Finally, apparently realizing that Representative Smith would not desist, Holder affirmed that whatever it was that the congressman was talking about (Holder would not pronounce the words), it was definitely not connected to the attacks to which Smith was referring.[1]

Holder's behavior before the House Judiciary Committee clearly reflected the position of the Obama administration on the terror war—a position that the administration had made conspicuously evident from the moment it took office. It would be the *Hear No Islam/See No Islam* position when it came to terrorism.

Whenever jihadists would strike, Jihad Denial would be the name of the game. This, of course, was central to the Left's cause, since denying jihad and its true roots helps to advance the progressives' goal of making America more vulnerable to jihad. And now the progressive dream had come true: the Left had its own Radical in Chief in the White House who was faithfully executing its destructive agenda.

Jihad Denial also came along with another sacred progressive goal: reaching out in solidarity to jihadists themselves—and the Obama administration didn't waste much time in getting down to business in that department, either. Obama's infamous Cairo speech in Egypt on June 4, 2009, set the tone perfectly for the administration's new path. In that address, Obama blamed the West for the terror war, portrayed the Islamic world as a mistreated victim, and made sure not to utter even one word about the doctrine of Islamic jihad. The underlying message of his talk came through loud and clear: the terror war could come to an end very simply—all the West had to do was start being nice to Muslims.[2]

Obama's foreign policy vision didn't just consist of being nice to Muslims, of course. It was also about being nice to organizations such as the Muslim Brotherhood, the leaders of which sat in the front row during his speech.[3] And that's why President Hosni Mubarak of Egypt didn't attend the speech, since he refused to appear with the leaders of the outlawed group—whom Obama had insisted on inviting.[4]

Obama's new path of Jihad Denial and romancing the Muslim Brotherhood took on devastating significance in October 2011, when his administration dutifully followed Muslim Brotherhood "requests" and purged all FBI and other intelligence agencies' training manuals of any mention of Islam and jihad.[5] The Department of Defense followed suit and enforced a purge of all individuals who didn't toe the new party line. New disciplinary action and reeducation was made mandatory for anyone in the government who dared to acknowledge Islam's role in the terror war.[6] Those who courageously told the truth about Islam, such as the scholar Robert Spencer, were removed from their positions as trainers of FBI and military personnel on the jihad threat and were replaced by members of Muslim Brotherhood front groups such as CAIR and ISNA.[7]

In the State Department, meanwhile, officials would be forbidden from asking Muslim immigrants about their views on sharia and jihad before approving their visa applications.[8]

A "counterterrorism" government guide would also tell officials that keeping Muslims out of the country for supporting sharia law violated the First Amendment.[9] All American officials and investigators were now permitted to consider only violent or criminal conduct in the terror war. Radical ideology was to be ignored, particularly if it had the veneer of "religious expression."[10]

The malicious intent of these new approaches launched by the Obama administration also revealed itself in the kind of people the administration brought into the fold. The mindset of these people was represented well by a Muslim named Mohamed Elibiary, who was given a plum position on the Advisory Council of Obama's Department of Homeland Security. The administration apparently couldn't find a better candidate than a Muslim Brotherhood sympathizer and an outspoken admirer of the Ayatollah Khomeini to serve on the DHS's Advisory Council. Elibiary was sworn in by Department of Homeland Security secretary Janet Napolitano in October 2010 and, shortly afterward, he became a senior adviser in the DHS's Countering Violent Extremism Working Group Department.[11]

Elibiary did not disappoint his employers, consistently using his position to stress that the U.S. was an Islamic country—by which he meant that the American Constitution was "Islamically compliant"—and to assure everyone that the return of the caliphate was "inevitable."[12] To make sure his message wasn't misunderstood, he incorporated the pro–Muslim Brotherhood hand signal, "R4BIA," on his Twitter profile.[13] Elibiary also *gained secret security clearance* via Napolitano and used this clearance, among other things, to download classified intelligence information that he subsequently shopped to a reporter, claiming that the department was promoting "Islamophobia."[14]

While Obama administration officials looked on approvingly at Elibiary's behavior, other Americans were extremely alarmed. Republican congressman Louie Gohmert was one of those Americans. In a July 2012 Homeland Security Oversight hearing held by the House Judiciary Committee, he questioned Napolitano regarding what she knew about Elibiary accessing classified information for sinister reasons. Napolitano stonewalled, maintaining that she was unaware that Elibiary had done anything of the kind and that she had also not been briefed on the issue.[15]

It remained a question of what was worse: the DHS secretary not knowing what her officials were doing with classified information, or knowing about it and not caring. The evidence, meanwhile, suggested that Napolitano *had* been briefed on Elibiary's activities. Terrorism analyst Patrick Poole confirmed that sources had informed him that Napolitano "had been fully briefed" on Elibiary having accessed classified information.[16] Napolitano, in other words, had lied to Gohmert.

During her deceptive performance in front of the Homeland Security Oversight hearing, Napolitano's body language conveyed obvious boredom, apathy, and contempt while she answered (or elected not to answer) Gohmert's questions.[17] It was significant that a Muslim Brotherhood sympathizer had used classified information to undermine U.S. security and yet the DHS secretary displayed a complete lack of interest in the matter—and a disdain for being asked about it. Moreover, Gohmert also asked Napolitano why, exactly, an Egyptian terrorist group had obtained U.S. visas and gained access to meet with top White House officials. Napolitano stonewalled on this line of questioning as well.[18]

Elibiary ended up resigning under mysterious circumstances in September 2014.[19] Suffice it to say that, during his years in his position, and under the approval of the Obama administration, this DHS "senior adviser" had used his appointment to openly support jihad and to make every effort possible to undermine the U.S. Constitution.[20] After his departure, Elibiary made sure to regularly remind everyone about his continued commitment to the cause. In May 2017, for instance, he publicly offered praise to Allah for the Islamic State's success in slaughtering Egyptian Christians, tweeting "how what goes around comes around."[21] His comment implied that the Islamic State's terror against Christians was some kind of karmic retribution for Copts killing/persecuting Muslims in Egypt, when the truth was the exact opposite, in terms of who was waging a genocide against whom.[22]

The Mohamed Elibiary episode exposed the Obama administration not only in terms of the kind of people it wanted in its ranks, but also in the context of what kind of agendas it wanted such people to serve. Indeed, Elibiary had been made a "senior adviser" to the DHS's Countering Violent Extremism (CVE) effort.

It soon became clear that countering "violent extremism" was the Obama administration's primary "focus" in the terror war. It served the administration's agenda perfectly because, at first glance, no one could point to what it was exactly that was being countered. There was no clear objective or identification of any specific enemy and, unsurprisingly, no mention of jihad or Islam. Countering "violent extremism" became one of those very vague and ambiguous goals to which the administration could refer when it came time to prove it was doing something about terrorism when, in fact, it was doing absolutely nothing at all.[23]

While the CVE strategy had its nebulous aspects, there was actually something that it very clearly sought to "counter." Indeed, it became quite evident that there were certain individuals, along with an ideology, that the administration regarded as "extremist" and that it wanted to block. And who were the guilty parties? The truth-tellers about jihad, of course. The counter-jihad movement represented the true "violent extremism" because, according to the administration, it was instigating all the terrible and racist hatred that was being displayed against Muslims everywhere.[24] The evidence substantiating this supposed reality proved nonexistent, but the notion prevailed nonetheless. And it was here that we saw the Left's upside-down inversion of who the good and bad guys really were: jihad had somehow become the victim, while the victims of jihad became the terrorists.

The administration's CVE charade was, in a nutshell, really all about one basic agenda: enforcing Jihad Denial and persecuting the dissidents who violated it. This situation yielded a disaster: the real threat facing America could not be named or labeled. In his book *Catastrophic Failure: Blindfolding America in the Face of Jihad*, author Stephen Coughlin documents how, under Obama, a dire threat was reduced to a "nameless abstraction." U.S. leaders and intelligence agencies ignored the most basic tenets of intelligence, which included the critical component of *threat identification*. The problem, notably, began in the Bush administration. Having worked himself in the Joint Chiefs of Staff Intelligence Directorate in the immediate post-9/11 period, Coughlin recalls how he discovered that,

> within the division there seemed to be a preference for political correctness over accuracy and for models that were generated

not by what the enemy said he was but on what academics and "cultural advisors" said the enemy needed to be, based on contrived social science theories.[25]

Under Obama, the situation went from bad to worse. Coughlin describes how Islamic supremacists became *completely aware* of the administration's calculated self-delusion and, consequently, felt arrogantly at ease in actually molding American leaders' thinking and policies. Our enemies, Coughlin writes, "successfully calculated that they could win the war by convincing our national security leaders of the immorality of studying and knowing the enemy."[26] As a result, they became overridingly confident in their ability to fulfill the Muslim Brotherhood's goal, which the Brotherhood boasted about in its own documents, of sabotaging the United States through the process of "civilization-jihad" and achieving this goal by Americans' own hands.[27]

Thus, America's suicidal disposition in the terror war reached a crisis level under Obama, when American officials actually started seeking advice and direction from *precisely those forces seeking to destroy the country.* As Coughlin shows, while the government identified certain individuals and organizations as providers of material support to terrorism, and as members or allies of the Muslim Brotherhood, it simultaneously sought out "those same people as cultural experts, 'moderates' and community outreach partners."[28]

With Obama in the White House, therefore, the enemy was, in effect, *advising Americans and formulating their policy* on how to promote their cause. Obama was also mischaracterizing the conflict America was in. "The public face of Islam in America," Coughlin notes, "was shaped by the Muslim Brotherhood." Islam in America, in turn, "took the form favored by the Brotherhood."[29] This catastrophe was compounded by the surreal fact that many officials in senior positions in the Obama administration *didn't even know anything about Islam* and were completely oblivious to the Islamic doctrines that justify and even mandate jihad against the West.[30]

Suffice it to say that, while threat identification is the foundation for any successful war effort and is, therefore, crucial to protecting Americans and enhancing our security, under Obama such identification was *impossible*. As Coughlin points out, "a postmodern form of relativism" had rendered America "incapable of recognizing existential epistemic threats and hence made it defenseless in the face of them."[31]

And it got worse. Not only did the Obama administration avoid recognizing the true threats that faced America, it spent a significant amount of time chasing around non-threats *on purpose*. Immense resources were wasted on investigating harmless non-Muslims *solely for the sake of appearing non-racist*. "Since 2009 we've opened investigations of groups we knew to be harmless," a Pentagon counterterrorism official revealed. "They weren't Muslims, and we needed some 'balance' in case the White House asked if we were 'profiling' potential terrorists."[32] In this way, the Obama administration could proudly maintain that it was not engaged in "Islamophobia."[33]

Meanwhile, the Obama administration was not content with solely silencing threat identification within the government. It would cause embarrassment, after all, if the media and American citizens could still talk openly and honestly about the ideology that posed a threat to America and the West. House Democrats, therefore, faithfully sprung to action and launched an effort to *criminalize* truth-telling about jihad in the country at large. Their effort produced House Resolution 569, which leading Democrats in the House of Representatives sponsored on December 17, 2015. Referred to the House Committee on the Judiciary, the resolution sought to destroy the First Amendment by condemning hateful rhetoric toward Muslims in the United States.[34] Conflating truth-telling about jihad with the supposed hatred of all Muslim people, the resolution sought to criminalize any attempt to accurately identify America's enemies and the ideology that inspires them. As Robert Spencer notes, the resolution used

> the specter of violence against Muslims to try to quash legitimate research into the motives and goals of those who have vowed to destroy us, which will have the effect of allowing the jihad to advance unimpeded and unopposed.[35]

The Left's effort with House Resolution 569 was an extension of UN Resolution 16/18, the effort pushed by the Organisation of Islamic Cooperation (OIC), the fifty-seven-nation alliance of Muslim states, to stifle free speech about Islam globally by implementing a UN rule against the so-called "defamation of religions." The real aim of UN Resolution 16/18 is, of course, to shut down "Islamophobia," which means to curtail any truth-telling about Islam and to impose Islamic blasphemy laws worldwide.[36]

Any law applied in the U.S. that is based on House Resolution 569 or UN Resolution 16/18 would be a violation of the U.S. First Amendment. But this doesn't concern leftists very much, since that is precisely their objective. This explains why Hillary Clinton *personally committed* the State Department to impose UN Resolution 16/18 on the United States in her meeting with the general secretary of the OIC in July 2011, while she was serving as secretary of state. Clinton also affirmed that, until the effort could become U.S. law, there would be action undertaken—by means of "peer pressure and shaming"—to intimidate Americans who engaged in the kind of speech that UN Resolution 16/18 sought to end. Then, tellingly enough, in June 2012, when Assistant Attorney General Tom Perez was asked by the chairman of the House Subcommittee on the Constitution to confirm that the Obama administration would "never entertain or advance a proposal that criminalizes speech against any religion," he refused to answer.[37]

While the Obama administration and its leftist loyalists were busy trying to impose Islamic blasphemy laws on the United States, other American progressive forces empowered Islamic supremacism in other realms. The leftist leadership of New York City, for instance, became busy accommodating Muslim Brotherhood directives by preventing the New York Police Department from focusing on Muslims in fighting jihad. The process started in 2012, when the Muslim Students Association (MSA), a Muslim Brotherhood front group, filed a federal lawsuit (along with a few other Muslim Brotherhood plaintiffs) against the NYPD. In its complaint, the MSA charged that the civil rights of Muslims were being violated by the NYPD's use of informants and plainclothes detectives to monitor various Islamic institutions—particularly MSA chapters—in the New York/New Jersey area.[38]

In early January 2016, New York City mayor Bill de Blasio and Police Commissioner William Bratton agreed to a settlement that would *exempt Muslims from NYPD surveillance*. The new guidelines explicitly barred police officers from basing any future law-enforcement investigations on race, ethnicity, or, as in the case of the MSA, religion.[39] As part of the settlement, New York City also deleted from the department's website an exhaustive NYPD report entitled "Radicalization in the West: The Homegrown Threat," which provided a crucial tutorial for all law-enforcement organizations seeking to understand how an individual is moved to Islamic radicalization.[40]

The NYPD's traditional practice of cultivating informants and using undercover investigators within the Muslim community had undeniably prevented many jihadist attacks.

But now, with more than thirty thousand worldwide Muslim terrorist attacks inspired by Islamic texts since 9/11,[41] with jihadist attacks on the rise globally, and with the FBI recently stating that it was investigating as many as nine hundred open cases on individuals suspected of being ISIS operatives,[42] it has become illegal for the NYPD to single out anyone in the Muslim community for surveillance and undercover operations. As writer Daniel Greenfield noted regarding this development, "if a successful terror attack occurs in New York, it will be because Bill de Blasio crippled the NYPD at the behest of Islamic groups."[43]

All of these events in America are a direct reflection of what is occurring in Western Europe—although the surrender there has already moved much further along. It is crucial to shed light on this catastrophic European situation, since it crystallizes the destructiveness of the leftist agenda and issues a dire warning to the U.S. about the American Left continuing to pursue its objectives.

Numerous leftist governments have spawned a catastrophe in Europe, enabling millions of Islamic migrants to swarm into the continent. This is how the Left abets "*Hijrah,*" the Islamic doctrine of *jihad by immigration*, whereby Islam conquers a non-Muslim territory through the weapon of demography.[44] And while Muslim "refugees" are colonizing an entire continent, European governments are preventing their populations from saying anything about the horrific consequences of this development by censoring and shaming them. The toxic phenomenon is represented best by the Muslim male immigrants' sexual assaults on European women and girls throughout Western Europe—and the pathetic inaction and silence with which it has been met by Western European leaders, authorities, and media.

In the infamous case of Cologne, Germany, on New Year's Eve, December 31, 2015, approximately one thousand Muslim migrants congregated at the city's main train station (after having carefully coordinated a plan to do so) and perpetrated mass sexual assaults on German women. Cologne mayor Henriette Reker's response was *to reprimand the victims*, suggesting that *they had asked for it*. She vowed to ensure that German women would change their behavior in the future, and that "online guidelines" would be published to teach the women how to avoid provoking any future sexual assaults by Muslim males.[45] This response was consistent with Islamic law, which sees sexual assault as the fault of the woman.[46]

The Cologne mayor's response was completely in line with the West's surrender to Islamic blasphemy laws in general, and with the stance of leftist feminists in particular. Feminist Naomi Wolf had already paved the way for Mayor Recker by praising the hijab, arguing that some kind of "thriving Muslim sexuality" is supposedly connected to it.[47] University of Oslo professor of anthropology Dr. Unni Wikan had also led by example with her solution for the high incidence of Muslims raping Norwegian women. Instead of punishing the rapists, Wikan counseled, Norwegian women needed to "take their share of responsibility" because they had to "realize that we live in a Multicultural society and adapt themselves to it."[48]

Mayor Recker's announcement, consequently, made total sense in the new utopian Europe constructed by the Left. That is why many Germans who dared to criticize Muslim refugees for raping women were punished. After Cologne's mass sexual assault incident, for example, German police fired water cannons at German demonstrators in the city who gathered *to protest* the rapes and sexual assaults committed by the refugees. To be clear: the water cannons *were not being aimed at the Muslim migrants who had committed sex assaults*, but at those who felt that what the migrants had done violated women's rights and Western values.[49]

It was not a big surprise, then, that when the New Year's Eve festivities in Cologne a year later saw a drastic reduction of violent crimes and rapes committed by Muslim migrants, leftists

condemned Cologne police for *stopping the rape of German women.*
The supposedly "racial" methods used to prevent the rapes were,
apparently, a bigger crime than the sexual assaults perpetrated the
previous year. According to the Left, the police were wrong to focus
their security efforts on the same groups that had been identified
as the main perpetrators of the 2015 attacks. Cologne police had
indeed successfully controlled thousands of so-called "Nafris"—
North Africans—as they attempted to enter the city center. In the
eyes of progressives, this was unconscionable.[50] In Europe, consequently, it has become clear that efforts to avoid rape by Muslim
refugees are now to be regarded as racist attempts to exercise white
privilege.[51]

In the United Kingdom, meanwhile, Muslim rape gangs run
wild—while child protective services, police, and the government
look the other way and then cover it up so as not to appear racist.[52]
In Sweden, there is a mass phenomenon of Swedish women and
girls being raped by Muslims, while the political leaders and the
media hide it as well.[53] While this madness transpires all across
Europe, leftist policies continue to facilitate Muslim migrants
flooding into the continent.

Thus, what we are witnessing is the Left's takeover of the
West and, in turn, the West's surrender to Islamic supremacism.
In America, we see how the Left succeeded through Obama in
enforcing Jihad Denial and in enabling the strength of Islamic
supremacist forces. In achieving this feat, progressives empowered
the advance of jihad and sharia in the United States, which made
the nation vastly more vulnerable to its enemy's attacks.

It is undeniable that the jihadist attacks that occurred on
American soil throughout the Obama years could have easily been
prevented. This fact will be heavily documented later in our story,
but for now we will cite just one illustrative example: the Boston
Marathon Massacre that the Tsarnaev brothers perpetrated on

April 15, 2013, which did not have to happen. The Russians, after all, had warned the FBI about the Tsarnaevs before the massacre, but the intelligence agency found nothing after its "investigation" of the two brothers. This is because the bureau had its hands tied behind its back with the Jihad Denial rules of the administration. It couldn't ask the right questions, nor pursue the right and necessary leads.[54]

Now that we have provided a brief glimpse into the catastrophic American surrender to Islamic supremacism, we can begin to move forward to unveil exactly *how* our enemy is taking over and how his victory is, essentially, *the story of the Jihadist Psychopath charming, seducing, and conquering his non-Muslim prey.* Before we get into the psychopathic elements of this tragic narrative, we first have to build the foundation to our story. It is necessary to initially identify and explain the Left as *a force*, what exactly it is, why it sides with our enemies, and why and how it has so easily seized power. The dissection of Jihad Denial, which we have already seen is one of the Left's strongest weapons, will feature prominently in this tale. We will then move on to our central thrust and unveil how Islamic supremacism's current victory over the West is the exact mirror image of how the psychopath conquers his victims. The Left, meanwhile, will be unmasked as the key minion of the Jihadist Psychopath.

We now take our next step and shine a light upon the *utopian virus*, which serves as the lifeline for the Left. We will learn why the utopian virus's message is so alluring and attractive, what allows it to gain so much power and influence, and why, in the end, it possesses so much potential to weave its tapestry of mayhem, destruction, and death.

CHAPTER 2

THE UTOPIAN VIRUS

Everything that exists deserves to perish.
> —KARL MARX, invoking a dictum of Goethe's devil
> in *The Eighteenth Brumaire of Louis Napoleon*.

It was the first lie, told by the father of all lies—and he came in the form of a serpent. It was the lie that would spawn the utopian virus: "You can be God."

One of the most powerful portrayals of Lucifer's seduction and destruction of Eve is found in John Milton's masterpiece, *Paradise Lost*, where Milton depicts the Serpent's shrewd temptation of Eve in the Garden of Eden. We see the Serpent's message of death camouflaged by the promise of life—as Eve is told that she can gain immortality and infinite knowledge and become godlike. The Serpent deceptively charms Eve and convinces her that he is acting in her best interests, while he is, of course, seeking her destruction. Taking the bait, Eve buys the lie.[1]

And so came the Fall. And with the Fall came the poisonous *utopian virus* that entered humans—inoculated into them by Lucifer himself.[2] The Fall enabled the utopian virus to root itself deeply into the DNA of man, engendering in him the passionate desire to become godlike. Humans were now tainted with the instinct to anoint themselves as social redeemers capable of engineering human "equality" and constructing a perfect world. It was the lie that Lucifer had intoxicated himself with—in his own quest to become like God and/or to replace God. It was a quest that led to his own fall, after which he zealously devoted his energy to passing down his formula for eternal damnation to humankind.

Lucifer desires to be God, but he cannot be God. While he grasps this eternal truth on some levels, he cannot accept it. This admixture of pride and denial sparks within him an inextinguishable rage and hatred and, in turn, the desire to pervert and destroy all of God's creation. Part of this rebellious and destructive agenda involves Lucifer's effort to infect humans with the virus that he had inoculated himself with—a virus that materialized from his own narcissism and pride. It was the *utopian virus.*

By succeeding in inoculating Eve with the virus, Lucifer had succeeded in infecting all of humankind with it. And, with the Fall, came humans' yearning to become gods themselves.

And so *the Left* was born.

While the utopian virus affects all of humankind generally, not every individual succumbs to it. There are, clearly, human beings who are capable of disabling the virus to large degrees within themselves, by means of such qualities as humility, the earnest pursuit of knowledge and truth, the discernment of imperfectability and hierarchy in the human condition, and an abiding faith in the Creator. The virus is also neutralized by the courage to endure slander and persecution for standing up for the truth—and by a rejection of the notion that humans can become autonomous from God. The virus is severely weakened, also, in humans who accept the limits of the possible and recognize that they cannot, on their own, make themselves perfectly equal and build a perfect planet.[3]

The humans who neutralize the utopian virus within themselves are individuals who can, generally, be categorized as "conservatives." They gauge and accept the limits of the human condition. They grasp that they cannot become gods—nor do they want to become gods. They also accept the reality of hierarchy in God's creation. And while conservatives can obviously be atheists, many are clearly and understandably religious people who want to be servants of God. They embrace the reality that redemption comes from above, rather than from the work of human hands.

Humans' rejection of the utopian virus is, in many respects, *the road less traveled*. It takes effort and bravery to fight it off. The easier path is to succumb to the virus's temptations, which feed the ego with false hopes and fairy tales. And this is precisely why the Left has such an advantage in the culture war, just as Lucifer had against Eve in the Garden. In the propaganda war, the utopian virus's lie is ever so alluring and attractive.

The falsehood at the heart of the utopian virus serves as the cornerstone of Marxist philosophy that, in turn, constitutes the foundation of the "progressive" movement. The virus pushes people to try to build the Tower of Babel, convincing them that they *can* and *should* build it. In perpetually trying to construct the Tower in our world, leftists are clearly those who have turned their back on God and who seek to make themselves into gods and build their own paradises. German Roman Catholic philosopher and theologian Dietrich von Hildebrand explains this phenomenon in his book, *The New Tower of Babel: Modern Man's Flight from God:*

> The mark of the present crisis is man's attempt to free himself from his condition as a created being, to deny his metaphysical situation, and to disengage himself from all bonds with anything greater than himself. Modern man is attempting to build a new Tower of Babel.[4]

At the root of this impulse to turn away from God, Hildebrand notes, is "the denial of man's condition as creature." In this belief system, man rejects the notion that he is a created being and a servant of God. Instead, man claims sovereignty, intoxicating himself with the illusion of complete and godlike self-sufficiency. He follows this delusion with the next step: believing that humans are on the road of unlimited and inevitable progress. This progress, in his view, will lead to paradise on earth—a paradise that, he believes, humans themselves can and will create with their own powers.[5]

The individual who clings to these fairy tales is labeled by this work as *the believer*.[6] The believer does not accept that his capacities are limited by the Fall in Eden (regardless of whether he believes that the Fall occurred). The key is that, as author David Horowitz has explained, *he believes that he can return there on his own*.[7]

Thus, believers appoint themselves as social redeemers. They seek to create human equality and *sameness*. They believe that they can change human nature and achieve *their own redemption* without God. And because they delude themselves into thinking that they do not need God for salvation, and that they are gods themselves, they are infested with pathological narcissism and self-adoration. This toxic disposition is well crystallized by the profound quotation that author Dietrich Heinrich Kerler puts into the mouth of the believer: "Even if it could be proven by mathematics that God exists, I do not want him to exist, because he would set limits to my greatness."[8]

The believer's obsession with his own imagined greatness and power to redeem the earth is interlinked, as already noted, with a tremendous rage and hatred. Passed down to man from Lucifer, this ferocious anger is focused on the human condition—and on the imperfection and hierarchy that is inherent in it. The believer, like Lucifer, is outraged at what he sees when looking at himself and humankind. Consumed with the *pretension to equality*, and yet constantly confronting the impossibility of building *the Tower*, the believer is engulfed by a torrent of rage and misery. Author Fr. Livio Fanzaga explains,

> Satan knows that God is God and that he is just a creature. He is conscious of it, but he does not accept it. He would like to be in the place of a Creator. This not being possible, he emits from his being an inextinguishable hatred.[9]

While Lucifer knows he cannot be God but at the same time is unable to accept it, so too the believer recognizes deep inside that he cannot be God and that humans cannot all be equal and the same. But he is unable—indeed, unwilling—to accept these realities. Thus, he appoints himself as a god and insists on pursuing the effort to build an earthly paradise—alongside other believers who have appointed themselves deities as well.

This is what *the Left* is all about. And in this context, we are able to grasp why there is so much hatred in the heart of the Left and why, while progressives camouflage their agenda with a smoke-screen of humanitarianism that allegedly wishes to foster equality and social justice, their engineering experiments invariably spawn mass murder and carnage. Hildebrand notes,

> The man who wants to be an absolute master, who renounces obedience to God, who believes himself able to create by his own forces a state of harmony without Christ, makes of this world a Hell, enslaves himself, and ends in a radical antipersonalism.[10]

The believer makes of this world a hell, indeed. And he makes of himself a slave absolutely. He also creates mass experiments in which millions are enslaved and suffer atrocious pain.

The believer's venture is ridden with catastrophe and destruction because it attempts to make humans into something they cannot be. The Marxist enterprise, by necessity, engenders killing machines and economic devastation in all of its physical manifestations. The *very socialist idea* itself is a call for murder. This is why the first murder in human history was itself a direct result of the utopian virus. Indeed, it can be argued that Cain's killing of Abel was, in its very essence, the first communist revolution. In the treatise on Christian hermeticism, *Meditations on the Tarot: A Journey into Christian Hermeticism*, the author gauges that Cain's murder of Abel was the "world's first revolution," since it was inspired by "the pretension to equality or, if one prefers, the negation of hierarchy."[11]

Cain's murder of Abel is a reminder of why terror is a *mandatory component* of the utopian virus' earthly incarnations. The attempt to engineer a classless order and to compel human equality necessitates terror. Once believers see themselves as gods, they hold themselves as the arbiters who get to decide which humans are *the anointed* and which are *the damned*. And since the old earth must, by necessity, be destroyed in order to build the perfect world upon its ashes, the blood of the humans who stand in the way of this process must be shed, and *the self-appointed redeemers are the ones who have to decide who they are*. In other words, as David Horowitz has noted, salvation on earth, orchestrated by human beings *alone*, by necessity "requires the damnation of those who do not want to be saved."[12] Horowitz makes a crucial observation about the believers in this context:

> They cannot live with themselves or the fault in creation, and therefore are at war with both. Because they are miserable themselves they cannot abide the happiness of others. To escape their suffering they seek judgement on all, the rectification that will take them home. If they do not believe in a God, they summon others to act as gods. If they believe in God, they do not trust His justice but arrange their own. In either case, the consequences of their passion is the same catastrophe. This is because the devil they hate is in themselves and their sword of vengeance is wielded by inhabitants of the very hell they wish to escape.[13]

We begin to discern, then, why every utopian enterprise to build heaven on earth ends in hell. The utopian virus inevitably spawns a murderous and suicidal quest. This is because the assumption that humanity is malleable and can be reshaped is fundamentally flawed. The feat is unachievable. The new human being, the *Soviet man*, that the believer seeks to construct, does not exist and cannot exist because man is, by nature, a woefully imperfect creature. Consequently, since what the believer is trying to achieve is impossible, the believer ends up being consumed with self-hatred, because he ultimately rejects man for what, and who, he is. The believer rejects himself and, consequently, *a death wish ensues*.

Even though the utopian experiment is a mythological delusion, the believer clings to it, and in his effort to bring it into practice, he not only must eliminate those standing in the way, but he must ultimately *lose himself* in the collective totalitarian whole that he simultaneously worships and seeks to create. The paradigm works in this way: The believer in the West rejects his own society, repudiating the values of democracy and individual freedom because they are anathema to him. And since he hates man for who and what he is, *he also hates himself*. He craves a fairy-tale world where no individuality exists, and where human estrangement is impossible. The believer, therefore, in rejecting who he is by nature, must also vanish in his quest as *an individual*.

In this light, we come to understand how and why the believer's overriding impulse is to dissolve his own individual and unwanted self into a totalitarian whole. In this quest for self-extinction in service of *the cause*, the believer gains what he perceives to be a self-made form of immortality. This is precisely why the leftist historical record is replete with examples of human lives being sacrificed on the altar of utopian ideals.[14] Here, we find a mutated Christian imagery. In the leftist's calculus, blood cleanses the world of its injustices and then redeems it—transforming it into a place where the believer will finally find a comfortable home. But the blood is not that of Jesus Christ; it is the blood of humans.[15] At this stage, we are reminded of George Orwell's *1984*:

> Alone—free—the human being is always defeated. It must be so, because every human being is doomed to die, which is the greatest of all failures. But if he can make complete, utter submission, if he can escape from his identity, if he can merge himself in the Party so that he IS the Party, then he is all-powerful and immortal. The second thing for you to realize is that power is power over human beings.[16]

Writer Daniel Greenfield comments on this phenomenon:

> The idealism of the Left is an inverted despair. Underneath its facade of optimism is always that darkness. Death is inevitable. It only has meaning in pursuit of totalitarian objectives. In that bleak world, subjugating and killing others for the greater good becomes the only available form of immortality.[17]

We begin to clearly see, therefore, what the Left's alliance with America's totalitarian adversaries is really all about. Believers are *longing for a tyranny they can worship*. Above and beyond rejecting God, trying to make oneself a god, and then striving zealously to create a perfect world, the leftist believer yearns to worship a secular tyrannical deity. As Hildebrand notes, "the man who turns away from God inevitably becomes the prey of an idol."[18]

Thus, the pathological narrative of the fellow travelers of the twentieth century becomes a totally predictable and logical tale in the context of leftist philosophy. It is that long and bloodstained story of Western leftist intellectuals traveling to communist hells to worship at the altar of their imaginary earthly paradises—only to be devoured by the tyrannies they came to worship. These political pilgrims, ultimately, knew very well—whether consciously or subconsciously—the fate that awaited them. In rejecting their own free societies and their own inner natures, they sought to strip themselves of their own unwanted selves. Their political journey was and is the leftist odyssey of the desperate longing for self-extinction.[19]

By surrendering to the totality in which he can achieve self-extinction, the believer fulfills his greatest calling: martyrdom for *the idea*. And here, we encounter the central theme of this book: *the believer actualizes his purpose by helping the adversarial totalitarian enemy conquer his host society*. This is why the believer so fervently allies himself with Islamic supremacism and seeks to facilitate its conquest of the West.

The vision of jihadists destroying Western civilization titillates the believer, for it is only on the ruins of his host society that the new paradise he envisions can be erected. And while the jihadist is busy trying to build a sharia-based utopia, the believer seeks to build a complementary utopia rooted in the elimination of all class distinctions. However different these two utopias may be, in terms of their core values and objectives, doesn't matter to the believer, because it is the destruction of the land of liberty and freedom (and therefore, by logical extension, of inequality and oppression) that serves as his overriding cause. Moreover, as explained above, the believer is well aware that, whether it is some sharia monstrosity or a Stalinist death camp that materializes in the nightmare he is enabling, it is all par for the course, since dissolving his individuality into the collective totalitarian whole is his top priority. He seeks to lose himself in the collective nirvana that the totalitarian enemy will bring.[20] This explains why leftists celebrated with such ecstasy when the 9/11 terrorists hit America; the ashes of Ground Zero represented the fertile soil on which they could begin to build their fairy-tale world—a world that would eventually, inevitably, consume them.[21]

The vital issue to stress here is that *the fellow travelers of this modern era continue in their quests,* and that their romance with communism has been replaced with their dalliance with Islamic supremacism.[22] This is the Unholy Alliance of our time.[23] In this new alliance, leftists no longer need to visit tyrannical hellholes as they did during the Cold War. The fellow travelers of today *have taken power in the West* and, because of that, they can now simply assist totalitarian monsters in infiltrating and destroying their own host societies. And, of course, the new fellow travelers know very well that they themselves will, ultimately, be devoured by these monsters, which will complete the last chapter of their journey in their political faith.

In light of these dark realities, it becomes evident what the true nature of the Left is and why, today, it is romancing the Jihadist Psychopath, who is the primary focus of our study. It also becomes transparent how and why the Left poses such a grievous threat when it is in power, since it shrewdly utilizes its influence to mold the thinking and circumstances in its own host society to aid and abet the Jihadist Psychopath's encroachment on our territory.

We are now much closer to unveiling the full story of how the Jihadist Psychopath is conquering us with the help of the Left. But we still have a bit of groundwork to lay. Now that we have learned exactly what *the Left is*, it is essential that we show *how the Left took power*, and *why it had such an easy time doing so.* This will equip us to understand why believers are able to sow as much destruction as they do—and why they are able to so successfully operate as minions in service of the Jihadist Psychopath.

In our next chapter, we tell a very crucial tale—the tale of the utopian virus in power.

CHAPTER 3

THE VIRUS IN POWER

As we learned in the previous chapter, the utopian virus gives birth to the Left and pushes it toward an alliance with the Jihadist Psychopath. It becomes clear, therefore, what a catastrophe the virus represents for the West, now that it has taken hold of its main institutions and power structures. Having seized power in both America and Western Europe, the Left is now actively facilitating Islamic supremacism's destructive encroachment on its own democratic host societies.

Trump's entry into the White House has brought hope that the progressive/Islamic supremacist tide can be halted on several fronts, but the problem remains that the Left has its forces deeply entrenched in the federal government and within the Trump administration itself.[1] The Left also remains extremely powerful, retaining control over the media, academia, Hollywood, and the culture at large. This chapter will examine the Left's dominion in each of these realms and reveal *how and why it got there*. In so doing, it will provide a concrete understanding of the Unholy Alliance's[2] strength and its inordinate ability to achieve power.

The leftist Obama administration ruled America for eight years and wreaked horrific damage in the process.[3] Now, while the Left's forces are still deeply embedded within the government and the Trump administration, the utopian virus also possesses a suffocating grip on the culture at large and, consequently, on the boundaries of what is presented to be permitted discourse.

In terms of the American media, the Left maintains almost complete control. While Fox News remains one of the conservative exceptions (with significant caveats), one only needs to watch MSNBC and CNN, or read the *New York Times* and *Washington Post*, to get a glimpse of how the Left rules U.S. media. No space exists in these outlets, for instance, for a real discussion about Islamic theology and how its texts inspire and sanction Islamic jihad. This is a telltale indicator of how the Left regulates language and thought in America.

There is, we should note, obviously an "independent" conservative media on the internet, just as there are various conservative websites. Web-TV stations such as The Rebel, InfoWars, and the CRTV network, and websites such as Breitbart, Frontpagemag.com, and JihadWatch.org are definitely part of a "resistance" movement that offers people information about Islamic supremacism that they will not find in the mainstream media. While these outlets are courageous in their dissident efforts, and while they are growing in strength and popularity, they still remain marginalized from the levers of power in the culture at large, and the malicious manner in which they are repeatedly slandered by the Left (as being racist, Islamophobic, etc.) helps to keep them on the periphery of the national discourse.[4]

With regard to academia, the situation today is an abomination. The Left completely controls the curricula and has brutally decimated free speech on campus. Leftist professors outnumber conservative professors roughly twelve to one at universities across America.[5] But although they are the overwhelming majority in numbers, leftists on campus now demand a "safe space" to shield them from any ideas they deem offensive—and cowardly university administrators surrender to them on a regular basis. Conservative faculty and students know they will be demonized and ostracized if they dare to break from the leftist party line. Prominent conservatives who dare to come speak on a U.S. campus face fascistic riots, violence, and threats.

The riots that prevented Milo Yiannopoulos from speaking at UC Berkeley in February 2017, followed by that university's blocking of Ann Coulter's and David Horowitz's attempts to speak there in April 2017, are just a few examples of the fascist Left's takeover of academia.[6] Additional examples abound, including the violent protests that aimed to prevent Ben Shapiro from speaking at California State University in February 2016 and the major uproar that occurred at Yale when ex-Muslim Ayaan Hirsi Ali was invited to speak there in September 2014.[7] All of these blatant illustrations of the Left's totalitarianism on American campuses reveal how "progressives" have taken over academia and stamped out all intellectual diversity—a phenomenon that David Horowitz has meticulously documented in many of his works.[8] It is no surprise, of course, that it is especially Islamic jihad and its true sources that cannot be discussed on a U.S. campus today, and the Unholy Alliance plays a central role in this narrative, seeing how the Saudi funding of American universities is heavy and has its obvious and intended results.[9]

In Hollywood, it is a given that we are dealing with uncontested leftist terrain. One could never imagine even *one movie* about the terror war that would honestly discuss Qur'anic texts in terms of how they inspire and sanction jihadists' war on the West. There are, to be sure, some rare exceptions where a film might dare to suggest that jihadists are the bad guys, such as *American Sniper.* But Hollywood does not allow any depiction of Islamic terrorism as a function of Islamic theology—and that is because the industry is ruled by the utopian virus. We know, of course, what Hollywood does allow: the propaganda that contends that "Islamophobia"—and not Islam—poses the real danger to the United States and to the world at large. And that is why anyone can be a terrorist in Hollywood movies—anyone, that is, except a Muslim. Instead, Muslims are always *the victims*. Films such as *Syriana, Traitor, Kingdom of Heaven,* and *Redacted* are perfect examples of this phenomenon.[10]

It is no coincidence, just like with the academic setting, that Muslim Middle Eastern countries are investing in Hollywood.[11] Muslim Brotherhood front groups also apply consistent pressure on the industry to produce Islam-friendly films. The Muslim Public Affairs Council (MPAC), for instance, which was founded by Muslim Brotherhood members,[12] has its own Hollywood Bureau that intimidates filmmakers on the subject of jihad and Islam, "offers" consultations for script approval, and gives out awards to those who portray Islam in the Brotherhood-approved way.[13]

Hollywood's deference to its Unholy Alliance masters also explains why, along with aiding and abetting Islamic supremacism, its movies routinely assail the Judeo-Christian tradition while promoting all other radical agendas.[14]

How did we come to this point, where the Left so thoroughly dominates the West's popular culture? The key to understanding this phenomenon is to grasp that the utopian virus infects the psychic DNA of its host with the impulse to wage perpetual war. The virus is, in and of itself, a form of *constant rebellion*. When the Serpent deceived Eve in the Garden, it wasn't a momentary mental lapse that he had, in the sense that he was bored and, to pass the time, he whimsically approached Eve and deceived her. And it was not as if, upon having completed his task, he just contentedly turned his attention to other mundane and benign activities. No, the Serpent is *always* at work in his rebellion against God. He is always at war, and his agenda is ferocious and destructive. And the progressive moment on earth is *his war in its earthly incarnation.*

The Left, in other words, *never sleeps.* Having inherited the utopian virus from the Serpent,[15] progressives are in a perpetual state of battle. Political war is their raison d'être, and their overriding goal is to destroy democratic-capitalist society and the Judeo-Christian tradition on which it is based.

No author has dissected and explained the Left's perpetual war better than David Horowitz. His scholarship thoroughly lays bare the Left's basic nature, its preferred tactics, and the reasons behind its victories in political battle.[16] He crystallizes how the Left's hatred and utopian vision inspires a missionary zeal that is *perfectly suited* to aggressive tactics and no-holds-barred combat. In illuminating this phenomenon, Horowitz also shows how conservatives are severally disadvantaged in fighting the Left because *they are not trying to transform the world*; they are not at war 24/7, the way the Left is. Conservatives are much more inclined to simply live their lives rather than to be engaged in endless crusades to transform society. For them, unlike for leftists, the personal can be separated from the political.

For these reasons, conservatives commonly fail to understand that there is a political war in process. Many of them even disapprove of their fellow conservatives engaging in political war when they perceive one. For the most part, conservatives just want to be nice; they prioritize being polite, having tidy and well-trimmed lawns, and avoiding conflict. They do not realize that the Left is out to destroy them and the society that they love. Consequently, they are severely handicapped in fighting political war. Horowitz's book, *Take No Prisoners: The Battle Plan for Defeating the Left*, makes this point with crystal clarity, showing exactly why the Left is so good at political warfare, why conservatives fail at it, and what the latter need to do to fight back and win.[17]

Another crucial factor that facilitates the Left's success in political battle is its shrewd focus on winning *the culture*. Italian Stalinist Antonio Gramsci played a pivotal role in teaching the Left this path to power. In his writings in the 1930s, Gramsci stressed that the Left had to put cultural institutions at the center of its revolutionary battle. In his vision, this meant infiltrating and taking over academia, the media, churches, the arts, and all other realms of culture.[18] By this process, progressive *ideas* would be introduced into the general culture and into the national discourse and, inevitably, people's thinking would be reshaped. The leftist vision would mold *the ruling ideas* and, eventually, produce the ruling political class. In other words: capture the culture and own political power. Authors such as David Horowitz and Barry Rubin have documented that it is precisely by this Gramscian prescription that the Left fought the culture war and subsequently captured power.[19]

In terms of political power itself, the Left has thoroughly infiltrated and taken control of the Democratic Party in America. As Horowitz has documented in his book *Shadow Party*, radical billionaire George Soros played a major role in this development by putting together a coalition of wealthy funders, radical activists, and political apparatchiks who eventually gained a lock on the Democratic Party's political apparatus, excluding moderates and molding party policies in a radical direction.[20] And the rest was history: after taking control of the Democratic Party, the Left captured the White House with the coming to power of Barack Obama.[21] Obama's entire political career, as Horowitz shows, was shaped, funded, and made possible by the Left's financial and political network.[22]

In his documentation of the workings of the Shadow Party, Horowitz dispelled the myth that conservatives and the Republican Party somehow represent the rich and powerful, while progressives and the Democrats are "the party of the people." Much to the contrary, Horowitz demonstrated that it is the Left that has successfully built the richest and most powerful political machine in American history. His work, *The New Leviathan*, exposed this influential and wealthy network and shows how the Left routinely moves radical ideas like Obamacare from the periphery of society, normalizes them, and then makes them the priority agendas of the Democratic Party.[23]

It is precisely in this way that the Left has succeeded in maneuvering America's entire national and social policy debate onto its own radical territory, thereby transforming the nation's political and cultural climate.[24] This is precisely why, as Horowitz has also demonstrated, Democrats and political leftists have controlled the governing councils and public schools of every major inner city in America for fifty years or more.[25]

The Left has actually achieved so much power, and is effecting such fundamental toxic change in America, that Horowitz felt it necessary to create an entire online encyclopedia of the Left, DiscovertheNetworks.org, which provides a map of all of its networks, funding, operatives, and agendas. The site identifies the purveyors of Islamic supremacism, lays bare the Left's alliance with them, and describes all the radical networks that surrounded the Obama administration and the Democratic Party leadership up till the present.[26]

Thus, it becomes clear how and why the Left has taken so much power in America and has gained control of the boundaries of permitted discourse. We can see why the Left has been so successful, by means of its Unholy Alliance with radical Islam, in enabling the Jihadist Psychopath to conquer us.

One of the main weapons that the Left has used in its position of power to aid and abet the Jihadist Psychopath is Jihad Denial. By making us unable to see, and speak about, the true threat and enemy we face, it has crippled our ability to defend ourselves. Jihad

Denial, therefore, is a vital component for us to explore and comprehend. And so we deconstruct and unveil its dark character and mechanisms in the next chapter.

CHAPTER 4

JIHAD DENIAL

The Left's war on its own host democratic society is greatly enabled by its consistent and focused empowerment of that society's enemies. As explained earlier, this is precisely why the Left sided with communism during the Cold War and why, today, it works collaboratively with Islamic supremacism within the Unholy Alliance in the terror war.[1] Islamic supremacism has simply replaced communism as the Left's ally against America and the West over the course of the past quarter-century.

The Left well understands that, in order to facilitate Islamic supremacism's assault on our society, it must suppress the ugly, discomfiting truth about this fascistic ideology and movement. Doing so is completely natural for the Left, which has routinely turned a blind eye to evil and to undesirable elements within adversary cultures, ideologies, and religions for decades. When Western citizens recognize an ugly truth about an enemy society, it poses a tremendous danger to the Left because (1) the conclusion can be reached that *Western society is better and, therefore, worth protecting and defending*; (2) the nature of the actual threat the enemy poses and a way to counter that threat can be discerned; and (3) the importance of preventing adherents of the enemy ideology from coming to live on the host society's terrain becomes plainly evident.

All of the above realizations are anathema to progressives, whose entire mission falls into ruins if citizens of their host society understand the evil of an adversarial system. The Left's goal of destroying its own society, and of constructing upon its ruins a utopia of perfect integration, equality, and sameness, simply crumbles if people take concrete steps to defend their own society from the enemy—which includes recognizing the destructiveness of immigration and refugee policies designed to import hostile populations.

Thus, we begin to understand why the Left is so unsympathetic to the victims of jihad and sharia—and why it consistently pushes them into invisibility. Their reality and suffering are *bad news* for the Left. When people witness the horrific ordeal of human beings tortured and murdered by the adherents of Islamic supremacism, they begin to see Islam for what it is. The Left is determined to stop this from happening, since its agenda cannot succeed if people understand the truth about the threat that they face. This is exactly why the Left engaged in Gulag Denial throughout the Cold War; denying the monstrous evils of communism was crucial for the Left's war on its own host society, and for its effort to help communists conquer that society.[2]

And so we have Jihad Denial—the Left's vehement effort to silence those who dare to tell the truth about Islamic supremacism. The Left has to keep Jihad Denial alive and healthy so that its plan of building its Tower of Babel on the ashes of its host society can move forward.[3] Most important for the Left is the tactic of *disconnecting Islam from Islamic terrorism*. As has been shown in Chapter 1, and as will be documented further in the ensuing chapters, the Left has succeeded brilliantly in this effort. Indeed, while controlling the culture and framing the national discourse on this issue, the Left has arrogated the moral high ground to itself when engaging in Jihad Denial, posturing as though it is working toward a society of social justice and fairness, while it paints all Muslims as victims of Western transgressions—*even during the height of an age that is replete with Islamic terrorism.*

Any person, meanwhile, who dares to whisper any sobering truth about Islam is now immediately shamed and dehumanized. Labeled a racist, bigot, and "Islamophobe" who supposedly hates all Muslim people and thinks that all Muslims are terrorists, this individual is caricatured as a mouthpiece of "hate speech" and an inciter of violence against Muslims. He is regarded as someone who needs to be silenced and, ideally, criminalized.[4]

One transparent example of this atrocious distortion that comes with Jihad Denial is the case of leading counter-jihadist Pamela Geller and the slanders leveled against her. Geller is perpetually cast by the Unholy Alliance as an "Islamophobe" and a "Muslim hater,"[5] when in fact, she is a noble humanitarian who is motivated, not just by the desire to defend Western freedom, but also by an impulse to protect Muslim people themselves—especially Muslim women and young girls who suffer under the vicious barbarities of Islamic gender apartheid. Geller has, for instance, done more on behalf of Muslim women than have any of her slanderers. Emblematic of her efforts was her fight on behalf of Aqsa Parvez, a sixteen-year-old Muslim girl who was murdered by her Muslim father and brother in an honor killing in Toronto in 2007. Geller brought attention to Aqsa's case and had a memorial grove successfully built in the girl's memory in Israel—after Aqsa's family and other Unholy Alliance forces had made it impossible for Geller to do so in Ontario.[6]

Geller's valiant efforts to bring attention to Aqsa's fate were part of her overall campaign to shine a light on the shameful practice of honor killings and on the suffering of all Muslim women under Islam in general. Such efforts are symbolized by the page on Geller's website titled "Honor Killings Grow in the West: Islam's Gruesome Gallery," which documents horrific cases in which Muslim women were subjected to honor killings and acid attacks.[7] It is worth noting that the members of the Unholy Alliance who smear Geller are the ones who are actually engaged in the hatred of Muslim people, since their assault on this counter-jihadist inevitably exonerates the Islamic ideology that inspires and sanctions the oppression of Muslims themselves—and leaves millions of them helplessly ensnared by the shackles of sharia. When the Unholy Alliance demonizes Geller, it actually *exacerbates* the suffering of Muslim people and depicts them as inferior, since it *lowers expectations of how Muslims should treat each other and non-Muslims*. This way of thinking holds Western societies to a higher standard of moral accountability, which confers an implied civilizational superiority on these societies and civilizational inferiority on Muslim societies. This is a dark form of leftist bigotry that is, with a few exceptions, never discussed in our media and culture.[8]

The Left used all of these same dirty tactics during the Cold War as well, labeling any conservative who tried to oppose communist aggression and infiltration as a "fascist," "McCarthyite," and "Red Baiter" (among other terms)—while making victims and martyrs out of many traitors who were in league with the communist enemy (e.g., the Rosenbergs, Alger Hiss, etc.).[9]

Jihad Denial, therefore, is a powerful mechanism through which the Left advances its malicious goals. It assists the Left, for instance, in bringing Islamic supremacist populations to Western shores through *Hijrah*—the process of jihad by immigration.[10] By importing masses of people who hate America and seek to destroy its way of life, the Left succeeds in severely damaging the United States and making it more vulnerable to attack. This explains why President Obama worked so hard to flood the U.S. with Muslim refugees[11] and why the Left is now so ferociously fighting Trump's efforts to protect America from refugees who hail from terror-infested nations.[12]

By denying the true character and roots of jihad and sharia through Jihad Denial, the Left prevents an evil enemy from being exposed and, in turn, enables that enemy. And the Left has been extremely successful in this feat, having imposed Jihad Denial on Western culture to such an extent that we are now seeing the virtual surrender of our civilization in the face of Islamic supremacism. Indeed, the West is now perpetually bending over backwards in its effort to silence any truth-telling about Islam and, of course, to disconnect Islam from every Islamic terror attack. Anyone who tries to point out unpleasant truths about Islam is either demonized or silenced. Many people are simply too scared to say what they see and think about Islam, because they are terrified of being called racists and suffering the consequences of being tarred with that word—consequences that may include stigmatization, marginalization, getting fired from one's job, being held back in one's career, being criminally charged, and much more.[13]

All in all, what Jihad Denial has achieved is to make the real perpetrators the victims, and the victims the perpetrators. Patriotism is now considered hatred—while self-defense is regarded as an incitement to violence against innocents. As a result, the effort to defend Western civilization from Islamic supremacism has been largely paralyzed.

Our next step in evaluating this disaster is to explore how Jihad Denial works as a machine. It is vital to lay bare the main arguments utilized by Jihad Denial, since they are extremely calculating, deceptive, and destructive. In the next chapter, we outline and discredit the specious facades of Jihad Denial.

CHAPTER 5

"NOT ALL MUSLIMS DO THAT!"

Now that we have learned how and why the Left perpetuates Jihad Denial, we move on to examine the key arguments within its toxic agenda. As will be demonstrated below, the entire gambit is a lie and a fraud.

It's Just the Extremists!

One of the most widely employed Jihad Denial arguments heard in our culture today is the infamous assurance that *it's not Islam, but the extremists!* This proposition is interwoven with the central foundation of the Jihad Denial matrix: *that it all really has nothing to do with Islam.* The thinking goes like this: even when jihadists quote their Islamic texts to justify their barbaric actions, *it is not because of Islam.* The terrorists, we are told, are just a very tiny minority of Muslims who have misunderstood and hijacked their own religion. They are, therefore, *not even real Muslims.*

The reality is that Muslims who perpetrate jihad do so because they are following the example of their prophet Muhammad and are abiding by the mandates of their faith.[1] This is precisely why they refer to their own texts to legitimize and sanction the violence they perpetrate. The "tiny minority" argument is also a complete falsehood, because (1) it is immaterial whether a large majority or tiny minority is involved, since a very small number of people can inflict a monumental amount of damage, and (2) the number of Muslims who are either involved in, or support, Islamic terror is actually extremely high.[2]

Not All Muslims Do That!

Another popular Jihad Denial argument is the *not all Muslims do that!* con job. In this case, when devout Muslims perpetrate a crime carrying out the directives of Islam, Unholy Alliance[3] members and followers dutifully proclaim: *but not all Muslims do that!* The bizarre assumption here is that because not all Muslims do something, it somehow makes the victims, and the problem of jihad and sharia, go away. But it is completely inconsequential whether *all* Muslims do something or not. It is a given that not *all* people in any one group do or see everything in the same way— and there are obviously some "good" people in most environments. What matters is that *Islamic law exists independently of whether Muslims follow it or not.* In other words, the fact that there may be Muslims who do not follow Islamic law does not make Islamic law disappear, nor does it erase the Muslims who follow it, or the people they hurt by doing so.[4] It is also crucial to keep in mind that when it comes to jihadists, they represent the military tip of the spear—and the military is always the minority of the population. As Daniel Greenfield points out: "Outside of Sparta, not everyone in a population fights."[5] Thus, not all Muslims might be carrying out the violent commands of Islam, but many of them may very well be supporting someone else doing it.

ISIS Kills Muslims Too!

Another much-used argument is the *ISIS kills Muslims too!* ploy. Here, we see the attempt to de-Islamize the Islamic State by noting that its victims include some Muslims. President Obama engaged in this charade on countless occasions.[6] But the proposition that Islamic terror cannot be Islamic if its victims include Muslims is simply erroneous. First, it completely ignores the reality of how totalitarian revolutions and systems *invariably devour their own children*. Indeed, the Islamic State kills Muslims *precisely because of Islam*, since *Islam by its very nature has to kill its own*. This is because the Muslims who are dying at the hands of the Islamic State are seen as *not the right kind of Muslims*. They are regarded as being either apostates or unbelievers. Islam creates these categories of subhumans and delineates the punishments that must be meted out to them. To be sure, Islam mandates that *devout* and *real* Muslims must punish, and in some circumstances kill, those Muslims whom they regard as neither legitimate nor properly devout.[7]

It would do well to point out that ISIS also fights other jihadist groups, such as Jabhat al-Nusra—which is an extension of al-Qaeda. Daniel Greenfield touches on this phenomenon, commenting: "If fighting ISIS or being killed by it makes you moderate, al-Qaeda is moderate."[8]

Criticizing Islam Means You Hate All Muslims!

Another deceptive ploy in this con game is that of *conflating all Muslims with Islam*. When a truth-teller points to a negative feature in Islam, the Jihad Denier will often immediately retort with the *not all Muslims do that!* charade. The assumption here is that the truth-teller has somehow said something bad about *all* Muslims. The denier then usually refers to some nice Muslim person he knows, as though this delegitimizes what the truth-teller has said. But the whole paradigm here, which involves a *conflation of Muslims with Islam*, is specious. The truth-teller never said anything about *all Muslims*; he was speaking about Islam.

Raymond Ibrahim, a leading scholar of Islam, has unveiled the monumental dishonesty that is involved in this conflation tactic. Noting that it is "an all too common approach" that is used to shield Islam from criticism, Ibrahim brings up the example that not every single Muslim alive today believes that the apostasy penalty should be upheld. But this reality, he stresses, "is not a reflection of Islam; it is a reflection of individual human freedom—a freedom that ironically goes against Islamic teaching."[9]

The conflation tactic is also severely flawed because it is based on a faulty Marxist collectivist premise that conflates an ideology with everyone who happens to be standing in the vicinity of its banner. The deniers who automatically accuse a person of hating all Muslims when that person has said something critical about Islam are actually projecting their own totalitarian Marxist thinking. The truth-teller about Islam is simply referring to *an ideology* that is dangerous, and to *the people who follow the ideology*. This by no means implies that every member of Islam accepts, knows about, or is carrying out these ideological teachings. But leftists automatically interpret truth-telling about Islam as hate speech against all Muslims, not only because it helps them achieve Jihad Denial, but also because *they themselves are totalitarians who cannot fathom the possibility of individuals existing outside of a group-think environment*. They simply cannot grasp that individuals can stand on their own and not have to conform to a party line, since it is not a reality that leftists themselves inhabit.

Look at All the Good and Peaceful Muslims!

There is also the trick of pointing to the "good" and "peaceful" Muslims in an effort to legitimize Islam. This also involves the tactic of conflating *all* Muslims with Islam. But it is irrational to associate "good Muslims" with the teachings of Islam, because their nonviolent behavior is not sanctioned by the Islamic texts that mandate totalitarianism and violence. In other words, there may be many Muslims who make up their own brand of Islam and believe in it and are, therefore, "good" Muslims *in our eyes*. But they are regarded as bad Muslims by Islam, because (1) Islam mandates Islamic law, Islamic supremacism, war against the unbelievers, sexual slavery, and many other barbarities,[10] and (2) *Muslims cannot be put on a higher pedestal of authority than Islam itself.*[11]

Another crucial fact to stress is that most Muslims are, obviously, born into Muslim environments and are not, therefore, given a choice as to whether they want to be Muslim or not. When they become adults, they may not agree with Islam or support or participate in jihad. But if they leave Islam, they risk being killed because of Islamic apostasy laws, which demand the killing of Muslims who abandon the faith.[12] These individuals are labeled "Muslim" nonetheless, but they are really Muslim *in name only*. Many of them live in the West and, therefore, have the luxury of not having to practice sharia and jihad—and some of them are even safe to reject both if they wish to. But it is precisely because of the West's influence, not of Islam's, that they are safe to do this.[13] These Muslims are, once again, a reflection of individuality and human freedom, not of Islam.

Others Do It Too!

Now we arrive at the popular *others do it too!* charade. This is when the denier hears about a crime committed by Islam and immediately brings up something that someone else has done that is allegedly similar. This tactic works very successfully in our culture, yet it is severely flawed. First, it is based on the false and bizarre assumption that a crime committed by a person in one place is somehow justified if another person does the same thing somewhere else. Second, the deniers in these instances always use fallacious parallels. For instance, when confronting the issue of Islamic rape, a denier will often equivocate by stating that rape is also committed by non-Muslims all across the United States. But the fundamental difference is that when a rape is committed in America, *it is illegal* and if the rapist is caught *he will be put in prison*. Where Islamic law prevails, *rape is legal.* A Muslim who rapes a non-Muslim female can point to Islam for justification and legitimacy.[14] And if a husband hits his wife in America, he will be charged with a crime. In Islam, the Muslim husband will not only *not* be charged, he will be seen as a good Muslim, since wife beating finds legitimacy in Islam.[15]

The Jihad Denier also draws a moral equivalency between Islam and other religions, especially Christianity and Judaism. When the denier is confronted by the verses in the Qur'an that promote jihadist violence, for instance, he instinctively retorts that the same teachings exist in other religions—*especially in the Old Testament*.

This tactic is also completely disingenuous. The Judeo-Christian tradition is built on the principle of trying to restrain humans from evil. Islam, meanwhile, on many levels, encourages its members to perpetrate evil: jihad, sex slavery, female genital mutilation, etc.[16] When the denier points to something Christians have done wrong, the argument is illegitimate because the behavior of Christians that may be "bad" *contradicts* Christian teachings. If Christians commit murder or engage in sex slavery, *they are acting in an un-Christian manner* because they are violating Christian teachings. But if Muslims kill unbelievers or force non-Muslim girls into sexual slavery, which the Islamic State and Boko Haram do on a daily basis, they can find justifications for this behavior in Islamic texts.[17] So there is no moral equivalency when it comes to Christianity and Islam.[18]

As far as the Old Testament is concerned, deniers often point to its "violent" texts to suggest that Judaism is no better than Islam when it comes to condoning violence. They like to display moral indignation about passages where God orders genocides, such as the order given to Saul against the Amalekites in 1 Samuel 15:3. But the command given to Saul, like others that may be found in the Old Testament, is not, like the Qur'an's teachings, *an open-ended command directed to all believers for all time and place.* Unless you are Saul or an Amalekite at that time and place, it doesn't concern you or anyone else. This is why, as Robert Spencer points out, there is not a single example of a Jew or a Christian committing an act of violence and justifying it by referring to the order given against the Amalekites.[19] And this is also why there are no Jewish or Christian fanatics anywhere who commit mass murder on the scale of 9/11 and justify doing so by pointing to their texts—the way the Muslim 9/11 attackers did with their texts.[20]

They Just Need Jobs!

Another argument in the Jihad Denial labyrinth blames poverty for Islamic terrorism (which, of course, also isn't really Islamic). This Marxist view was put on full, pathetic display in February 2015 when Obama's State Department spokeswoman, Marie Harf, infamously suggested that one of the main root causes of Muslims joining groups like ISIS is "lack of opportunity for jobs."[21] In this leftist line of thinking, Islamic "extremism" stems from poverty and oppression, which, in turn, are caused by capitalism, American imperialism, etc. This paradigm achieves the leftist objective of absolving jihadists—because *the devil made them do it*. And the devil is us. *We are at fault because we forced their hand.*

Empirical reality and historical evidence, of course, completely discredit the *poverty causes terrorism* fantasy. Many jihadists and jihadist leaders come from the most educated, wealthy, and Westernized backgrounds.[22] Osama bin Laden was the son of a billionaire businessman, Ayman al-Zawahiri is a physician, and Khalid Sheikh Mohammed has an engineering degree. One of the San Bernardino shooters, Syed Farook, held a good job in environmental health,[23] and the Chattanooga shooter, Muhammad Youssef Abdulazeez, had a degree in electrical engineering.[24]

Close to 60 percent of Palestinian suicide bombers have attended college; they are not the children of economic despair and hopelessness.[25] As scholar Daniel Pipes affirms, "suicide bombers who hurl themselves against foreign enemies offer their lives not to protest financial deprivation but to change the world."[26] And no wonder that a 2016 report found that, contrary to Marie Harf's wisdom, Islamic State recruits were not driven by poverty and were above average in education.[27]

Despite the evidence, however, the Left continues to believe in and regurgitate this toxic nonsense. And that is why this particular Marxist assumption molded American policy throughout the Obama years. In September 2013, for instance, Secretary of State John Kerry launched a new global "counter-terror" fund. At a New York meeting of the Global Counterterrorism Forum (GCTF), he spoke of the importance of "providing more economic opportunities for marginalized youth at risk of recruitment." He and his Turkish counterpart, Ahmet Davutoglu, unveiled a two hundred-million-dollar initiative designed to leverage public and private funding in support of "countering violent extremism" (CVE) efforts, the disastrous approach to terror practiced by the

Obama administration discussed in Chapter 1.[28] Known formally as the "Global Fund for Community Engagement and Resilience," the purpose of the group was to support local communities and organizations to counter "extremist" ideology and promote "tolerance."[29]

The problem with all of these efforts, of course, is that there are many rich Muslims who support terrorism, and there are many poor people who do not support or engage in terrorism. Robert Spencer asked the appropriate question in the context of John Kerry and the GCTF:

> Is it poverty and a lack of economic opportunities that leads the fantastically rich House of Saud to finance that jihad worldwide? If Kerry were correct and terrorism is simply a byproduct of poverty, why isn't Haiti a terrorist state? Why isn't the world plagued with Bolivian suicide bombers?[30]

Shillman Fellow Bruce Thornton has made a similarly profound observation exposing the fundamental flaw of the *poverty causes terrorism* Marxist charade:

> Left unexplained is the fact that billions of other people around the world even more impoverished and hopeless have not created a multi-continental network of groups dedicated to inflicting brutal violence and mayhem on those who do not share their faith or who block their visions of global domination.[31]

Indeed, many people around the world have suffered and been humiliated, but they have not turned to terrorism. One thing for sure in terms of Kerry's GCTF, however, was that, as Spencer warned at the time, some or most of its funds would end up financing the jihad terror it was purporting to try to stop.[32]

All They Need Is an "Arab Spring!"

Another Jihad Denial gambit involves the fairy tale that claims that once the bad, corrupt dictators in the Islamic Middle East are removed and the people are given a "democratic alternative," Islam will democratize and everything will be fine. This is how the West projects ridiculous leftist assumptions onto Islam and deceives itself.

A perfect example of this distorted way of thinking was found in the so-called "Arab Spring"—which the West convinced itself was a democratic movement driven by the philosophies of Thomas Jefferson and Thomas Paine. The "Arab Spring" was, in reality, just a simple impulse toward an Islamist Winter. Its main objective was to construct and impose sharia as a ruling legal system. Anyone with common sense could have easily understood this from the start, since in all of the "Arab Spring" demonstrations there was not one speech, or one placard, that could be found stating "Down with Sharia" or "Separation between Mosque and State." Author Nonie Darwish pointed out this gargantuan elephant in the room:

> As I watched the TV coverage of the massive protests, I was desperately searching for a brave poster proclaiming something new and daring—a poster that demanded reformation of the system and not merely removal of the dictator, along with slogans of freedom and democracy—but I could not find any. This is what I wanted to see: "Separation of mosque and state," "Removal of sharia from the Egyptian constitution," "Equal rights for all," or "Equal rights for women"—better yet, "The beating of women is not a husband's right." To my disappointment, I did not see any signs like this.[33]

Darwish was absolutely right, but the West needed to convince itself that the "Arab Spring" was a yearning for democracy, even though everything that was transpiring suggested the exact opposite. Consequently, leftists nurtured the fairy tale that there was a democratic impulse in a region and a belief system where a large percentage of Muslims advocate jihad, hate Jews, and support the stoning of adulterers, the killing of apostates, female genital mutilation, and many other brutal aspects of sharia law.[34] Consequently, the "Arab Spring" amounted to precisely what it was intended to amount to: more jihad and sharia. And that is why it created the Islamic State.[35]

Don't Be Racist!

Another crucial component of the Jihad Denial scam is the argument that anyone who says anything critical about Islam is a racist. And since most people in the West now dread being labeled such, this slander has silenced the society at large in terms of the truth about Islam. This leftist tactic has succeeded because, as writer Daniel Greenfield has noted, the Left has achieved the *racialization* of Islam—even though Islam is not even a race.[36] Referring to this con job as the "Big Lie," Robert Spencer writes about its spurious charges and his own efforts to fight them:

> I have repeated more times than I could possibly recall: "What race is the jihad mass murder of innocent civilians again? I keep forgetting." I've pointed out almost as often that Muslims who believe that their god is commanding them to wage war against and subjugate those who don't believe as they do come in all races, and that race has nothing to do with their imperatives.[37]

These simple truths, unfortunately, have not made a dent in the Unholy Alliance's tactic on this score. And the Obama administration empowered the whole charade by launching the effort to make "Middle Eastern and North African" a race.[38] Since the principal beneficiaries of this move would be Muslim Arabs, the intent was obviously to give Muslims special privileges—and to bolster the charge of "racism" against anyone daring to tell the truth about jihad or sharia.[39]

Thus, because Islam has surreally acquired racial status, it is now considered racist to criticize Islam, a protected status that Islam, and no other religion, possesses. The absurdity of the whole thing becomes obvious when looking at the Unholy Alliance's treatment of *ex-Muslims*, whom leftists freely criticize without the slightest worry that their condemnations may be inherently "racist."

It would be important, at this point, to reflect on a theme stressed by author Shelby Steele in his masterpiece *The Content of Our Character*, where Steele focuses on white people's need *to feel innocent* in the struggle over race in America.[40] He discusses this issue in the black-white context, but his point is extremely relevant to Jihad Denial today. Indeed, since the Left has succeeded in racializing Islam, we begin to understand better why so many Americans surrender to the Unholy Alliance's bullying on this issue: *because they want to feel innocent in the face of accusations of racism*. They are, therefore, terrified to say anything about Islam that the Unholy Alliance might frown upon.

Steele also reveals how, in race relations in America, *white guilt has translated into black power*.[41] The Unholy Alliance knows this all too well—and now that it has racialized Islam, it has successfully translated white guilt into Islamic power.

White People Can't Understand Islam!

Connected to the *you are racist!* slander is another farcical smear: *that white people can't understand Islam*. By this point, we begin to witness so much pathology and contradiction that it is difficult to keep track of it all. But let us try:

The Unholy Alliance lectures truth-tellers about Islam that they must not paint all Muslims with the same broad brush, because *not all Muslims do that!* And yet, the truth-tellers are simultaneously told that they can't understand Islam anyway because Muslims are actually one big racial group within which everyone is the same—and presumably dark-skinned. The illogic here is represented best by journalist and novelist Rula Jebreal, who adamantly insists that non-Muslims are all white and simply cannot understand Islamic culture, which apparently consists of exclusively dark-skinned Muslims.

As a guest on a segment on "CNN Tonight" with Don Lemon, Jebreal lectured former CIA analyst Buck Sexton about Islam, telling him that because "white people like yourself" don't understand "the language, culture, and religion" of Islam, they are incapable of understanding the Islamic State. While Jebreal's chastisement of Sexton might have been a bit confusing for many Unholy Alliance members who insist that the Islamic State has nothing to do with Islam, her position became more intriguing when she continued her reprimand of Sexton: "You need to understand what is appealing—what is the message that ISIS actually is selling in these prison cells. And what they are selling online."[42] Here Jebreal implied that there *was*, lo and behold, such a thing as an Islamic "culture" after all. And, in her view, there was something "appealing" about it to many Muslims—all of whom, apparently, are part of one race—that white people simply can't understand.

To summarize the twisted logic here: a white person cannot understand all the dark Muslim people who find Islamic terrorism appealing—but Islam has nothing to do with terrorism. Robert Spencer made the heroic effort to untangle this mystery wrapped inside an enigma. Wondering about Jebreal's thesis, and all the white people who just happen to be Muslims, he notes:

> That there are "white people" who are fervent believers in Islam, such has Hamas-linked CAIR's Ibrahim Hooper, the late al-Qaeda jihadi Adam Gadahn, the Marin County Taliban John Walker Lindh, North Carolina jihad plotters Justin Sullivan and Donald Ray Morgan, would-be Wichita jihad bomber Terry Lee Loewen, Boston Marathon jihad bombers Tamerlan and Dzhokhar Tsarnaev, UK "Sharia patrol" leader Jordan Horner,

Brandeis Professor Joseph Lumbard, and so very many others, escapes her, and demonstrates the hollowness of her analysis—and CNN's.[43]

On the same theme, Daniel Greenfield affirms:

Also Islamist groups love to drag out white American converts as fronts. Like Ibrahim Hooper of CAIR or Ingrid Mattson of ISNA. So according to Rula Jebreal, Hooper and Mattson also don't get Islam. But presumably they're useful idiots for the Islamic cause.[44]

Greenfield also observes that those who don't understand Islam include Rula Jebreal's Jewish banker husband. That might be horrifying to Jebreal herself, Greenfield points out, because:

Arabs like Rula Jebreal, who originally comes from '67 Israel, are classified as white by the census bureau. They've demanded a special minority classification MENA, because in real life, minority privilege beats that imaginary "white privilege" that leftists love to rant about. (If you're lobbying to be classified as a minority, you know white privilege is a myth.) Which would mean that Mohammed was white.[45]

And so perhaps it all ends up making sense why terrorist Muslims are not really authentic Muslims after all. "If white people don't understand Islam," Greenfield notes, "that would include its founder. That must be why Arab Muslims keep misunderstanding their religion."[46]

There Is No Islam!

All of these Jihad Denial strategies are, in the end, intentionally doing one basic thing: painting Islam as *never doing anything at all*—unless it can be praised by Muslims and the Left. In other words, when Islam maims and oppresses, it *never stands for anything.* Spencer has referred to this Jihad Denial tactic, making the crucial point that, "For Leftists and Islamic supremacists, it is a cardinal sin to *essentialize* Islam—that is, to dare to suggest that it actually teaches and stands for anything in particular."[47]

We Need to Have Religious Freedom!

While deniers insist, on the one hand, that Islam doesn't stand for anything and, therefore, cannot be essentialized, they contradict themselves by maintaining that it stands for a great deal—since it is actually a religion and, therefore, cannot be touched. This is because religious freedom is guaranteed in the U.S. Constitution and also because, according to leftists, no faith propagates hatred and violence—a mantra that Obama repeatedly maintained throughout his administration to exonerate Islam.[48]

Suffice it to say that, while the Unholy Alliance defends Islam by maintaining that no faith sanctions violence, it spends a considerable amount of time alleging that Christianity and Judaism do exactly that. In any case, many people are afraid to say anything negative about Islam because it is a "religion" and it is assumed that all religions must be "good" and cannot possibly sanction hatred and violence. The problem, of course, is that Islam is not so much a religion as a *political ideology.*[49] Moreover, and again, *it does* preach hatred and violence.

Thus, Islam is able to continue its malicious agenda in the U.S. because it receives protected status under freedom of religion statutes within the country (while not standing for anything at all). Because of this protection, Muslims are also able to continue building and congregating in their mosques without any questions or even government surveillance.[50] And yet, the empirical evidence demonstrates that Islamic mosques are often covers for violence and jihad.[51]

In the end, when we examine all of these different arguments that are used to sustain Jihad Denial, we find not only a shrewd deception, but also a ruthlessness and heartlessness. The whole paradigm is a reflection of the Left's callous disregard for the victims of jihad and sharia, victims who include Muslims, such as Muslim girls and women who suffer immensely under Islamic gender apartheid, where they are afflicted by every barbarity from female genital mutilation to forced marriage, forced veiling, and forced segregation.[52] Mantras such as *not all Muslims do that!* do absolutely nothing to defend these victims—or future victims. And they do absolutely nothing to protect the world from Islamic jihad and stealth jihad. To the contrary, they enable our enemy.

Now that we have understood the nature and agenda of Jihad Denial, we move on to demonstrate how it manifests itself and spawns an environment that invariably turns a blind eye to the connection between Islam and Islamic terrorist attacks. The next chapter unveils real-life stories about a civilization that is under attack by Islam, while it simultaneously engages in suicide by seeing no Islam at all.

CHAPTER 6

SEE NO ISLAM, HEAR NO ISLAM

At roughly 10:00 p.m. on Saturday night, June 2, 2017, a white van plowed into a group of pedestrians on the London Bridge in London, United Kingdom. Three men then immediately jumped out of the vehicle and began stabbing civilians, while screaming "This is for Allah!", "This is for Islam!", and "Stop living this life!"[1] The assailants murdered seven people and injured roughly forty-eight—before they themselves were killed by police.[2]

One of the jihadists who perpetrated this mayhem had been influenced by the Islamic teachings of Sheikh Ahmad Musa Jibril, a Palestinian Muslim cleric in Dearborn, Michigan, who has a degree in sharia law from the Islamic University in Saudi Arabia and is popular with al-Qaeda and ISIS jihadists.[3] Jibril, in turn, was inspired by Salman al-Awdah, a Saudi sheikh who was greatly admired by Osama bin Laden. Jibril's internet website told Muslims that their "heart must contain nothing but HATE to all kafers [non-Muslims]...Not just plain hate it must be the peak of hate," and "Give them a knife and a bulletful of gun."[4]

The ring leader of the trio who murdered the pedestrians on the London Bridge, Khuram Butt was featured in a documentary about jihadis in Britain, where he was shown unfurling an Islamic

State flag in a park. He had also been reported twice to police for "extremism."[5] But while counter-jihad activists Robert Spencer and Pamela Geller had been banned from Britain for supporting Israel,[6] Butt was free to roam the streets of the UK until he embarked on his murderous killing spree for Allah.

When Western leaders and the establishment media beheld the jihadist bloodbath on the London Bridge, the Islamic nature of the crime somehow eluded them. British Prime Minister Theresa May represented this disposition well, coming out with tough talk that had no substance behind it. She blustered that "enough is enough," that there was "far too much tolerance of extremism in our country," and that "when it comes to taking on extremism and terrorism, things need to change." How they were going to change exactly remained a bit mysterious, however, since the prime minister also pleaded for everyone to understand that the ideology that had inspired the London Bridge attackers and other Islamic terrorists was "a perversion of Islam."[7]

Across the ocean in America, MSNBC anchor Richard Lui also had a hard time detecting any trace of Islam in the London Bridge jihad. He was far more worried about much more serious things, such as the "risk of overreaction" by British authorities responding to the jihadists' murders.[8] U.S. "moderate" Muslim Reza Aslan, meanwhile, also had bigger priorities than to ruminate about why the jihadists on the London Bridge were referring to Islam during the commission of their atrocities. In Aslan's mind, President Donald Trump was the real problem to be addressed, since he had responded to the terrorist mayhem by stressing the importance of resisting jihad. This step by the leader of the Free World was simply over the line for Aslan, who then tweeted out that Trump was a "piece of s**t."[9] Notably, Aslan had never used such strong language to denounce Islamic jihad mass murderers themselves.[10] It was only an American president who wanted to resist the jihadists that warranted this reaction from Aslan. And that is why Aslan had additional things to say about the U.S. president, calling him an "embarrassment to America," a "stain on the presidency," and an "embarrassment to humankind."[11]

Eleven days earlier, on the evening of May 22, a jihad massacre hit an Ariana Grande concert in Manchester, killing twenty-two people and injuring approximately forty-eight. A suicide bomber, twenty-three-year-old Salman Abedi, detonated an improvised explosive device at the end of the concert, causing mayhem among the twenty thousand fans flooding out of the arena.[12] It was the deadliest terror attack in Britain since the July 7, 2005, suicide bombings in London that had killed fifty-two people and injured more than seven hundred.[13]

Shortly after the bombing, the Islamic State took responsibility for the attack, boasting that a "soldier of the Khilafah [caliphate]" had carried it out.[14] That "soldier," Salman Abedi, was known to British authorities as a terror threat, and had been in touch with a recruiter for the Islamic State.[15] He had been described by his friends as a "devout" Muslim who had memorized the entire Qur'an. His parents had emigrated from Libya and his father was a pillar of the mosque the family attended.[16]

When it came time for Western leadership and the establishment media to comment on what had happened in Manchester, however, they somehow couldn't hear or see Islam anywhere. Theresa May was her usual self, full of baffled confusion, stating: "We struggle to comprehend the warped and twisted mind that sees a room packed with young children not as a scene to cherish but an opportunity for carnage."[17] Germany's Chancellor Angela Merkel was also rendered clueless, announcing: "It is unbelievable that somebody has used a joyful pop concert to kill or seriously injure so many people."[18] Why any leaders of nations would be incapable of comprehending what had occurred, or would find it unbelievable, was baffling in itself, given that even a beginner's course in world history would quickly make one aware that totalitarian death cults—such as Islam, Nazism, and communism—are saturated with the tradition of infanticide, practicing child sacrifice regularly and with relish.[19] There was really nothing hard to believe about what happened in Manchester.

Nonetheless, across the Atlantic, the *New York Times* was also very confused, struggling to figure out what could have possibly led Abedi to do what he did. "No one yet knows," its editorial asserted, "what motivated him to commit such a horrific deed."[20] A quick call to a few scholars of Islam not infected by Jihad Denial would have cleared up the mystery quite quickly. But no such calls were apparently made by the writers of the *New York Times* editorial. The UK's *Independent* also shared the *Times'* disorientation, but it made sure to take the extra step of advising that nothing be done to stop the jihad terror. "We're not actually equipped to do that much at all," writer Andrew Buncombe wrote, "other than to try to carry on, to not allow ourselves to be terrorized, to stop living our lives."[21] Robert Spencer responded to Buncombe's sentiment by pointing out that, well, there was actually "plenty that we can do. We can stop lying to ourselves and to each other about what is happening and why."[22] Buncombe issued no response to Spencer's suggestion.

The mayor of Greater Manchester, Andy Burnham, also jumped on the Jihad Denial bandwagon, adamantly professing that the suicide bomber who had attacked Ariana Grande's concert did not represent Muslims. In fact, Burnham insisted, *Abedi wasn't even a Muslim.*[23] Abedi would have probably been a bit perplexed by this characterization of himself if he had heard it before he blew himself up, just as all of his friends who considered him a devout Muslim were undoubtedly confused when they heard of Burnham's explanation. Robert Spencer cut to the core of Burnham's mindset:

Any Muslim who commits an act of violent jihad becomes, simply by virtue of doing so, not a Muslim. Islam is thus always preserved as good and benign, no matter what crimes are committed in its name, and politicians such as Andy Burnham are free of any responsibility to understand the motives and goals of those who have vowed to destroy us.[24]

It was true: In the eyes of British politicians and the establishment media, the motives and goals of jihadists like Abedi were not the important issue. The real issue was the "backlash" that could happen against Muslims *after* a jihadist attack. And so Muslims became the real victims after the Manchester terror, as they do after every Islamic terror attack. That's why *Newsweek* and ABC News both decided that the most important angle to stress in covering the Manchester terror was not the Islamic doctrine that motivated the suicide bomber but the potential "anti-Islamic backlash" to what Abedi did.[25]

Thus, after Manchester, the priority—even for the police—was not to crystallize the terror and what caused it, but to *not call the terror by its name* and, most urgently, to call for "diversity" and to oppose "hatred." This is why Greater Manchester chief constable Ian Hopkins described what happened as a "despicable act" rather than as terrorism, and emphasized that:

We understand that feelings are very raw right now and people are bound to be looking for answers. However, now, more than ever, it is vital that our diverse communities in Greater Manchester stand together and do not tolerate hate.[26]

The hate Hopkins referred to was, obviously, not the Islamic hatred for the unbeliever, mandated by Islamic texts,[27] that drove Abedi to do what he did. No, the hate was Islamophobia.[28]

The Islam that couldn't be detected by Jihad Deniers in Manchester on May 22, 2017, and on the London Bridge on June 2, 2017, also couldn't be detected by them six months earlier, on the morning of November 28, 2016, when a Somali refugee and Ohio State University student, Abdul Razak Ali Artan, set off a fire alarm in a building on his campus and then got into his car. As a crowd of students began evacuating the building, Artan drove his vehicle into the students and then jumped out and began stabbing them with a butcher knife. If the London Bridge jihadists had been searching for a jihadist attack to emulate, they had surely found it in Abdul Razak Ali Artan. After having injured eleven students, Artan was shot and killed by campus police before he could succeed in taking anyone's life.

Artan left several clues about what had inspired his jihad by car and knife on the morning of November 28. He had earlier appeared in Ohio State University's newspaper, *The Lantern*, in a feature entitled "Humans of Ohio State," in which he spoke about what a victim he had become, since he was, as he described, "scared" about performing his Islamic prayers in public. For some reason, he had felt that people were nervous about seeing Muslims praying.[29] The cause of that apparent nervousness became quite obvious on November 28.

In a Facebook message that he had posted before the attack, Artan referenced jihad terrorist leader Anwar al-Awlaki while issuing his own expression of how "sick and tired" he was of seeing his "fellow Muslim brothers and sisters being killed and tortured everywhere"—and how he couldn't "take it anymore." America had to stop "interfering with other countries," he insisted, if it wanted "Muslims to stop carrying [out] lone wolf attacks." "By Allah," Artan boasted, "I am willing to kill a billion infidels."[30]

In the context of these inspiring messages, one couldn't help reflecting on the Islamic State's directive to its faithful worldwide to use all sorts of imaginative methods of killing the unbelievers, including slaughtering them with a knife or running them over with a car.[31]

Thus, it appears that Islam just might have had something to do with the journey that Abdul Razak Ali Artan embarked on that Monday morning of November 28, 2016. But that is not how leftists on the Ohio State University campus saw it. In fact, lo and behold, they could detect no Islam at all, no matter where they looked in examining Artan's rampage and pronouncements. Instead, they saw the occasion as a perfect time to reissue yet another call for *gun control*—and they did so at a rally to mark Artan's terror attack.[32] The fact that Artan had used a knife and not a gun didn't seem to make any impression on the student demonstrators. Logic, it appears, just couldn't be permitted to get in the way of a leftist crusade.

Leftist students also used the occasion to *blame the police* and to hold them culpable for what Artan had done. In another rally that was held in response to the terror attack, activists on campus asserted that Artan was *the actual victim* and that he had been wrongly killed because justice could never "come from a cop's bullet."[33] One of the demonstrators suggested that the greatest misfortune of all was the fact that "right-wing pundits" were exploiting the attack in order to make the case that Columbus, Ohio, was a city awash in "Islamophobia and xenophobia."[34]

Roughly eleven months earlier, a devout Muslim by the name of Edward Archer appeared to be inspired by the same ideas that had moved Abdul Razak Ali Artan to action. On the evening of January 4, 2016, twenty minutes before midnight, dressed in Islamic garb, Archer ambushed Philadelphia police officer Jesse Hartnett in his police car at 60th and Spruce Streets, shooting him three times in the arm with a semiautomatic 9mm pistol—a police-issued firearm that had been stolen from an officer's home in 2013. Though wounded and bleeding heavily, Hartnett not only survived the shots but managed to pursue and shoot Archer in the buttocks as he fled the scene. Archer was apprehended by authorities and subsequently confessed to investigators that: "I follow Allah. I pledge my allegiance to the Islamic state. That is why I did what I did." The Muslim shooter also stressed that he believed that police-enforced laws were illegitimate because they ran contrary to the Qur'an.[35]

It appears that it wasn't only the Qur'an that had inspired Archer to try to kill a police officer. Archer happened to spend quite a bit of time at Masjid Mujahideen, a mosque in west Philadelphia headed by Imam Asim Abdur Rashid. Immediately following Archer's shooting of Hartnett and the subsequent news report that Archer had attended Masjid Mujahideen, Rashid emphatically maintained that he had no idea who Archer was and that he was unaware if Archer had ever been to his mosque. And then, mysteriously, as evidence began to surface revealing that Rashid and Archer were actually *personal friends*—and that, not only had Archer attended Masjid Mujahideen, *but he was actually a devoted regular there*—Imam Rashid suddenly recovered from his bout of amnesia and remembered that, yes, after all, he did know Archer. And lo and behold, he also recalled that Archer had actually attended morning, midday, and evening prayers at his mosque on a regular basis.[36]

The police, meanwhile, received information indicating that Archer was part of a larger terror cell. Curiously, this fact had somehow eluded Imam Rashid. More curious still was the question of how, if Islam was a religion of peace, Archer had missed that peaceful message while reading Islamic texts and listening to the sermons inside Masjid Mujahideen.

While this script of smoke and mirrors played out, some curious developments were transpiring in the "investigation" that political and law-enforcement authorities were conducting into Archer's shooting. In a press conference that took place shortly after the shooting, Democrat Mayor Jim Kenney called Archer a "criminal" and then, out of the blue, surprised everyone with his remarkable—and until then unknown—expertise in Islamic theology. He assured everyone that Archer's actions had *nothing* to do with Islam, emphasizing profusely that:

> In no way, shape, or form does anyone in this room believe that Islam or the teaching of Islam has anything to do with what you've seen on the screen.... It is abhorrent. It is terrible and it does not represent the religion or any of its teachings. This is a criminal with a stolen gun who tried to kill one of our officers. It has nothing to do with being a Muslim or following the Islamic faith.[37]

One couldn't help but wonder, upon listening to Kenney's pronouncement: How exactly did the mayor know what *everyone* at the press conference thought about Islam and its connection to Archer's shooting of Hartnett? Did he have ESP? Had he checked with everyone about the matter beforehand? Was everyone at the conference an expert on Islamic teachings, thereby rendering their opinions highly consequential?

Let us suppose, for a moment, that *almost everyone* in the "room" did, by some strange coincidence, believe what Kenney said they believed. Hypothetically, what if one person there actually thought something different and had articulated his dissent to Kenney? Knowing this, would Kenney have pointed out, during his conference, the dissident opinion in the room—and explained what it was based on? Or let us suppose, conversely, that the dissident didn't exist, and *everyone* really did believe what Kenney said they believed. What if they were wrong? And what if Kenney had been shown evidence, before the press conference, of all the Islamic texts that proved that his view—and supposedly everyone else's—was incorrect? Would he have said the opposite in his statement? And what if everyone else in that room had disagreed with him upon his supposed consultation? Would he have announced that fact but still stuck to his own position? And, perhaps most importantly: Did it matter at all what Archer himself thought about why he shot Officer Hartnett?

One highly significant question that the mainstream media unsurprisingly never even bothered to broach was this: Was the mayor of Philadelphia really some kind of expert on Islam? If he was, where, when, and how did he get his training? And why was it so important for him to emphasize the supposed un-Islamic nature of Archer's shooting—when Archer himself had emphatically verbalized how very Islamic it actually was?

The mindset that had motivated Edward Archer to go on his jihadist expedition in Philadelphia appeared to have something very much in common with what had inspired the devout Muslim husband-and-wife team of Syed Rizwan Farook and Tashfeen Malik a month earlier. On December 2, 2015, Farook and Malik opened fire on Farook's municipal government workmates at a Christmas party in San Bernardino, California. The massacre left fourteen people dead and twenty-one wounded. The couple fled after perpetrating their atrocity but were killed several hours later in a shootout with police.

Before the attack, Malik had used her social media to express her love of ISIS and to pledge her undying devotion to Islamic State leader, Abu Bakr al-Baghdadi. Authorities' investigation into Malik's background soon uncovered her ties to a jihadist mosque in Pakistan. She was, in the words of one of her teachers, "a religious person" who often exhorted people "to live according to the teachings of Islam."[38] Farook, meanwhile, had cultivated relationships with several Muslim terrorist organizations. Days after the attack, the Islamic State's official radio station praised Farook and Malik and described them as "supporters" of their group. When the duo's townhouse in Redlands, California, was searched, authorities found thousands of rounds of ammunition and a dozen pipe bombs.[39] Farook's father, also named Syed, affirmed that his son was an open supporter of the Islamic State and that he (son Syed) hated Israel.[40]

Rafia Farook, Syed's mother, also played an intriguing role in the family. She lived with the couple and just happened to be an active member of the Islamic Circle of North America (ICNA), an organization that openly supports sharia and the caliphate, and has links to the Muslim Brotherhood and to the Pakistani jihad group Jamaat-e-Islami.[41] She was, according to her husband and Farook's father, "very religious" like Farook.[42]

Did this "very religious" Muslim woman know what her son and his wife were up to while living with them? Absolutely not, pleaded David Chesley and Mohammad Abuershaid, two of the Farook family lawyers, who issued a statement declaring that, while Farook's mother resided with the couple, she "stayed upstairs" and was stunned when she found out about what her son and Malik had done, as was the rest of the Farook family. As Chesley stated after the massacre: "None of the family members had any idea that this was going to take place. They were totally shocked."[43]

Did Rafia Farook really not know what was going on and was she really shocked? Robert Spencer asked some pertinent questions regarding this matter:

> Farook's mother didn't notice the twelve pipe bombs and well over 4,500 rounds of ammunition because she "stayed upstairs"? Was she an invalid, then, who never ventured downstairs at all? If so, why did the couple leave their six-month-old daughter in her care when they went off to shoot Infidels for Allah?[44]

Spencer was on to something. As the evidence poured in, it turned out that Rafia Farook had somehow managed to venture downstairs from time to time, and that she may have occasionally bumped into some pipe bombs and rounds of ammunition after all. Curiously enough, FBI agents discovered an empty GoPro package, shooting targets, and tools inside a Lexus that was registered in *her* name.[45] It is worth remembering that Farook and Malik had worn GoPro cameras on their body armor during their shooting spree.[46] Rafia Farook *could also drive* and was pulled over in her son's SUV after the massacre.[47] She could even make it by herself to ICNA meetings.[48]

Despite these facts about the Farook family, all of which were ascertained quite quickly, President Obama responded to the attack in a manner that was to be expected only of an Unholy Alliance leader.[49] First, he ordered federal officials not to publicly link Islam to what Farook and Malik had perpetrated. Second, instead of discussing what had clearly inspired Farook and Malik, he blamed their attack *on guns.* The problem, in Obama's view, was gun ownership in America, and the solution was to have a law passed that would block individuals on the "No Fly List" from legally purchasing firearms—a measure, incidentally, that would violate the Constitution. Attorney General Loretta Lynch, meanwhile, weighed in by threatening to prosecute any Americans who dared to make anti-Islamic statements in response to the San Bernardino massacre.[50]

Because of these boundaries that the Obama administration placed on the range of permissible thoughts, the FBI was initially reluctant to investigate the mosque that Farook had attended. The president went on to state, falsely, that there was no intelligence showing that Farook and Malik had received guidance or money from terrorist groups overseas.[51] The Department of Defense and Special Operations Command's Threat Finance Agency had, in fact, concluded that "Malik and Farook most likely received funding from terrorists abroad." And that is why it "issued alerts to the appropriate banking institutions to flag financial transitions from specific banks accounts."[52]

In his eventual "official" speech on the attack, Obama, unable to deny the evidence any longer, finally admitted that the San Bernardino massacre was terrorism. But he stressed that Farook and Malik were "self-radicalized"—even though the label is a complete myth[53]—and maintained that their attack was not part of a "broader conspiracy." Thus, he denied an ISIS connection and the words "Islam" and "jihad" did not pass his lips. Obama did concede that "an extremist ideology has spread within some Muslim communities," but he claimed that Farook and Malik were only "embracing a perverted interpretation of Islam that calls for war against America and the West."[54] As always, he failed to explain how, exactly, their interpretation was "perverted" and why so many millions of Muslims around the world were drawn to it.

Most disturbingly, it turned out that the Obama administration had actually shut down an investigation that would have almost surely led authorities to Farook and Malik and thereby could have prevented the attack in the first place. Investigator Phil Haney, a former Department of Homeland Security agent, revealed that the government had closed a surveillance program that he had created to identify global networks that were smuggling jihad-friendly Muslims into the United States. The database investigated groups that had ties to Farook and Malik as far back as 2012. But the State Department and the DHS Office for Civil Rights and Civil Liberties believed that Islamophobia was at play and that the "civil rights" of the Muslims under observation were being violated, even though an overwhelming majority of them were not even American citizens. In any case, the administration officials accused Haney of profiling Muslims, removed his security clearance, and terminated his program, destroying all sixty-seven records of information that he had gathered. One of those records included an investigation into an organization with ties to the Riverside, California, mosque that Farook had attended.[55]

Haney himself emphasized that if his work had been allowed to continue, it could very well have prevented the San Bernardino massacre. He affirmed that,

> Either Syed would have been put on the no-fly list because association with that mosque, and/or the K-1 visa that his wife was given may have been denied because of his association with a known organization.[56]

Haney also stated that he was looking into Tablighi Jamaat, a Sunni Islamic group tied to the fundamentalist Deobandi movement—a movement that has ties to the Pakistani school attended by Malik.[57] An investigation into that school would eventually have turned up Malik's name, which subsequently would have been entered into the proper databases.

A neighbor of Farook and Malik, meanwhile, had observed very suspicious activity at their apartment, but the fear of being called a "racist" kept him silent.[58] This tragedy evokes the memory of a certain young man, Brian Morgenstern, who worked in a Circuit City outlet in New Jersey back in January 2006 and also felt fear when two Muslims approached him in the shop and asked to have a VHS tape transferred to DVD. While carrying out their request, Morgenstern discovered that the tape showed men shooting weapons and shouting "Allahu akbar." He initially thought about calling the police but then hesitated, asking his coworker if his concern about what he had seen was "racist"—even though the Muslims in this case were white Europeans from the former Yugoslavia. Fortunately, the coworker advised Morgenstern to call the police, which he did. It turned out that the Muslims in question were plotting a jihad mass murder attack at Fort Dix, and the jihadist plot was foiled.[59]

Brian Morgenstern's initial hesitation was a sign of something afoot in America, a certain pressure that was in the air—a pressure connected to the leftist student demonstrators on the Ohio campus who just couldn't see Islam in Abdul Razak Ali Artan's jihad-by-car-and-knife expedition, and to President Obama's delusional claims about the un-Islamic nature of the San Bernardino massacre. This work has crystallized what this pressure is and from where it emanates. It is a pressure that, catastrophically, Farook's and Malik's neighbor could not overcome. It is a pressure to which many other Americans are surrendering, thanks to the Unholy Alliance's successful imposition of a Jihad Denial framework that paints all concern about jihad as Islamophobia, racism, and bigotry.[60]

The "pressure in the air" in the Farook-Malik case also had a great deal to do with the fact that the husband-wife jihad team, despite all the evidence of their nefarious connections and views, had *never* been questioned or put under any kind of surveillance or on any watch list.[61] Malik, a Pakistani national who had lived for years in Saudi Arabia, actually passed *three* background checks by U.S. immigration officials when she moved to the United States from Pakistan. None of the checks had discovered that she had written *openly and extensively* on her public social media accounts about her ardent desire to wage jihad and to achieve martyrdom in the name of Islam. The discovery was not made because, during that time period, *immigration officials were forbidden* to review social media as part of their screening process. The Obama administration had banned any examination of the social media posts of immigration applicants. John Cohen, a former acting undersecretary at DHS for intelligence and analysis, explained that this rule was in place because of the fear of a "civil liberties" backlash and "bad public relations" for the Obama administration.[62]

Thus, Tashfeen Malik was granted her green card in July 2015. It also turns out that her visa was improperly approved. The U.S. allowed her an entry visa even though *she never provided the extra evidence requested by an immigration official*. This occurred because, as House Judiciary Committee chairman Bob Goodlatte pointed out, the Obama administration refused "to take the steps necessary" for a more thorough vetting.[63]

This whole disastrous mentality of political correctness, as we know, has been observable in the events surrounding every jihadist attack in the United States and the West. The facilitation of terror and the subsequent denial of the terror itself all transpired, for instance, in exactly the same manner in the jihadist attacks in Chattanooga on July 16, 2015,[64] at the Boston Marathon on April 15, 2013,[65] and in Fort Hood on November 5, 2009.[66]

This whole *See No Islam/Hear No Islam* mass psychosis is now the standard in America and the West. It faithfully follows the pattern of the surreal press conference given by Philadelphia mayor Jim Kenney on the evening of January 4, 2016, that we documented above. Kenney pleaded with everyone to believe that Edward Archer was no jihadist, even though Archer insisted that he was—and all of the evidence indicated that Archer was telling the truth.

Commenting on the Kenney/Archer affair, Robert Spencer laid bare the willful blindness that now predominates in our culture:

> Poor Archer! What does he have to do to get taken seriously as a jihadi? If shooting a police officer multiple times and pledging allegiance to the Islamic State, which has called on Muslims in the U.S. to attack police officers, won't do it, what will?[67]

Spencer has asked the crucial and painful questions. What will indeed convince the West's leaders and the establishment media that Islam might have something to do with Islamic terrorism? As we have explained thus far, and as we will continue to demonstrate in the pages ahead, with the Unholy Alliance in control of our culture, we can only expect more of the same—and the body count of unbelievers will continue to mount as the West's surrender to Islamic supremacism continues.

The *See No Islam/Hear No Islam* virus is now in complete control of our society. The situation has become so bad that even sharia law can no longer be criticized in the West without repercussions. If you have a problem with sharia, you are deemed a racist.[68] What happened to Ben Carson during his 2016 GOP presidential campaign serves as a clear example of this phenomenon. When he dared to state that sharia law was not compatible with the U.S. Constitution, Carson became the target of hysterical denunciation and slander from the establishment media and from many public figures—including even GOP presidential candidates. The attacks on Carson were only to be expected, of course, since he had violated the tenets of Jihad Denial, and such a violation was now considered a thought crime. We will examine this important case at greater length in our next chapter, for it crystallizes the extent to which the Unholy Alliance and Jihad Denial have constricted the boundaries of discourse in order to achieve their malicious objectives.

CHAPTER 7

BEN CARSON'S SHARIA THOUGHT CRIME

On Sunday, September 20, 2015, GOP presidential candidate Ben Carson appeared on NBC's *Meet the Press* and affirmed that because sharia law was incompatible with the U.S. Constitution, he personally would not support a Muslim in the role of U.S. president. Later that evening, in an interview with *The Hill*, Carson followed up by stating that he would make an exception for a Muslim who had "publicly rejected all the tenets of sharia and lived a life consistent with that."[1]

In reality, there was nothing controversial about what Carson had said. Sharia is one of the most barbaric and totalitarian systems on earth—and reserves its greatest cruelty for women.[2] The problem, of course, was that Carson's statements were spoken in a culture that is now controlled by the Unholy Alliance,[3] which, in turn, regulates the boundaries of permitted discourse in that culture.[4] And since the Unholy Alliance's sacred cow is Jihad Denial,[5] and sharia mandates jihad, while jihad's primary purpose is to establish worldwide sharia,[6] a public outcry against Carson ensued quite predictably. Within the blink of an eye, the usual suspects stepped forward and dutifully denounced Carson, painting him as a racist (even though he is black), bigot, and Islamophobe.

The establishment media, for example, got to work quickly. Paul Waldman led the way with a piece in the *Washington Post*, labeling Carson's comments as "extreme and unsettling" and as representing an "Islamophobic" epidemic that sought to install "Christian supremacy."[7] CNN also faithfully fulfilled its Unholy Alliance obligations, with anchor Anderson Cooper inviting Reza Aslan, a "moderate" Muslim, onto his show to portray Carson as a racist. Aslan affirmed how "natural" it was for Carson to speak this way, since "xenophobia" and "Muslim bashing" are, in Aslan's view, rewarded by GOP voters.[8]

The *Washington Post* went an extra lap to prove its Unholy Alliance credentials, taking issue with a reference Carson had made to "taqiyya" during his discussion of sharia. *Taqiyya* is an Islamic term for the notion that Muslims are morally justified in lying to unbelievers in order to deceive them—and Carson had accurately explained what *taqiyya* was.[9] The *Post* quickly approached Islamic apologists to whitewash *taqiyya*, which the apologists did by *lying about it*. In other words, the *Post* encouraged Islamic deceivers to engage in *taqiyya* about *taqiyya* in order to slander Carson.[10]

The *Huffington Post*, meanwhile, ran a hit piece titled "Ben Carson Walks Back Anti-Muslim Comments with More Anti-Muslim Comments," which was full of predictable smears and implied that Carson uniformly hated all Muslims. This was clearly the Unholy Alliance's *conflation* tactic at work, which, as explained in Chapter 5, disingenuously blurs Islam with all Muslim people for the purpose of slandering those who tell the truth about Islam as haters of Muslims.[11] The reality in this case, of course, was that Carson had never made any anti-Muslim comments at all, since he was talking about an ideology and its adherents, *not about all*

Muslim people. He had also never "walked back" anything; he had simply followed up on his earlier statements by explaining his legitimate concern about a totalitarian belief system that is incompatible with the American Constitution.[12]

Sen. Harry Reid (D-NV), like most of his Democrat colleagues, did not seem too interested in the technicalities of sharia law during this controversy. Instead of reflecting on the pain and anguish that sharia has brought, and continues to bring, to hundreds of millions of people around the world, Reid called Carson's remarks "disgusting" and stated that "shameful intolerance and bigotry should have no place here."[13] Some GOP presidential candidates—including Ted Cruz, Carly Fiorina, Marco Rubio, and Jeb Bush—also took shots at Carson.[14] Former New York governor George Pataki jumped aboard the defend-sharia bandwagon as well, comparing Carson's statement to anti-Catholic campaigning against John F. Kennedy in 1960.[15]

The vicious and defamatory reactions of the establishment media and politicians to Carson's truth-telling about sharia were so widespread that talk radio host Mark Levin came out denouncing them, stating that there should be a backlash from Americans.[16] Carson was, of course, completely correct in asserting that Islamic law is incompatible with the U.S. Constitution. To be sure, sharia infringes on myriad freedoms through its mandate of theocracy, including the freedom of speech and women's freedom. Sharia also commands the Muslim faithful to regard non-Muslims as inferior.[17] In Islam, as opposed to the Declaration of Independence, all men are *not* created equal. The Qur'an describes Muslims as "the best of people," and they are considered to be decidedly superior to non-Muslims.[18] Muslims are expected to emulate Muhammad and pattern their lives after his, since he is their example. As author William Kilpatrick notes,

The imitation of Muhammad leads to unequal treatment of believers and non-believers, to child brides, polygamy, wife beating, stoning for adulterers, the murder of apostates, and various other, shall we say, un-American activities.[19]

Slavery, under Islamic law, is also legal, which explains why Islamic slavery continues to be practiced in Africa *to* this day.[20]

One would think that Carson's critics would have felt obligated to face these facts and to demonstrate how, in their view, sharia was compatible with the Constitution.[21] But with the Unholy Alliance in charge, the critics and slanderers of Carson were not held accountable for their statements by the establishment media.

It was telling that Carson's denouncers spent zero time discussing or criticizing the Muslim leaders who themselves consistently emphasize that Islam and democracy are incompatible.[22] Also, intriguingly enough, the Muslim Brotherhood cast itself as the "voice of reason" against Carson. The Council on American-Islamic Relations (CAIR), for instance, demanded that Carson withdraw from the presidential race because of his statement. A Muslim Brotherhood front group that is linked to Hamas and has been designated a terror organization by the United Arab Emirates, CAIR was an unindicted coconspirator in the Holy Land Foundation terrorism-financing trial in 2007–2008. More than a dozen of its leaders have either been convicted of, or investigated for, involvement in terrorist activity.[23] But the organization was highly respected by the Obama administration and, therefore, claimed the moral high ground in condemning Carson. "I think his remarks should be repudiated by everyone on the political spectrum and that he should withdraw," Ibrahim Hooper, one of CAIR's leading spokesmen, told the *Washington Examiner*.[24]

It would do well to note that Hooper himself has affirmed that he would ideally support replacing the U.S. Constitution with sharia.[25] "I wouldn't want to create the impression that I wouldn't like the government of the United States to be Islamic sometime in the future," he told the Minneapolis *Star Tribune* in a 1993 interview. Ten years later, in 2003, Hooper stated that if Muslims were ever to become a numerical majority in the U.S., they would likely seek to replace the Constitution with Islamic law (sharia), which they view as divinely inspired and thus superior to all other legal systems.[26]

Meanwhile, Huma Abedin, Hillary Clinton's infamous right-hand assistant at the time, attacked Carson on Twitter, stating: "You can be a proud American, a proud Muslim, and proudly serve this great country. Pride versus prejudice."[27] This tweet came from an individual who has extensive connections to the Muslim Brotherhood, the wellspring of numerous Islamic terrorist organizations.[28] But the establishment media, of course, has never focused on these connections, nor did it call Abedin out on them after her tweet. Neither has the establishment media ever focused on Abedin's mother, Saleha Abedin, who is the director of a Muslim Brotherhood group that advocates the implementation of strict sharia law and opposes Egyptian statutes that currently ban marital rape, female genital mutilation, and child marriage.[29] Thanks to the success of Jihad Denial, daring to question Huma's mother about her views, or to ask Huma Abedin about *her thoughts* regarding her mother's views, is now considered racist and Islamophobic.

The Carson-sharia saga demonstrated that if an individual in our contemporary culture has a problem with sharia law, he is routinely smeared as a hater and a bigot. This phenomenon was on full display in early June 2017 when "March Against Sharia" rallies were held across North America and *they were confronted* by counter-protests that were equal in size or even larger. The pro-sharia activists hollered with moral indignation and called the anti-sharia demonstrators "racist" and "Islamophobic."[30] The magazine

Teen Vogue represented the leftist disposition well by labeling the counter-protests as "hate speech."[31]

Now that we have demonstrated how Jihad Denial successfully shuts down any truth-telling about sharia, we shall move forward to tell another crucial part of our story: how the success of Jihad Denial is connected to a strong and fundamental human instinct that our enemies discern and maliciously use against us. This is the instinct that leads people to delude themselves when they are under siege by a threat over which they have little or no control. This work follows the lead of author Bill Siegel in calling this instinct the *Control Factor*, which is the title Siegel chose for his book on the subject.[32] The Control Factor is directly connected to our surrender in the terror war because it molds many people's desperate need to embrace Jihad Denial as a way of psychologically coping in the hopeless situation they find themselves in—*and have often put themselves in.*

It is vital that we understand the Control Factor and how exactly it works, since the Jihadist Psychopath, who will soon make a grand appearance in our story, studies it very meticulously for the purpose of exploiting it and using it against us. This is a crucial dynamic for us to grasp if we are to fully comprehend the reasons for the West's surrender to the Jihadist Psychopath. We therefore explore the Control Factor in our next chapter.

CHAPTER 8

THE CONTROL FACTOR— AND THE CON

Humans can go to incredible lengths to deceive themselves—especially in situations where they face grave danger and, moreover, where they have no control over that danger. In such scenarios, many people trick themselves into believing that they are *part of the script*—that they are, in other words, somehow influential in what their haters think and that they can therefore minimize the danger they face, when in fact they can do no such thing. But these individuals' self-deception consoles them, just as it disarms them in the face of the enemy and prevents them from taking the actual actions that could protect them from the threat confronting them.

Author Bill Siegel labels this dynamic in the context of our terror war as "the Control Factor," which is the title of his book analyzing the issue.[1] He demonstrates that this factor is the element in humans' psychology that induces them to deceive themselves in certain dangerous situations, and that it is precisely this element that is today causing the West to embrace Jihad Denial and, by logical extension, its own surrender. Siegel documents how our culture, media, and political elites are voluntarily fooling themselves into believing that they are somehow part of the script in terms of how Islam views us, when, in fact, they are not part of the script at all. But because they cannot tolerate the notion that the situation is out of their control, they convince themselves that they are in control.

This phenomenon is related to Stockholm syndrome—the psychological condition in which captives feel and express empathy and sympathy toward their captors and abusers, often to the point of defending and identifying with them.[2] Siegel shows how this syndrome works in the context of Jihad Denial, where many people are simply unable to accept the truth about Islam and the threat it represents because of their own emotional and psychological incapacity. It is too depressing and frightening for them to acknowledge what Islam really is and the threat that it actually poses.

The people who embrace the Control Factor are primarily on the Left and they come in two basic varieties. The first variety, which we will label "Type I," are the leftists who willfully embrace Jihad Denial because they are completely aware of what their membership in the Unholy Alliance entails.[3] They seek to utilize Jihad Denial to aid and abet Islamic supremacists' agenda to destroy the West, since it serves their own desire to destroy their host society and to build their vision of a classless utopia on its ashes.[4] The second variety, which we will call "Type II," are the leftists who are relatively uncertain about the malice and destruction behind the Unholy Alliance's agenda, but they support it, and allow the Control Factor to shape their thoughts and behavior, because they cannot accept certain basic truths about the human condition and the threat that Islam poses. Too much knowledge about Islam will shatter the fairy-tale world that they need to believe in and will undermine their faith in the utopia that they think they—and/or their leaders—are building.

Thus, when Type II leftists are confronted, for instance, by the truth about the threat posed by Muslim refugees within the reality of *Hijrah* (jihad by immigration),[5] it completely threatens their belief in the possibility of human progress and the creation of a society where perfect equality and uniformity of thought reign. Consequently, these leftists must deny this reality about the refugees and they allow the Control Factor to rule their psyche. This facilitates their embrace of Jihad Denial and convinces them that the Muslim refugees just need hugs and jobs and then everything will be all right.[6]

It becomes clear, therefore, that for Type II leftists and for a large percentage of people overall, it is simply unbearable to acknowledge the threat posed by Islam for what it really is. To confront the reality that jihadists simply hate non-Muslims and want to subjugate and/or kill them because of what Islamic texts say—and that there is nothing one can do to change their minds—is too agonizing for many people to accept. It is too horrifying for them to reconcile themselves with the powerless feeling they experience when confronted with this fact and with its resultant implication that *they cannot change Islam,* nor the dire situation it presents to unbelievers. And so the Control Factor comes to the rescue and takes away their feelings of despair and incapacity, offering them the Jihad Denial that will provide a soothing—and yet temporary—tranquilizer.

Siegel documents how the West has become engulfed by the Control Factor, and reveals the mental gymnastics it is now engaging in to delude itself from the threat we face. The Control Factor, Siegel explains, is "that effort our minds engage in order to keep us blind." In so doing, Siegel notes, "we falsely convince ourselves that we are in control of a battle that is rapidly getting beyond our control."[7] He points out that:

81

> It is that creative part of our minds that actively and continu-
> ously seeks to assure us that the threat we feel, see, hear, and
> think about is largely under our control, when it in reality is not.[8]

The Control Factor greatly facilitates the Unholy Alliance's quest to impose Jihad Denial onto the culture and into people's consciousness. There is a vicious cycle at work in this process: the Unholy Alliance willfully nurtures and exploits the Control Factor, and the multitudes who are brainwashed and enslaved by it help the Unholy Alliance to increase its power. This, in turn, continues to feed the influence of the Control Factor.

What is happening in this cycle involves the phenomenon of human gullibility and people's need to believe in the myths fed to them by their deceivers—and, in this case, to their own detriment. This dynamic also involves another powerful human trait: the deep-rooted need in many people to believe in the good nature of others. It is precisely this need that often places people in great peril. It is crucial that we elaborate here upon this facet of the human condition, because it is central to our story of how the Jihadist Psychopath is deceiving and steering us toward our own suicide.

In her book *The Confidence Game: Why We Fall for It...Every Time*, Maria Konnikova masterfully analyzes and documents the phenomenon of the art of *the scam* and delineates the dynamic of deceiving and being deceived.[9] Though Konnikova's book does not deal with jihad, the terror war, or anything connected to the Jihadist Psychopath, her analysis of *the scam* very much sheds light on our narrative about the relationship between the Jihadist Psychopath and the unbelievers he is deceiving and conquering.

Konnikova shows how humans are hardwired to believe *what they wish to be true*, and how this leads them into the trap of con artists who shrewdly perceive and exploit this yearning in their victims. She illuminates people's vulnerability to deception and explains why so many of them fall into the hands of tricksters. And she unveils the scary codependent relationship between the con artist and the victim, emphasizing a particularly profound truth:

> The truth of our absolute and total need for belief from our earliest moments of consciousness, from an infant's unwavering knowledge that she will be fed and comforted to an adult's need to see some sort of justice and fairness in the surrounding world.[10]

This disposition, Konnikova explains, makes things very easy for the con artists in our midst, because,

> We've done most of the work for them; we want to believe in what they they're telling us. Their genius lies in figuring out what, precisely, it is we want, and how they can present themselves as the perfect vehicle for delivering on that desire.[11]

Thus, there is a cooperation—and a form of courtship—between the perpetrator and his victim.

Konnikova elaborates:

> The true con artist doesn't force us to do anything; he makes us complicit in our own undoing. He doesn't steal. We give. He doesn't have to threaten us. We supply the story ourselves. We believe because we want to, not because anyone has made us. And so we offer up whatever they want—money, reputation, trust, fame legitimacy, support—and we don't realize what is happening until it is too late. Our need to believe, to embrace things that explain our world, is as pervasive as it is strong.[12]

Here, Konnikova's words resonate powerfully for us, since they relate directly to our own narrative in the context of the Jihadist Psychopath, to whom we are giving up our freedom, security, and civilization with full complicity. To be sure, as we will demonstrate in the following chapters, Konnikova's description of the con game is the mirror image of the Jihadist Psychopath's relationship with his prey. The dynamic is also directly connected to the deadly history of the fellow travelers who made pilgrimages to communist hells. They searched eagerly for utopian paradise, and their communist hosts fooled them with phony Potemkin villages[13]—which the fellow travelers looked upon with awe in their desperation to be deceived.[14] Konnikova writes:

> Con artists, at their best and worst, give us meaning. We fall for them because it would make our lives better if the reality they proposed were indeed true. They give us a sense of purpose, of value, of direction.... Ultimately what a confidence artist sells is hope.[15]

Just as Konnikova explains how the con artist knows exactly whom he can deceive, so too—as we shall reveal in the following pages—the Jihadist Psychopath *knows exactly* who are the unbelievers he can persuade to participate in their own self-destruction. As Konnikova notes, it's what the grifters (the con artists) "are particularly good at: looking at a sea of faces and finding the one who, at this point in time, would be the perfect mark. It's the first step of the confidence game, the put up..."[16]

In the following chapters, we will demonstrate how the Jihadist Psychopath knows exactly how to play this game, and *with whom*—and how he is well aware that many of his victims will enthusiastically participate in their own demise. This is precisely why the Muslim Brotherhood boasted in its infamous internal document, the *Explanatory Memorandum*, that it will destroy our civilization from within *by our own hands*.[17]

It is crucial to emphasize that many victims in the con game possess a tremendous narcissism, since in needing to believe that they are part of the script and can *actually change it*, they incubate a pathological and self-destructive ego. Author Shelby Steele has identified this form of narcissism in the context of *selfish white guilt* in American race relations. Pointing to the narcissism behind victim status and the white leftist's embrace of it, Steele notes: "Selfish white guilt is really self-importance. It has no humility and it asks for an unreasonable, egotistical innocence."[18] Steele's analysis helps shed light on our subject, for it crystallizes leftists' willful blindness toward the jihadist threat and how it is molded by their desire to see themselves, and feel *about themselves*, in a certain way.

It becomes evident, therefore, that leftists view themselves as being important and powerful enough to change the world. In the context of Islamic supremacism, they actually believe that their own utopian fantasies can transform not only Islamic doctrine but also how Muslims interpret it. At the same time, they want to see themselves as open-minded, cool, and "good people." The dominant leftist culture has indoctrinated them to believe that the only way they can be those things is to not be racist—*and that seeing Islam in Islamic terrorism makes you racist.*[19] Thus, consumed with their self-centeredness—and craving the material and cultural rewards of being "good" in a leftist culture—these individuals choose *the road more traveled by*: Jihad Denial. It's clearly the most convenient and safest card for them to play.

Thus, while the Unholy Alliance is so obviously malicious in its destructive agenda, it also inhabits, as noted above, a component of "brain dead" (Type II) leftists who simply want to avoid being called "racist" and who yearn to be "on board" with the crusade for "social justice" and "equality." They are desperate to ingratiate themselves with the leftists who shape the permitted boundaries of discourse, and they dread the prospect of being ostracized and punished for thought crimes.[20] They don't know anything about Islam and they don't want to know anything about it. They only want to belong to the Left and to feel good about themselves. As author Daniel Greenfield puts it: "The liberal defenders of Islam have chosen not to read the Koran. They know next to nothing about Islam except that it's a minority group. And that's how they like it."[21]

Consequently, we see how the reality of the jihadist threat is simply too much for leftists—and for many people in general—to bear. To preserve their own emotional equilibrium and their own self-perception as "good" people, the individuals who comprise this large segment of society allow the Control Factor to dominate their worldview. And so they embrace and dutifully regurgitate all the different variants of Jihad Denial arguments that are offered to them by the Unholy Alliance, which knows all too well the lies they so desperately need to be fed.[22]

Now that we have laid the groundwork for understanding the Control Factor and the con game transpiring between Islamic supremacism and its non-Muslim victims, the Jihadist Psychopath and his modus operandi enters our tale. In the next chapters, we will immerse ourselves in the world of the psychopath. We will lay bare his psychology and outline how he utilizes his charm and deception to ensnare and devour his victims. In so doing, we will also illuminate the disposition of the psychopath's victims, as we demonstrate how they are often complicit in their own abuse and enslavement. This sets the stage for us to explore and understand the Jihadist Psychopath himself, and how he is successfully persuading the West to commit suicide—as he hands it the noose which it is now willingly wrapping and tightening around its own neck.

PART 2

Dancing with the Jihadist Psychopath

CHAPTER 9

PSYCHOPATH

A psychopath seeks to destroy and conquer. He is spiritually empty inside and needs to steal the life force of others to sustain himself. He is an energy bloodsucker. His strategy is ruthless, cunning, and wise. He charms, deceives, and manipulates—and when he gauges that the moment is right, he entraps and devours his prey.

In this chapter, we will unveil the world of the psychopath, and as we lay bare his impulses and tactics, it will become transparently clear that it is a carbon copy of what Islamic supremacism is currently perpetrating against America and the Western world.

First, we must make note about our term *psychopath*. The psychopath is also known as a sociopath, but for our purposes, we call him a psychopath. As psychopathy expert Thomas Sheridan notes, a "compelling reason" to use the term "psychopath"

> "is that most psychopaths—due to their warped egocentric grandiosity—prefer to be called either sociopaths or narcissists because they think these terms may make them seem less insane. Appearances are everything to the psychopath."[1]

On this score, let us take note how important labeling is—and how vital it is for us to call our ideological enemy in the terror war *by his real name*, and not by the name that he and his propagandists want us to call him. Just like we don't want to do the psychopath any favors, nor do we want to make the Islamic supremacist comfortable in any way. We want to tell the truth about the evil that threatens us and *we want to make the truth hurt.*

It is also important for us to stress that while this work's understanding of psychopathy credits the superb work of experts such as Sheridan and others who are mentioned and cited throughout the text, this book's association of Islamic supremacism with psychopathy is made *by this author alone* and it is not discussed by any of the experts referenced here, nor were any such comparisons made by them.

And so we begin:

The psychopath is out to deceive, exploit, and subjugate people. While he is going about his business, he has no shame about it, because he has *no conscience.* He feels no guilt, remorse, affection, or compassion. He does not possess any sense of obligation to others, nor does he grasp what it means to be concerned about other humans' welfare. He is completely "freed from the morality and empathy that shackles the rest of society."[2] At the same time, he is very adept at *pretending that he possesses these traits.* Thus, when a psychopath has intelligence and craft (and this is often the case), he can take control of people and rise to power very easily. Along with his lack of conscience, the psychopath also has no notion of responsibility. He will, therefore, never accept that anything is his fault and, most importantly, he *never apologizes.*[3]

Psychopaths know exactly whom to manipulate and deceive, because they can recognize non-psychopaths—especially the virtuous and gullible ones—quite quickly. As Stout writes,

> the shameless know us much better than we know them. We have an extremely hard time seeing that a person has no conscience, but a person who has no conscience can instantly recognize someone who is decent and good.[4]

Once the psychopath finds his target, his war begins—and the war involves a constant game of deception. His *entry phase* features a calculated and relentless offensive of charm and seduction. He focuses intensely on nurturing a sense of closeness with his victims and indoctrinating them with the belief that *he is acting in their best interests.*[5] He also emphasizes to his targets that *he and they are a lot alike.*[6] Expert on psychopathy Martha Stout explains (she calls it sociopathy):

> When a sociopath identifies someone as a good game piece, she studies that person. She makes it her business to know how that person can be manipulated and used, and, to this end, just how her chosen pawn can be flattered and charmed. In addition, she knows how to promote a sense of familiarity or intimacy by claiming that she and her victim are similar in some way. Victims often recall statements that affected them even after the sociopath was gone, such as, "You know, I think you and I are a lot alike," or "It's so clear to me that you are my soul mate."[7]

These components of the psychopath's charm offensive explain why psychopaths are often experts at faking sincerity. They have to be, since they need *to get in the door* and *stay inside* in order to achieve their purposes. Citing an experiment that studied the psychopath's acting skills, psychopathy expert Kevin Dutton notes that psychopaths were "far more convincing at feigning sadness when presented with a happy image, or happy when looking at a sad image, than were non-psychopaths."[8] This is because psychopaths have, as Dutton affirms, not only "a natural talent for duplicity," but they also feel the "moral pinch" considerably less than others.[9] In one of his studies, Dutton analyzed a psychopath who had joined the British MI5 (the British equivalent of the FBI). One of this individual's colleagues told Dutton that even if this psychopath "had a telephone cord wrapped around your neck, he'd be charming the bloody pants off you." The colleague continued:

"He'd strangle you with his own halo, and then put it put it back on as if nothing had ever happened."[10]

Thus, the deception game the psychopath plays in order to *gain entry* is often extremely successful. Once *he is in*, the takeover begins. The moment the psychopath has a firm grip on his victims, he begins employing a wide variety of shrewd, malicious strategies to entrap them and to make sure they are unable to untangle the web he has woven. He keeps his prey constantly on the defensive—making sure they feel frightened and guilty, and that they find it difficult to think for themselves and take action for their own self-determination. During the psychopath's takeover and ultimate devouring of his victim, the former not only feels absolutely no shame about, nor takes any responsibility for, what he is doing, but *he poses as the victim who needs to be pitied*. That's right, *he* is the loving and caring party who has been *hard done by*, and his victims are the ones who owe him, not only an apology, but the surrender of their very lives to set things right.

To be sure, the psychopath carries out his "pity me" charade with precision, and this gambit effectively disarms his victim. He will especially amplify the crocodile-tears routine in situations where his prey might be onto him and getting ready to confront or leave him. Stout explains,

> Crocodile tears from the remorseless are especially likely when a conscience-bound person gets a little too close to confronting a sociopath with the truth. A sociopath who is about to be cornered by another person will turn suddenly into a piteous weeping figure whom no one, in good conscience, could continue to pressure."[11]

A psychopath plays the pity card because he knows that good people will let him get away with anything *as long as he can get them to feel sorry for him*. Indeed, when people feel sorry for someone, they usually become defenseless vis-à-vis that person.

As Stout observes, "any sociopath wishing to continue with his game, whatever it happens to be, should play repeatedly for none other than pity."[12] This is because, as Stout explains,

> More than admiration—more than even fear—pity from good people is carte blanche. When we pity, we are, at least for the moment, defenseless...our emotional vulnerability when we pity is used against us by those who have no conscience.[13]

As one typical psychopath (whom we quoted in the preface) told Stout in an interview, "What I like better than anything else is when people feel sorry for me. The thing I really want more than anything out of life is people's pity."[14] A powerful example of how the psychopath succeeds in this particular field is when other humans fall in love with him/her. Psychopathy expert Sandra L. Brown demonstrates how the male psychopath, for example, targets the hyper-empathetic woman by playing his "empathy" card to hook her.[15] In other words, he gets her to feel sorry for him. In this way, the psychopath *captures the monopoly on victimhood* in his relationship with his victims. And acquiring victim status garners a person (or an ideological movement) an enormous amount of power in many of the right circumstances.

The psychopath also utilizes his own feigned indignation to deter his victim from zeroing in on him and recognizing his true agenda. As Stout notes, the opposite of the crying tactic comes into play: "Sometimes a cornered sociopath will adopt a posture of righteous indignation and anger in an attempt to scare off her accuser."[16] Along with this indignation will also come *groundless accusations*.[17] This keeps the victim on the defensive and apologetic—while the psychopath's faults and overall goals are whitewashed and ignored.

Throughout this ordeal, to further tighten his grip on his prey, the psychopath unleashes the *unappreciated card*. He is the one who *has done so much*, while others have neither recognized his sacrifices nor *paid him his due*. This tactic explains why the psychopath always has *a tremendous sense of entitlement*. And to validate this whole illusion, he often creates an *invented fake past* so that he can more easily draw pity, appreciation, awe, a sense of debt, and trust from not only his victims, but also from onlookers—many of whom become his victims as well.[18]

The psychopath applies a deadly dual strategy. On the one hand, he plays the *feel sorry for me* tactic; on the other, he inflicts terror into his victims, who become so scared of him that they simply don't dare have any other perspective than to see him as the victim and to defend him to others. They dread the consequences of thinking and acting in any other way. Thus, when the psychopath abuses his victims and engages in other pathologies, his victims usually end up *making numerous excuses* for his behavior and *blaming themselves and others*.

At this point, it is crucial for us to emphasize that many average people become ensnared in the psychopath's web because they assume that the psychopath *is just like them* and has a conscience and similar goals. This is because they need to believe that everyone has the same objectives and that all people have some good in them.[19] They have difficulty accepting—and often cannot accept—that some people do not fit this mold. They therefore project their own worldview onto the worst of people who intend them harm. This is the fertile soil in which the psychopath sows his seeds of psychological manipulation, and it is precisely the environment in which con artists function.

When victims project their own values onto a psychopath, they are engaging in suicidal behavior. Here, it is vital to stress that, when victims engage in this behavior, as we have previously discussed, they are involved in an extreme form of self-centered egoism since they are acting: (1) out of the narcissistic belief that they can change the nature of the threat and be *part of the script*; (2) to maintain their own peace of mind because their emotional incapacity does not allow them to face the harsh reality of the situation they face; and (3) out of fear of losing their identity and belonging in their communities.[20]

Thus, the victims suppress their own concerns and intuition about the very real threat they face. They fall for the psychopath's tricks and get trapped in his cage because they need to believe in their own value system *no matter what*. How they see the world is central to their own narrative about themselves, which often involves *the arrogant delusion that they can change others*. And so, the archetypal victims of the psychopath often have strong traits of narcissism—which ultimately become their own undoing.

Fully cognizant of his prey's narcissism, the psychopath *exploits it*. He knows that his victims often have a strong instinct to remain in denial throughout the entire ordeal of their own destruction by his hands. Along these lines, Mary Stout crystallizes the thought processes of people manipulated by psychopaths:

> Why are conscious-bound human beings so blind? And why are they so hesitant to defend themselves, and the ideals and people they care about, from the minority of human beings who possess no conscience at all? A large part of the answer has to do with the emotions and thought processes that occur in us when we are confronted with sociopathy. We are afraid, and our sense of reality suffers. We think we are imagining things, or exaggerating, or that we ourselves are somehow responsible for the sociopath's behavior.[21]

Throughout this whole ordeal of conquering his prey, the psychopath perfects and strengthens his game by molding and influencing *the view of others*. To be sure, psychopaths are especially preoccupied with controlling how people think and see. As Sheridan notes, "The key thing all psychopaths have in common is power over the perception of others."[22] For the psychopath, there is always a propaganda war at play and he is an expert at it. The average person, meanwhile, is generally not engaged in any propaganda war, nor is he an expert in fighting one, and so this puts him at a severe disadvantage if he is in the crosshairs of a psychopath. One reality that compounds the average person's disadvantage is the fact that he, like most people, very much cares what others think—which the psychopath is constantly shaping. And the average person has the desire to appear innocent.[23]

Now that we have dissected the psychopath's aggression and his success in conquering his victims, we must examine why the psychopath is engaged in this war on others. Yes, in general, we recognize that the phenomenon of evil is an undeniable reality. But we must also stress that the psychopath is dominating and subjugating others, in part, because he is suffering from *attachment disorder*; in most cases, he was deprived of proper bonding and love after birth and in his childhood with his parents.[24] This kind of deprivation experienced by a person often leads to *a nonexistent self* and, therefore, a nonexistent identity that is interwoven with that person's lack of a sense of responsibility and empathy.

What we must highlight here is how this lack of self leads to the psychopath's aggression and his quest to subjugate and conquer others. The dots connect here because *a lack of identity often leads to a need to control, humiliate, and consume others.* Because the psychopath has no inner self, he has to create a self by conquering and devouring the "self" of others. He needs the energy of others to sustain himself because there is an eternal black hole inside of him. Sheridan notes that "psychopaths are never satisfied because all psychopaths have this sense of emptiness inside of them and an insatiable hunger to dominate others."[25] Stout explains that whenever there is a lack of self and identity, and a void in a sense of responsibility and emotional attachment, there is inevitably a need to control people and take over their lives.[26] She writes:

> As a psychologist, I can tell you that the absence of an inter-vening sense of responsibility based in emotional attachment is associated with an endless, usually futile preoccupation with domination, and results in eventual life disruption and eventual deterioration.[27]

This emptiness also explains the complete lack of interest that the psychopath has for things like the arts, history, literature, music, and intimate relations with others. Indeed, anything that represents the beauty, excellence, and joy that most of humankind is quite capable of appreciating sparks zero passion in the psychopath. American physician and expert on psychopathy Hervey Cleckley explains this phenomenon in his book *The Mask of Sanity*, where he analyzes the psychopath's incapacity to feel and appreciate the essence of life the way that normal humans do. In one profound passage, he writes how the psychopath:

> is unfamiliar with the primary facts or data of what might be called personal values and is altogether incapable of under-standing such matters. It is impossible for him to take even a slight interest in the tragedy or joy or the striving of humanity as presented in serious literature or art. He is also indifferent to all these matters in life itself. Beauty and ugliness, except in a very superficial sense, goodness, evil, love, horror, and humor have no actual meaning, no power to move him. He is, further-more, lacking in the ability to see that others are moved. It is as though he were color blind, despite his sharp intelligence, to this aspect of human existence. It cannot be explained to him because there is nothing in his orbit of awareness that can bridge the gap with comparison. He can repeat the words and say glibly that he understands, and there is no way for him to realize that he does not understand.[28]

Dutton refers to this quote by Cleckley, adding that "the psychopath, it's been said, gets the words, but not the music, of emotion."[29]

And so, we have now been able to gauge the psychology of the psychopath—and how he entraps and conquers his victims. For those of us who know a little bit about Islam and jihad, something eerily familiar comes to our minds when we read the text above. Indeed, as we behold the psychopath's mindset and his craft, it becomes quite obvious that the method by which the psychopath imposes his will on his victims is a mirror image of how Islamic supremacism is currently subjugating the West. And so now we move forward to tell that story—the tale of how the Jihadist Psychopath is using all of his psychopathic tactics to charm, seduce, ensnare, and devour a frightened, brainwashed, and surrendering America and Western world.

CHAPTER 10

JIHADIST PSYCHOPATH

Like any psychopath, the Jihadist Psychopath seeks to destroy and conquer. While he is following his religion's mandates, he is spiritually empty inside. He therefore needs to steal the life force of the non-Muslims he victimizes—so he can temporarily sustain himself. His strategy is ruthless and cunning. He charms, deceives, and manipulates—and when he gauges that the moment is right, he entraps his non-Muslim victims and devours them.

To demonstrate how the Jihadist Psychopath is today achieving success in his malicious quest, we will now enter and unveil his morbid world. We encourage our readers to keep the previous chapter handy and to have its key themes in mind, for as we outline the Jihadist Psychopath's main characteristics and his strategy for conquest, it will become clear, element by element, how his agenda is a mirror image of the traditional psychopath's world—only with a Jihadist twist.

In his quest to subjugate non-Muslims, the Jihadist Psychopath has his obvious weapon of violent jihad, but he also has an equally—if not more—powerful weapon in his arsenal: the ploy of deception. It is vital for us to launch our story by examining this tactic, for it serves as the essential foundation for the Jihadist Psychopath's warfare.

Our study of the Jihadist Psychopath's trickery begins with the fact that Islam is, at its very core, a religion/ideology rooted in deception. The God of Islam, who goes by the name of *Allah*, proudly refers to himself as the *greatest deceiver* several times in the Qur'an.[1] If Allah is the father of lies, it becomes understandable why Islam teaches that lying is *an obligation* for Muslims *if it serves the benefit of Islam*. Islamic authorities have even created actual religious doctrines that mandate and justify lying. One of these doctrines is known as *taqiyya*, a principle that allows Muslims to lie to non-Muslims for the sake of subjugating them and empowering Islam.[2] Muslims are also encouraged to break their oaths if doing so will advance the cause of Islamic supremacism.[3] The prophet of Islam, Muhammad, who is considered the ideal model to be emulated by all Muslims,[4] led by perfect example in this department, breaking numerous oaths and treaties, including those he had made with the Jewish tribes known as the Banu Qaynuqa and the Quraysh. Muhammad violated the treaty of Hudaybiyya with the Quraysh, for instance, by refusing to return a woman of the tribe, Umm-Kulthum, back to Mecca.

Allah and Muhammad both laid out examples of deception for their followers to emulate. And while they commanded Muslims to deceive non-Muslims, *they also deceived fellow Muslims themselves*. Indeed, the Islamic paradise that is promised to Muslims if they die while waging holy war against non-Muslims is in itself a deceptive scheme manufactured by Muhammad, in Allah's name, for the sake of luring Muslims into jihad.[5] Islam enforces jihad as an obligatory duty for all Muslims and, not withstanding Islamic supremacists' *taqiyya* about what jihad is really about,[6] *it is meant to be violent*. In Islamic texts, jihad is clearly defined as "war with non-Muslims to establish the religion."[7] As a result, Muslims are tricked and forced into fighting jihad. And not only do they have to kill and die for Allah, but it is highly problematic for them to try to escape this fate, since Muhammad commanded the killing of any Muslim who leaves the religion.[8]

What we have here is a structure in which Muslims are instructed to deceive non-Muslims *while they themselves are deceived*. To compound the pathology of this paradigm, Muslims are also commanded to take control of non-Muslims and to shame them, while Allah controls and shames Muslims themselves in the process.[9] Indeed, Allah is constantly threatening and humiliating not only his enemies, but also *his followers.*[10] Islamic law, after all, has extremely rigid religious rules, which include the mandate of praying and fasting, by which everyone *must* abide. Muslims are accountable to one another in this context, and a perpetual atmosphere of dread and terror hovers around the obligatory following of these rules. In societies that are governed by sharia, for example, a Muslim can easily be sentenced to death if he/she is caught not fasting properly during Ramadan.[11] What we basically have in this paradigm, therefore, as writer Daniel Greenfield points out, "is a hierarchy of deception and oppression with the Muslims being, first and foremost, slaves of Allah."[12] As a result, Muslims are under perpetual pressure to control one another, while their main duty is to wage holy war. The end result is that sharia is imposed on everyone (who isn't murdered), and no individuality or freedom remains.[13] A small loophole is sometimes left for those non-Muslims who refuse to convert but agree to live as second-class "dhimmis," paying taxes and abiding by very strict rules.[14]

Thus, we begin to gauge how humans' highest purpose in Islam is to sacrifice their lives for Allah—whereas conversely, in Christianity, God sacrifices His only son, Jesus, for humans.[15] The scholarship of author Nonie Darwish on this stark contrast between Islam's Allah and the God of the Bible powerfully illuminates the physical and mental slavery in which Islam's followers find themselves trapped. As Darwish documents, the Islamic faith confers absolutely no intrinsic self-worth upon Muslims. That is, Muslims have no "relationship" with Allah, nor any kind of two-way conversation with him. They are not welcome to approach Allah to discuss or confess what is in their hearts and minds. They are not entitled to any freedom of conscience or to use their own powers of reason. On this one-way street, a mean, angry, and sadistic Allah simply tells Muslims what to do and what not to do. Unquestioning obedience to Allah, therefore, under penalty of death and hellfire, is the core message of Islam. In the Bible, by contrast, God is a loving father with whom an individual can have a relationship and personal conversation—and through whom he can find salvation.[16]

These facts are crucial for us to digest in our study of the Jihadist Psychopath because they explain how and why jihadists are like robots that lack any humane or civilized human qualities, including conscience. Jihad is their main mission and, as Darwish reveals, jihad "is the ultimate tool for controlling others."[17] The whole Islamic objective, therefore, is *control*. Greenfield also offers a profound reflection on this phenomenon:

> Islam is fundamentally about power, not an interior life. It's a collective relationship rather than a personal one. Power validates Muslims. Since Islam is spiritually empty, the only validation is power and power is a hollow and unsatisfying validation. The truth of Islam is demonstrated through the Muslim oppression of non-Muslims.[18]

As the Jihadist Psychopath pursues his goal of conquering his victims through deceit, violence, and control, he is also constantly *shaming and blaming* his victims—*as a means of establishing his control*. The Jihadist Psychopath's philosophy is clear: his victims are bad, and he is good. This jihadist mindset emanates directly from Allah's and Muhammad's teachings that *all non-Muslims are sinners*, while *Muslims are not sinners*. In Islam, even if Muslims might sin, *it doesn't matter*—as long as they make up for their transgressions by waging jihad. This reality serves as the fertile soil to the jihadists' monopoly on victimhood, which, in turn, serves as a key gateway for the Jihadist Psychopath's conquering path. We now take a closer look at this dynamic:

In Islam, non-Muslims are seen as evil and perverted trans-gressors. Muhammad made this message very clear by waging war on unbelievers and relentlessly condemning Christians and Jews for rejecting Allah.[19] As Darwish notes:

> Islam is the only religion that dedicates the majority of its scrip-tures not to its own followers but to condemning whole groups of people outside the religion as cursed, doomed, and unfor-given sinners.[20]

To be sure, Islam defines unbelievers as the very worst of people, *the guilty*. Muhammad, meanwhile, as noted above, is seen as the role model of exemplary behavior, and *his followers are inherently innocent*. Islam sees itself as perfect, and it regards Muslims as "the best of people" who are never wrong in any way when persecuting non-Muslims.[21] Moreover, unlike for Jews and Christians in the Bible, to whom confession brings forgiveness, grace, and redemption, confessing sins in Islam *is not a blessing*. This is because, again, Muslims are not seen as sinners in Islamic theology, and if they do sin, *they are not to confess their sins, but to conceal them*.[22] For those Muslims *who are* guilty of wrongdo-ing, there is only one way to be forgiven, and that is to wage war on non-Muslims in jihad.[23] And so, since most Muslims are aware, in their own private conscience, that they are, in various ways, sinners, they know what they have to do about it. Consequently, jihad is really, in the end, all about purifying oneself not only with the blood of others, but also with one's own blood.[24] Algerian militant Ali Benhadj crystallized this central tenet of Islam, which maintains that death and blood purify the earth:

> If faith, a belief, is not watered and irrigated by blood, it does not grow. It does not live. Principles are reinforced by sacrifices, suicide operations and martyrdom for Allah. Faith is propagated by counting up deaths every day, by adding up massacres and charnel-houses. It hardly matters if the person who has been sacrificed is no longer there. He has won.[25]

The reality that emerges in this pathological paradigm is that Muslims are, essentially, taught to bring about the death of the unbelievers, and of themselves, through holy war. And they are instructed to *change others*, not themselves. So when anything goes "wrong," it cannot be the fault of a perfect doctrine acted upon by the best of people, it must be the fault of non-Muslims. When jihad is waged on the non-Muslims, *it is their fault*, because they provoked the war on themselves by being sinners and rejecting Allah.[26] The non-Muslims are always blamed, and Muslims *must never* take responsibility.

Islamic theology provides yet another reason for Muslims to never be held accountable for anything in relation to the non-Muslim: unbelievers' disbelief is regarded as being *worse than murder*. That is, non-Muslims' rebellion against Allah is considered to be a greater transgression than even an act of murder committed against them.[27] *The very existence of non-Muslims* is regarded by Islam as offensive, and as a provocation to justifiable violence.[28] Thus, Islam is, by *its very nature*, a victim. As ex-Muslim writer Abu Kasem has documented, Islamic theology inspires the notion that Islam itself is offended and persecuted by any un-Islamic activities carried out by unbelievers anywhere at any time. He provides numerous examples, from a female unbeliever venturing outdoors without a hijab, to unbelievers drinking alcohol or going to a stage theatre. Anyone doing anything, anywhere, that is against what Allah wants, represents an affront to Islam. Consequently, Islam views itself as the only religion to which every person on earth must submit, and the failure to submit is considered an act of defiance against Islam.[29] And while the Jihadist Psychopath *convinces us that he is the real victim, he must also convince himself.* As Iranian ex-Muslim Ali Sina explains:

> Islam is the religion of permanent victimhood. Victimhood justifies revenge. If you are a Muslim, jihad is prescribed on you against those who oppress you. This oppression need not be real. It can be as imaginary as perceiving insult on your belief. Criticizing Islam is consequently perceived as oppression and therefore, Muslims feel compelled and justified to take their revenge.[30]

Throughout the entire time that jihadists are oppressing unbelievers, therefore, *they believe that they are the ones who are being oppressed.* And the jihadists engaged in this behavior cannot be sinning, since, again, there is no sin in Islam and *no need for Muslims to ever be contrite for their actions.* Thus, we find the Qur'an giving permission to the oppressed to fight against their oppressors,[31] and the Islamic justification for jihad to eliminate disbelief.[32]

At this juncture, we are able to decipher numerous psychopathic traits that surface in the world of jihad, especially this fundamental one: *never having to say you're sorry.* The Jihadist Psychopath never apologizes. Unsurprisingly, Muhammad led by example in this regard as well. Indeed, when Allah's messenger hurt innocents, *he never apologized* and always painted his victims as deserving of their punishment. When he committed war crimes, Islamic theology *sees him as innocent.* When he had six to nine hundred male Jews of the Banu Qurayza tribe beheaded, they had, in the Islamic vision, asked for this fate by refusing to convert to Islam.[33]

And so, an integral element in the Jihadist Psychopath's play-book is crystallized right before our eyes: the *I am victim* charade. Indeed, while pushing the notion that the victim has brought Islamic aggression upon himself, the Jihadist Psychopath perpet-ually paints himself as the party that is being wronged. And yes, again, Muhammad led by example here as well, since he played the victim at every stage of his war against unbelievers. In the beginning of his mission, for instance, when Muhammad and his followers were just a small-numbered group in Mecca, and their chances of conquering unbelievers were zero, Allah's messenger posed as a persecuted and victimized minority whose message was one of peace and tolerance (i.e., Qur'an 109:1–6: "You shall have your religion and I shall have my religion"), while also proclaiming *a future* vengeance against his non-Muslim persecutors.[34] This set a rule of thumb for all Muslims: when you are in the minority in a country or a population, be deceitful by preaching a message of tolerance and promoting your own victim status as an oppressed minority; when you eventually grow in number and become pow-erful, take to the sword, as Muhammad and his followers did when they grew in number and gained power.[35]

Once Muhammad had grown in strength and was capable of subjugating unbelievers, jihad entered a violent stage, and so Muhammad waged ruthless holy war, which included his ordering of political assassinations. But even when Muhammad engaged in this terror, he still positioned himself as the victim. After all, the Jewish tribes against which he perpetrated jihad still refused to convert to Islam, and such a refusal was seen by Muhammad as an act of oppression against him and his followers—and as violence against Allah.[36] This is why Islamic commentators on Muhammed's brutality against the Jews always stress the victim-hood of the Muslims and the treachery of the Jews.[37] Author Mark Durie notes how Muhammad played the victim card:

One of the themes of Mohammed's program was an emphasis on the victimhood of Muslims. To sustain the theological position that conquest is liberation, it becomes necessary to seek grounds to find the infidel enemy guilty and deserving of attack. Also, the more extreme the punishment, the more necessary it becomes to insist upon the enemy's guilt. Since, by divine decree Muslims' sufferings were "worse than slaughter," it became obligatory for Muslims to regard their victimhood as greater than whatever they inflicted upon their enemies. The greater victimhood of Muslims became a doctrinal necessity, a feature of the "compass of faith" for Muslims.[38]

As a result, even when Muhammad commanded his followers to kill various people, he was always the victim, professing that the people whom he murdered had not only wounded him personally, but also had hurt Allah. The terrible fate of poetess Asma bint Marwan was typical in this regard. When she wrote verses criticizing Muhammad's murder of another poet, Abu 'Afak (who was one hundred years old), Muhammad cried out about the pain she was *causing him*, asking: "Will no one rid me of this daughter of Marwan?" One of Muhammad's followers, Umayr ibn Adi, immediately went to Marwan's house the same night, where he murdered her and her baby while she was nursing the infant in her arms. Muhammad commended him: "You have helped God and his apostle, Umayr!"[39]

Now that we see how the fundamental ingredients of the psychopath's mindset are inherent in the personas of both Allah and his messenger Muhammad, we begin to behold the foundations of the Jihadist Psychopath's world. We now move on to outline the other key characteristics of psychopathy that are found in the Jihadist Psychopath, and to examine how they enable him to subjugate his victims:

From the realities illuminated above, it becomes clear why, with the lack of any sense of wrongdoing, the Jihadist Psychopath possesses absolutely no shame and, in turn, absolutely *no con-science*. He feels no guilt, remorse, affection, or compassion. He especially does not have any sense of obligation to non-Muslims, nor is he concerned about their welfare. He is, like every psychopath, oblivious to any notion of morality, empathy, or responsibility. It is important to stress here that Islam is, as scholar Mark Durie has pointed out, *an actual attack on the human conscience itself*, and that it ultimately blunts any feelings of shame and guilt in its prac-titioners regarding the violence that their texts command them to carry out.[40] This is why the Jihadist Psychopath *never apologizes*. In fact, we have never seen any Muslim leaders or groups apologiz-ing to the West *for anything*. Not one prominent Muslim religious or political leader, for example, has ever apologized for 9/11 or for any other jihadist attack.[41]

Meanwhile, just as the psychopath is proficient in *pretend-ing* that he has a conscience and that he is a saint while wreaking his havoc, so too the Jihadist Psychopath engages in this charm offensive as well. This charade transpires through the Jihadist Psy-chopath's minions—the Muslim "civil rights" groups in the West who don the *nice guy mask* and claim that *they are separate* from violent Islamic terror and totalitarian sharia jihad, and that, in so doing, they represent *the real Islam*. Behind this veneer, of course, these Muslim pretenders wholeheartedly support what the Jihad-ist Psychopath is doing *because he is fulfilling Islamic obligations*.

The Jihadist Psychopath's whole matrix now comes into clearer focus: he perpetrates terror and possesses malicious goals vis-à-vis non-Muslims, while his spokespeople *to the West*—Muslim Broth-erhood front groups such as the Council on American-Islamic Relations (CAIR), the Islamic Society of North America (ISNA), and the Muslim Students Association (MSA)—throw dust into the eyes of the non-Muslim public. They camouflage their reli-gion's violence and its true aims with the pretense of wanting to safeguard Muslims' "civil liberties," combat so-called Islamophobia, and rescue unbelievers themselves from their destructive and misguided un-Islamic ways.[42] In other words, these Muslim deceivers posture as though they are acting out of compassion and empathy, and, most importantly, *in the unbeliever's own interest*, the same way that the psychopath pretends he is acting in his victims' interest—and the same way that the Serpent pretended to act on Eve's behalf.[43]

We see, therefore, how when brave truth-tellers dare to identify the theological root cause of a jihadist attack, a certain section of what Nonie Darwish has termed the *Islamic Terror Orchestra* screams and whines: "We are not like that!"[44] Darwish explains how this orchestra has worked out a whole cunning symphony, with each section knowing exactly what notes to play, and at what time. She outlines how it works:

> ...when Islamic terrorism and beheadings anger the world and turn public opinion against Islam, that orchestra starts playing a different tune to confuse and prevent the world from uncovering their coordinated handy work. While one group proudly takes credit for the terror, another publicly denounces it. But most groups, while enjoying the power and attention the terrorists have bestowed on them, stand by with a look of victimhood saying: "I am a victim too because you condemn me and my peaceful religion when I did not do anything. That is not Islam and you are an Islamophobe."[45]

It goes without saying, of course, that there are moderate Muslim individuals who do oppose the Jihadist Psychopath and are honest about Islamic sources of terror. Author Christine Douglass-Williams has interviewed a distinguished group of these Muslim individuals in her book, *The Challenge of Modernizing Islam: Reformers Speak Out and the Obstacles They Face.*[46] Some of these reform-minded Muslims deserve the West's support. But they are, unfortunately, small in number and remain exceptions to the rule.[47]

It also goes without saying that the argument of this work is, obviously, *not* that all Muslims are psychopaths. They are clearly not. As we discussed in Chapter 5, "Not All Muslims Do That," there are many good and peaceful Muslims. The key issue here is that their peacefulness says something about *their freedom and dissociation from* Islam. In other words, this book's focus is on the devout Muslims who follow Islam's violent commands with fervent dedication.[48] Nonetheless, no matter how many times this work will emphasize this point, the Jihadist Psychopath's minions within the Unholy Alliance[49] will definitely smear this book, alleging that it somehow labels all Muslims as psychopaths—when it is doing no such thing. This type of slander is, of course, only to be expected, since it is part of the Jihadist Psychopath's propaganda war, which includes the tactic of making false and ungrounded accusations, which we will explore in Chapter 12.[50]

It would also be important to point out here that while many "moderate" Muslim groups pay lip service to denouncing Islamic terror and terrorist organizations like ISIS, few of them ever really actually do anything concrete about it. As author Robert Spencer has noted, we have yet to see any prominent "moderate" Muslim leaders in the United States set up, in their mosques and institutions, any honest, transparent, and inspectable programs that teach adherence to the U.S. Constitution and a rejection of jihad, sharia, and Islamic supremacism.[51] The nonexistence of such programs reveals what attitude is really at hand in a large section of the Muslim community.

All of these ingredients of the Jihadist Psychopath's mindset make it clear that the *I am victim* charade is at the core of his war on unbelievers. Islamic supremacists' manipulation of the term *Islamophobia*, which supposedly means an "irrational" fear of Muslims, is a central feature of this ploy. They crudely exploit this term to portray themselves as victims, while they perpetrate their aggression, and it works perfectly. Indeed, anyone who carefully observes jihadist attacks will witness that right after jihadists launch a strike, the actual victims—non-Muslims—end up bending over backwards to apologize to the Muslim world. This is because once any brave voice points to a jihadist attack and identifies its Islamic inspirations, the designated section of the aforementioned Islamic Terror Orchestra screams, "We are not like that!" and "You are an Islamophobe!" Many non-Muslims immediately get petrified, recoil, and distance themselves from the truth-tellers, profusely apologizing to their Muslim accusers so that they can prevent the labels of "racism" and "hate speech" from being affixed to them. A toxic relationship of codependence ultimately forms here, as Muslim abusers and their surrendering victims form a toxic bond. As Greenfield explains: "Muslims use victimhood and violence to create a dependent relationship in which their victims are convinced that the violence inflicted on them is caused by that victimhood."[52]

It becomes clear why, immediately after every jihadist attack, the narrative within the West's establishment media is quick to claim that the root cause of Islamic terror—which is not called by its name—is *discrimination against Muslims*. We hear endless discussions about how Muslims are the real victims, and how Islamophobia has to end because it is causing the violence.[53] Muslim Brotherhood front groups help pull the strings to enable the whole process, thereby fulfilling their role as revealed in the Muslim Brotherhood document *Explanatory Memorandum*, which outlines the Islamic supremacist strategy to defeat the West and the U.S. by our own hands.[54]

Some Islamic supremacists are completely open about this *I am victim* strategy. At the Islamic Circle of North America (ICNA) annual conference in Baltimore, Maryland, in June 2016, Shaykh Omar Suleiman, a member of ICNA's Shariah Council, boasted in his keynote session speech "Quran and Islamophobia": "Alhamdulilah [Praise be to God] for Islamophobia! ...Thank God for Islamophobia that causes us to grow and develop a strong Islamic identity[.]"[55] Suleiman made it clear that the real Islamic supremacist agenda is to push Islamophobia in order to empower Islamic identity, ideology, and, therefore, power. It is important to keep in mind here that Suleiman is one of ICNA's leaders, that the conference at which he spoke was the largest annual Muslim gathering in the U.S., and that his comments were tweeted out to over 56,000 followers.[56]

This dark feature of Islamophobia is, essentially, the Jihadist Psychopath's central propaganda ploy for silencing those who would tell the truth about him.[57] The whole Islamophobia charade has succeeded to such an extent that now a campaign in the UN, led by the Organisation of Islamic Cooperation (OIC), is making headway in its quest to criminalize any truth-telling about Islam through UN Resolution 16/18.[58] Author Stephen Coughlin has documented how Islamic supremacists exploit Islamophobia in the context of the OIC. That organization, he writes:

> has taken control of the term's usage and retains control of its application for use in hostile information campaigns. The term Islamophobia has become, in effect, a brand that is managed by the OIC."[59]

Islamophobia, therefore, is the principal vehicle through which the Jihadist Psychopath exploits his victim status to gain power, and it enables his aggression toward unbelievers. As Coughlin notes,

> When we see the word Islamophobia we should instantly be aware that it represents an OIC campaign package that seeks its

implantation internationally as well as in America, with support from the Brotherhood through front groups that, as the Explanatory Memorandum says, "adopt Muslims' causes domestically and globally...and support the global Islamic State wherever it is."[60]

Dr. Mahathir Mohamad, the ex-prime minister of Malaysia (known as a "moderate Muslim"), crystallized this whole jihadist victimhood game perfectly when, in the tenth summit of the Organisation of the Islamic Conference in 2003, he stated: "We are all Muslims; we are all oppressed; we are all being humiliated." Therefore, the solution to this problem, he stated, was for Muslims to acquire "guns and rockets, bombs and warplanes, tanks and warships" with which to wage war on non-Muslims.[61] Ali Sina offers keen insight into the psychological dynamic involved here:

> Muslims must feel victimized. The doctrine of victimhood is essential to the survival of Islam. It is the glue that binds the ummah, the entire Muslim world into one nation. Without it they will tear each other apart. With it they direct their enmity at others. As a result, peace with Muslims is impossible because the doctrine of victimhood is fundamental to their faith.[62]

Thus, after every jihadist attack today, we see how the Jihadist Psychopath's team takes pains to stress that *Muslims are the true victims*. And Western leaders and media desperately embrace this deceit—hook, line, and sinker. The examples are endless: after the Orlando terror attack of June 12, 2016, *Time* magazine made sure to portray the jihadist perpetrator, Omar Mateen, as *the victim*, because he allegedly had been bullied by his coworkers.[63] *Time* failed to explain why no other human being in America who had been bullied didn't go on to perpetrate the worst terrorist attack in America since 9/11. Then, a month later, after the Nice terror attack in France in mid-July 2016, the BBC reported that *Muslims* were the "real victims" of that attack as well. This was because the BBC had learned that local Muslims were claiming to have perceived a great deal of Islamophobia among non-Muslims after the attack. One Muslim reported the horror: "People who yesterday would embrace me warmly are now cold towards me."[64]

And so, it becomes transparently evident that the Jihadist Psychopath is a carbon copy of the traditional psychopath—only with an added ideological component. And it likewise becomes crystal clear how Islamic supremacism's leaders and warriors are psychopaths themselves, while their non-Muslim victims surrender to them in exactly the same manner as the victims of the textbook psychopath surrender to him.

Now that we have deciphered how the Jihadist Psychopath is the mirror image of the textbook psychopath—especially with regard to how he attempts to wield a monopoly on victimhood— it is essential that we examine further this jihadist victimhood charade, since it is at the epicenter of our enemy's war against us. We therefore now move forward to study several specific cases of how the Jihadist Psychopath has successfully exploited the victim card to carry out his con game and lead us into his deadly trap.

CHAPTER 11

ISLAM: THE ETERNAL VICTIM

On September 29, 2015, at United Nations Headquarters, President Obama stood in front of the "Leaders' Summit on Countering ISIL and Violent Extremism." He was there to tackle the problem of the Islamic State and its terrorism. As he began to speak, it quickly became apparent that the Qur'anic verses that ISIS members invariably cite to justify what they do were not in the forefront of the president's mind. Nor did the president seem at all interested in the importance of labeling the West's enemy with the name that it must be called. Instead, Islamophobia was foremost on his agenda. And so he stated:

> [W]e have to commit ourselves to build diverse, tolerant, inclusive societies that reject anti-Muslim and anti-immigrant bigotry that creates the divisions, the fear, and the resentments upon which extremists can prey.[1]

Referring to the Islamic State as "ISIL,"[2] Obama also made sure to go out of his way to stress the notion that ISIS is un-Islamic, and to underscore the fact that the Islamic terror group kills Muslims as well as infidels. The president stated that ISIS was:

[A] band of terrorists that kills innocent Muslim men, women, and children. We're working to lift up the voices of Muslim scholars, clerics and others—including ISIL defectors—who courageously stand up to ISIL and its warped interpretations of Islam.[3]

This entire display by the leftist U.S. president was a typical performance of Jihad Denial by an Unholy Alliance[4] member and figurehead. Indeed, as we demonstrated in Chapter 5, the fact that ISIS kills Muslims is actually completely consistent with the pure Islamic nature of ISIS.[5] But Obama would never, obviously, admit such a thing, since enforcing Jihad Denial and making Muslims *the victims* in the terror war had to be his priority.[6]

It is important to note here that during his UN talk, Obama, in a manner that was typical for him, barely touched upon the non-Muslim victims of ISIS and jihad. By minimizing their suffering, the president further fulfilled his Unholy Alliance obligations, since pushing into invisibility the millions of Christians who are facing genocide, sexual exploitation, and mass abductions and displacements at the hands of jihadists is a crucial component of Jihad Denial. To be sure, turning a blind eye to such victims helps keep the focus on Islamophobia and distracts people from looking at the Islamic texts that inspire and command jihadists to wage war on Christians and other non-Muslims.[7]

Overall, therefore, Obama's behavior at the "Leaders' Summit on Countering ISIL and Violent Extremism" was a typical performance by a leftist minion of the Jihadist Psychopath. And he did his duty well: he separated Islam from Islamic terror and painted Islam as the victim of ISIS—when, in fact, it is Islam that gives life to ISIS. In carrying out his deception, the president promoted the *Islam is the victim* charade that is today being successfully advanced by the Jihadist Psychopath and his helpers. As we have already demonstrated, this con job is a central tactic in the Jihadist Psychopath's war on his un-Islamic prey. Because of the centrality of this tactic in the Jihadist Psychopath's arsenal, this chapter will now provide several case studies of how it is manifesting itself in the terror war.

We begin with a look at the buffoonish antics of Rep. Keith Ellison in fellow congressman Peter King's House hearings on Islamic radicalism in early 2011. Ellison is the first Muslim to have been elected to the U.S. House of Representatives and, among the many intriguing things about him, *his hajj to Mecca was paid for by the Muslim Brotherhood.*[8] It did not come as a great surprise, then, that, during his testimony, Ellison focused on the bad things that supposedly racist Americans had allegedly said about Mohammad Salman Hamdani, a Pakistani-born Muslim American who died in the collapse of the World Trade Center on 9/11 while assisting in rescue efforts. Sobbing during his testimony, Ellison stated that:

> After the tragedy some people tried to smear his [Hamdani's] character solely because of his Islamic faith. Some people spread false rumors and speculated that he was in league with the attackers only because he was Muslim. It was only when his remains were identified that these lies were fully exposed. Mohammad Salman Hamdani was a fellow American who gave his life for other Americans. His life should not be defined as a member of an ethnic group or a member of a religion, but as an American who gave everything for his fellow citizens.[9]

It is, of course, tragic that Hamdani died, and he truly was a hero—among many heroes who died that day in New York. But Ellison's tears were not merely expressions of his supposed empathy for Hamdani. He shed them, clearly, to signify that *Muslims were the real victims* of 9/11. He said nothing about the non-Muslim victims of 9/11, nor about the ideology that spawned it. And aside from the curious nature of Ellison's tears, there were a few other things that likewise seemed askew about the congressman's conduct and pronouncements in the hearings that day:

To begin with, six weeks after 9/11, before Hamdani's remains were identified, Congress signed the PATRIOT Act into law with this line included: "Many Arab Americans and Muslim Americans have acted heroically during the attacks on the United States, including Mohammad Salman Hamdani, a twenty-three-year-old New Yorker of Pakistani descent, who is believed to have gone to the World Trade Center to offer rescue assistance and is now missing."[10] Hamdani was, in other words, clearly singled out for particular high honors among the thousands of victims of the September 11 attacks. Moreover, the identities of the people who had supposedly called Hamdani all those racist names, and who had allegedly associated him with 9/11 because he was a Muslim, remained a mystery, since no evidence of anyone insulting Hamdani was produced by Ellison or anyone else.[11]

None of the facts about Hamdani were of any interest to Ellison, whose only real concern was to portray Muslims as the victims of 9/11. And so, not surprisingly, a few days after his tearful performance, Ellison gave a speech in Michigan in which he attacked three witnesses who had appeared at King's hearings. Denunciations of jihad and its sources, however, didn't find their way into his speech.[12]

This twisted con game of the Jihadist Psychopath transpires in every killing field where jihad spills human blood. Muslim convert Marmaduke Pickthall unintentionally shed light on this deceptive scheme in his influential 1927 lecture "Tolerance in Islam," where, in reference to the Armenian genocide, he emphasized that "before every massacre of Christians by Muslims of which you read, there was a more wholesale massacre or attempted massacre of Muslims by Christians."[13] Professor Ahmad bin Muhammad, Algerian professor of religious politics, regurgitated this theme when he faced Dr. Wafa Sultan in a debate on Al Jazeera TV on July 26, 2005. Enraged by Sultan's truth-telling about Islam, Muhammad shouted: "We are the victims! ...There are millions of innocent people among us

[Muslims], while the innocent among you...number only dozens, hundreds, or thousands, at the most."[14] A certain picture emerges quite clearly for us in the pronouncements of Marmaduke Pickthall and Ahmad bin Muhammad: there are always *more* Muslim victims—and *Muslims always suffer more*, no matter how much pain they inflict on their victims.

The genocide that Islam is routinely perpetrating against Christians serves as a perfect example of this whole *Islam is the victim* deception. We see it being played out tragically today in the horrifying suffering of Coptic Christians at the hands of jihad in Egypt. The Muslim Brotherhood perpetually terrorizes the Copts—killing them; burning down their churches; kidnapping, raping, and forcibly converting their girls; and oppressing them in myriad other vicious ways.[15] Yet once the Unholy Alliance is finished constructing the narrative, the perpetrators and victims switch labels. Indeed, even when Coptic churches are burned to the ground at the behest of the Muslim Brotherhood, it is still the Copts who are painted as the perpetrators, since it is they who have, allegedly, brought the persecution upon themselves.[16]

The figure of Mohamed Elibiary is a typical example of this blame game in the persecution of the Copts. A Muslim Brotherhood sympathizer, Elibiary is the Muslim "cleric" who served on the U.S. Department of Homeland Security's Advisory Council under President Obama and who, among other things,[17] used his Twitter account during his time in the administration to blame the Copts for the oppression they were suffering—because they had, in his view, fanned the flames of "Islamophobia."[18] Author Raymond Ibrahim explains how this upside-down world—in which Muslims blame Christians for their own persecution under Islam—is completely normal in the Islamic narrative, because it is crucial for Islam to always turn history into victimology:

Today, whether as taught in high school or graduate school, whether as portrayed by Hollywood or the news media, the predominant historic narrative is that Muslims are the historic "victims" of "intolerant" Western Christians."[19]

In light of this, Elibiary's behavior becomes totally understandable and reveals how the jihadist psychopathic dynamic transpires in Egypt, where Christian Copts are terrorized by Muslims because they are Christians, but it is the Muslims who end up being portrayed as the victims.

Another hot spot on the international stage where we find the jihadist *I am the victim* charade being played out is in Iran, where the Islamic Republic consistently demands that *the U.S. apologize* for how it has abused the Islamic revolution. In November 2015, for instance, President Hassan Rouhani stated that ties with the U.S. could only be repaired if the U.S. were to express remorse for its past mistreatment of Iran.[20] Indeed, even though it is the Islamic Republic that has declared war on the American "Great Satan," has been killing Americans for years,[21] and regularly holds protests against the U.S. where Iranians chant "Death to America" and burn U.S. flags, it is Iran that claims to be the victim in the whole narrative.

And Iran's leftist minions in the West do all they can, in turn, to make sure that everyone understands the importance of feeling the Islamic Republic's pain. President Obama was especially busy with this task, basing American policy on it. In a typical speech, he pleaded that:

> Part of the psychology of Iran is rooted in past experiences, the sense that their country was undermined, that the United States or the West meddled in first their democracy and then in supporting the Shah and then in supporting Iraq and Saddam during that extremely brutal war....So part of what I've told my team is we have to distinguish between the ideologically driven,

offensive Iran and the defensive Iran that feels vulnerable and sometimes may be reacting because they perceive that as the only way that they can avoid repeats of the past.[22]

In this context, it becomes understandable why the Jihadist Psychopath's relentless *I am the victim* con game takes on a number of bizarre and surreal manifestations. Consider, for instance, how the Unholy Alliance paints Palestinian women as victims for *not* being raped by IDF soldiers. That's right, you read that correctly, and we repeat: Palestinian women *are victims* because they *are not* raped by Israeli soldiers. This is how the twisted paradigm works:

When there are zero Muslim victims, Muslims *are still the victims*. This is what Hen Mazzig, a young former IDF soldier, learned when he traveled throughout the U.S. Pacific Northwest in early 2013, speaking at college campuses, high schools, and churches to educate Americans about Israel. Mazzig's military service was in the IDF COGAT unit, which tries to promote Palestinian civil society and attends to the needs of Palestinian civilians. During Mazzig's trip, anti-Israel activists showed Mazzig their gratitude for his efforts by making groundless accusations against him and the country he represented. One of the accusations was that Mazzig was a rapist, although he had never raped anyone. On one particular occasion, a female professor asked Mazzig if he knew how many Palestinians had been raped by IDF forces. Mazzig answered that, as far as he knew, there were none. This prompted the professor to react with indignation, as Mazzig recalls:

> She triumphantly responded that I was right, because, she said, "You IDF soldiers don't rape Palestinians because Israelis are so racist and disgusted by them that you won't touch them."[23]

This intriguing reasoning inspired quite an interesting academic paper produced by then-graduate student Tal Nitzan, under the tutelage of her PhD advisers led by Zali Gurevitch. The abstract of the paper explains that its original purpose was to find instances of rapes of Palestinian women by the IDF, but that it failed to find what it was looking for. The decision was made, therefore, that the paper should instead show that "the lack of organized military rape is an alternate way of realizing [particular] political goals." Thus,

> In the Israeli-Palestinian conflict, it can be seen that the lack of military rape merely strengthens the ethnic boundaries and clarifies the inter-ethnic differences—just as organized military rape would have done.[24]

In summation, Tal Nitzan could not find any cases where IDF soldiers had raped Palestinian women—even though Palestinian media constantly accuse Israeli soldiers of perpetrating this crime. Clearly dejected by these findings, Nitzan had to twist her thesis so it still cast Israelis as perpetrators and Palestinians as victims who were viewed as inferior.[25] That's right, if Israelis perpetrated rape, then they were clearly racist, but since the evidence revealed that they didn't perpetrate rape, then it also proved they were racist. And, of course, Nitzan herself had, by this time, also become a victim. How, you ask? Her thesis had been criticized by some observers and commentators, and those criticisms were, yes, you guessed it: tantamount to her being raped as well.[26]

When it comes to Muslims raping non-Muslims, by contrast, a completely different set of values comes into play. With the Unholy Alliance in charge of *the spin*, in such cases *the Muslim rapists are the victims*, and the rape victims are the perpetrators. This is how the process works:

When the reports poured in about the many 2016 New Year's Eve Muslim sex assaults in Germany, Austria, Switzerland, Finland, and other European countries, the Unholy Alliance quickly got busy advancing its psychopathic paradigm.[27] As we discussed in Chapter 1, Cologne mayor Henriette Reker did her leftist duty and reprimanded *the victims*, suggesting that *they had asked for it*. She vowed to make sure that women would, in the future, change *their* behavior, so as not to provoke Muslims to sexually assault them anymore. This would all be made easy, she assured everyone, because there would now be published "online guidelines" for women to read so that they could sufficiently educate themselves.[28] It wasn't clear at that time if it would be the burqa or the niqab that would be the solution of choice, or if the "guidelines" would involve staying at home and only leaving the house with a male guardian and being completely covered up.

In any case, it appears that Henriette Reker had probably been inspired by leftist feminist Naomi Wolf, who found the hijab "sexy" during her political pilgrimage to the Islamic Middle East in early 2008,[29] and also by University of Oslo professor of anthropology Dr. Unni Wikan, whose proposed solution for the high incidence of Muslims raping Norwegian women is not for the rapists to be punished, but for Norwegian women to "take their share of responsibility" for the rapes, since Muslim men find their manner of dress provocative. Norwegian women must, in Wikan's worldview, "realize that we live in a Multicultural society and adapt themselves to it."[30]

And so, perhaps it should have been no great surprise when German police fired water cannons at German demonstrators who gathered in Cologne to protest the rapes and sexual assaults committed by the Muslim refugees during the New Year's Eve celebrations of 2016.[31] *The hoses were not aimed at the Muslim migrants who had committed sex assaults*, but at those who felt that what the assailants had done was wrong and took a stance against it. This is because, as has become quite clear by now, Muslim molesters and sex offenders are always *the real victims*.

Leftist feminist Gaby Hinsliff made herself the poster girl for this Unholy Alliance dysfunctional con game in her January 2016 essay in the *Guardian* where she painstakingly explained that the Muslim rape mobs in Cologne, whom she made sure to benignly call "refugees," were really the "oppressed," and that the women they had assaulted were essentially members of a privileged class whose inherent sense of entitlement had actually provoked the violence of the mobs. This, Hinsliff explained, was why some of the victims' valuables were stolen. The sexual assaults, in other words, weren't really about rape, but about the poor, the oppressed, and downtrodden taking what was owed to them.[32] So it was really all about class warfare and about the have-nots trying to acquire what they were being deprived of by the greedy capitalists.[33] Once again: the Muslim rapists were the victims.

This whole convoluted and bizarre tale gets even stranger and more toxic when the victims of Muslim rape and assault happen to be Unholy Alliance members themselves. Indeed, when leftists are sexually abused and violated by Muslims, they often cover up for and defend their abusers—and even flat-out label themselves as the perpetrators and their abusers as the victims. Consider, as an example of this madness, how the Norwegian left-wing activist Karsten Nordal Hauken was consumed by an overwhelming sense of guilt after he had been anally raped by a Somali migrant refugee. When his rapist was subsequently deported in 2016, Hauken described himself to a Norwegian documentary crew as an ardent "feminist and anti-racist" who was deeply saddened to see his rapist forced out of the country. He emphasized that the violator was "not responsible for his actions," because he was "a product of an unjust world" and "of an upbringing marked by war and deprivation." In short, Hauken maintained that his violator was the victim, and that the rape *wasn't even about the sex*. Being raped by a Somali refugee, therefore, in no way prompted Hauken to rethink his left-wing worldview, nor to reconsider his enthusiastic support for immigration policies that would continue to flood Norway with additional hordes of Muslim migrants. Said Hauken:

> I stand rock solid in my opinion that people like him need our help. I want us to continue to help refugees with such a background...For I am a human being first, and not a Norwegian. No, I'm part of the world, and the world is unfortunately unfair.[34]

A young female leftist activist volunteering at a migrant camp on the French-Italian border was yet another of the many feminists who shared Hauken's mindset about the sexual abuse they had suffered at the hands of Muslim migrants. Gang raped by a group of African males, this woman's main worry afterward was that her attack might be used by political figures and social activists to discredit the reputation of migrants. So she covered up her own rape.[35] That's because, yes, you guessed it again: her rapists were the real victims. In the wake of a series of coordinated suicide bombings that killed nearly three dozen people and wounded at least three hundred others in Brussels on March 22, 2016, author Daniel Greenfield touched on this *Islam is the victim* phenomenon in his Frontpagemag.com article "Aftermath of Muslim Terror Attacks Always a 'Difficult Time for Muslims.'" Stating sardonically that "I know it's always a difficult time for me, right after I punch someone in the face," Greenfield added:

> We really need to stop wasting time protecting cities from Muslim terrorists and focus on protecting Muslim hurt feelings afterward. We should create a whole special department to manage this imaginary backlash which Muslims constantly whine about, but never actually materializes.[36]

One can't talk about Muslim victims in America, of course, without mentioning the one and only Linda Sarsour, the notorious Palestinian-American political "activist" who was one of the organizers of the 2017 Women's March. Over the July 4 weekend in 2017, she just happened to be in the mood for jihad, so in an infamous keynote address to the Islamic Society of North America, she issued a call to her fellow Muslims to wage jihad against President Trump. As a self-identified devout and knowledgeable Muslim, Sarsour is obviously aware that the Qur'an, Hadith, and Islamic law all acknowledge that jihad involves warfare. Indeed, there is no ambiguity about this in Islamic texts, which clearly define jihad as "war with non-Muslims to establish the religion."[37] Islamic tradition also records Sarsour's prophet as stating: "I have been made victorious through terror" (Sahih Bukhari 4:52.220). And yet, when some Americans dared to express concern about Sarsour calling for a jihad against the American president, Sarsour and her Unholy Alliance comrades became indignant. Indeed, how dare anyone see any religious significance in the jihadist attacks that struck in cities like Orlando, Boston, and San Bernardino?

And so, before you knew it, Sarsour, too, became the victim. Leftist publications, from the *Huffington Post* to ThinkProgress, quickly came to poor Sarsour's defense, attacking and mocking her critics for not understanding *what jihad really meant*. Only the ignorant and racist, they argued, would think that jihad had something to do with violence.[38] Sarsour herself said that jihad really was all about fighting for racial and economic justice.[39] Apparently, for some reason, ISIS, al-Qaeda, and Hamas never got this message.

Sarsour was so upset about the criticism she received after calling for jihad against President Trump that she ended up threatening on Twitter: "Just know that I am taking names of those who have lied about me to defame my character. I may be quiet now but not for long. I am working." She then added, "I have a running document of the lies & who is putting them out there. This is not about setting records straight, it's who will pay 4 lies?"[40] This was quite ominous, but how exactly the evil Islamophobes were going to pay for their "lies" remained a mystery; what was clear, however, was that Sarsour was the victim in it all. Robert Spencer described Sarsour's awful suffering:

> Here is a woman who is a darling of the Left and the establishment media whining because she has faced some justified criticism. She got a platform in the Washington Post to clarify her "jihad" remarks, and recently gave the commencement speech at CUNY. She is lionized and hailed everywhere in the mainstream, while her critics are shut out of the mainstream, shouted down and physically menaced when we speak at colleges and universities (if we get invited at all), and excoriated everywhere as "racists" and "Islamophobes."[41]

With the Jihadist Psychopath's monopoly on victimhood now entrenched so firmly in the West, it appears that even corrupt and incompetent Muslims who work in U.S. law enforcement are immune from criticism. Consider, for instance, the tragic fate that befell Justine Damond, a forty-year-old Australian woman who resided in Minneapolis. In July 2017, Mohamed Noor, the first Somali Muslim on the Minneapolis police force, shot and killed this unarmed woman for incomprehensible reasons. While Noor subsequently refused to speak with investigators, the empirical evidence and the account of events that Noor himself relayed to friends, revealed that his nervousness and pronounced lack of respect for women were the cause of Damond's death.[42] Noor was simply not cut out to be a policeman. Minneapolis mayor Betsy Hodges' reaction to the incident, meanwhile, spoke volumes. She *did not* state that the Minneapolis police force would reconsider its willingness to hire incompetent Muslim police officers just to please multiculturalists. And she *did not* encourage a reflection on how leftist efforts to socially engineer police forces just might cost innocent people their lives. Instead, she stressed that after this shooting, *Islamophobia would not be tolerated.*[43]

And so the lesson in Justine Damond's murder by a Muslim cop was transparent: *Muslims are always the victims*. One couldn't help but wonder what kind of announcement Mayor Hodges would have made if a non-Muslim officer in her city's police department had shot an unarmed Muslim woman.

With all of the Islamophobia purportedly in the air, it became evident why, back in March 2016, lawyers in Vancouver, Canada, had no choice but to launch a free, confidential "Islamophobia Legal Assistance Hotline" that Muslims could contact when they felt victimized.[44] This provided great inspiration for the city of Boston, which had suffered the Boston Marathon Massacre at the hand of jihadists on April 15, 2013, and needed to do something to prevent future recurrences of terrorist violence. And so, in July 2017, Boston authorities made the decision to hang fifty posters around the city that would address "Islamophobia." That's right. "What to do if you are witnessing jihad terror" was a statement that didn't make it onto the posters, but "What to do if you are witnessing Islamophobic harassment" did.[45]

At this stage, it is important for us to introduce a crucial element in the Jihadist Psychopath's *I am victim* charade: transference. This is the process, first described as a psychological phenomenon by Sigmund Freud, by which the Jihadist Psychopath projects his own crimes onto his victims. In his new book, *The Big Lie*, author Dinesh D'Souza masterfully demonstrates how leftists engage in transference by calling their conservative opponents "fascists"—when, in fact, the leftists are themselves the actual fascists.[46] "Through a process of transference," D'Souza writes, "leftists blame their victims for being and doing what they themselves are and do."[47]

Transference applies directly to our story because, whenever one observes the elements of the Unholy Alliance's propaganda, one always finds the Unholy Alliance accusing its victims of the behavior that it itself is perpetrating against them. Moreover, it labels its victims with the names *that belong to itself.* For instance, we constantly witness anti-Semites calling Jews "Nazis" and accusing them, among myriad things, of treating the Palestinians the way that the Nazis once treated the Jews.[48]

And so now in our terror war, while the Unholy Alliance refuses to call jihad by its true name, it actually uses that very word to describe *the victims* of jihad and those who are fighting to confront it. An example of this crude transference *by proxy* was on display when the Los Angeles *Jewish Journal* ran a cartoon on October 11, 2013, comparing conservative Tea Party activists to Islamic jihadists. The cartoon likened people who want to reduce government intervention and government spending to terrorists who engage in mass murder.[49] This tendency is found among many Democrats, who routinely call Republicans all kinds of names, including "jihadists," "arsonists," and "terrorists." We witnessed this behavior during the government shutdown in the fall of 2013.[50] Interestingly enough, evidence surfaced that this strategy was devised by Obama's top adviser, Valerie Jarrett.[51] This practice of transference by the Unholy Alliance is vital for us to keep an eye on, for it is directly connected to the Jihadist Psychopath's practice of ascribing victim status to himself and perpetrator status to his victims—and he does it all with the collaboration of his leftist lackeys.

Now that we have observed how the Jihadist Psychopath functions in his *I am the eternal victim* costume, we begin to gauge what a crucial role the victim charade plays in the world of Islamic supremacism. To be sure, there is little more important for the Jihadist Psychopath than to whimper after punching his victims in the face (or killing them). This is why the Unholy Alliance creates its *Cry-Bully,* the agitator/aggressor among leftists and Muslims that gets to whine and complain after perpetrating violence against his victims. In understanding the Cry-Bully better, we also begin

to comprehend why members of the Unholy Alliance have fabricated so many hoax hate crimes. The Cry-Bully and the hoaxes that
accompany his con game are explored in our next chapter.

CHAPTER 12

THE CRY-BULLY AND THE VICTIMS WHO WEREN'T

The Jihadist Psychopath portrays himself as a victim in order to deceive and ultimately conquer unbelievers. The Unholy Alliance,[1] which serves as the Jihadist Psychopath's minion, has manufactured its own special *Cry-Bully* as part of this *I am victim* strategy to help its master get what he wants. The Cry-Bully, as writer Julie Burchill has aptly dubbed him,[2] is the leftist/Islamic aggressor who cries and whines after he has perpetrated violence and imposed some form of totalitarian control on his victims.[3] As part of its Cry-Bully tactic, the Unholy Alliance creates myriad *hoax victims* to promote the *Islam is the eternal victim* narrative. This chapter will demonstrate how the Cry-Bully tactic and man-ufactured "hate crimes" against Muslims are together enabling the Jihadist Psychopath to achieve his sinister objectives.

Unholy Alliance members target the American university campus as one of their favorite territories upon which they can unleash the Cry-Bully on their victims. Part of this agenda includes the demanding of a "safe space" for the Cry-Bully. The reasoning that the Unholy Alliance manufactures here is that whoever dares to think differently from the Cry-Bully becomes a thought-criminal who is engaged in "hate-speech" and is, therefore, provoking violence. Thus, when anyone dares to say—or even think—anything contrary to the Left-Islam view of the world, the Cry-Bully immediately declares that he does not "feel safe" and, therefore, needs a "safe space." This means, of course, that the thought-crime perpetrator must be silenced altogether.

The Jihadist Psychopath is making tremendous gains through this sinister "safe space" tactic.[4] Indeed, the strategy is silencing all truth-telling about Islam in the culture at large and on the American campus in particular. There is no mystery, for instance, about what dark forces were behind the riots that prevented Milo Yiannopoulos from speaking at UC Berkeley in February 2017, or what forces caused that same university to block Ann Coulter's and David Horowitz's attempts to speak there in April 2017.[5] And it is self-explanatory why such a huge uproar occurred at Yale when ex-Muslim Ayaan Hirsi Ali was invited to speak there in September 2014.[6] Horowitz has meticulously documented how this Unholy Alliance fascism has stamped out all intellectual diversity in academia.[7] And it is no surprise that American universities receive substantial amounts of funding from Saudi Arabia, just as it is no secret what the intended objectives of such funding are.[8]

Writer Daniel Greenfield has profoundly deconstructed how this whole Unholy Alliance agenda works in the figure of the Cry-Bully. He reveals how the Left, just like Islamic supremacism, weaves the victimhood tapestry: "The left is a victimhood cult. It feeds off pain and fetishizes suffering as a moral commodity to be sold and resold in exchange for political power."[9] Greenfield calls this leftist charade "victimocracy" and illustrates how its foot soldier, the Cry-Bully, personifies the "abuser-victim."[10] The Cry-Bully, he explains, is the abuser who pretends to be a victim. His arguments are his feelings. He comes armored in identity politics entitlement and is always yelling about social justice or crying social justice tears. If you don't fight back, the Cry-Bully bullies you. If you fight back, the Cry-Bully cries and demands a safe space because you made him feel unsafe.[11]

Greenfield continues:

> It's impossible to have a rational conversation with a crybully because it doesn't want to talk to you; it wants to loudly broadcast its feelings. As one Yale crybully wrote, "I don't want to debate. I want to talk about my pain." My pain. Me. Stop arguing with me and start paying attention to me right now.[12]

The Cry-Bully, Greenfield writes, is "an oppressed oppressor. An abusive victim. A self-righteous hypocrite. A loudmouth censor. A civil rights activist who wants to take everyone's rights away."[13] The Islamophobia charade is, of course, a central part of this con job. Greenfield explains:

> Islamism is the ultimate Cry-Bully cause; on one hand stamping around murdering anyone who doesn't agree with you, on the other hand yelling "ISLAMOPHOBIA" in lieu of having a real adult debate about the merits of your case.... The British-born Islamist recently sentenced to twelve years had no problem posing with severed heads ("Heads, kaffirs, disgusting") and asking friends back home to send him condoms which he planned to use raping women captured as "war booty" but then claimed to be having nightmares and suffering from depression in order to escape jail.[14]

A significant component of this phenomenon is the Unholy Alliance members' morbid dread of freedom. Author Shelby Steele has written on this issue, analyzing how freedom is too threatening to many victim-minded people because it entails individual accountability. He demonstrates how the "victim," in an effort to escape the demands of freedom, makes all manner of accusations to absolve himself of potential failure.[15] We undoubtedly witness this reality playing itself out in the Cry-Bully's tactics in American culture in general and on the American campus in particular. Making endless accusations (i.e., about racism, Islamophobia, etc.) and demanding his need for safe spaces, the Cry-Bully reveals his cowardice; in actuality, he cannot live up to the demands of individual responsibility, nor can he honestly acknowledge the illegitimacy of his own cause.

Greenfield profoundly sums up the whole Cry-Bully scam in the image of the prophet Muhammad, who, as we demonstrated in Chapter 10, invariably cast himself as the victim despite all the violence he perpetrated.[16] "Someone always 'made' Mohammed do it," Greenfield writes. "Someone got him so frustrated and upset that he had no choice but to rape and kill."[17]

The Cry-Bully reveals to us how psychopathic the Unholy Alliance truly is, and why its members are so driven to carry out the victim scam. And that is exactly why the Left-Islam axis creates so many *hoax* hate crimes. Greenfield explains:

> If crybullies can't safebait you, they will manufacture threats by faking hate crimes against themselves or phoning in bomb threats to validate their need for a safe space in which no one is allowed to disagree with them. Surviving their own fake crimes turns crybullies into social justice heroes.[18]

Thus, it becomes quite apparent why the establishment media consistently refuse to even contemplate the Muslim community's obligation to make Americans feel safe (e.g., by repudiating Islamic texts that inspire and sanction violence against unbelievers), and instead, perpetually amplify the narrative that *Muslims are the ones who are afraid* and that it is *non-Muslim Americans who need to make Muslims feel safe*. Robert Spencer illuminates this upside-down madness, revealing why Muslim Brotherhood front groups such as CAIR so desperately need to promote the notion that hate crimes against Muslims are commonplace:

> The Hamas-linked Council on American-Islamic Relations (CAIR) wants and needs hate crimes against Muslims, because they're the currency they use to buy power and influence in our victimhood-oriented society, and to deflect attention away from jihad terror and onto Muslims as putative victims.[19]

All of this is precisely why we are now seeing so many fabricated "hate crimes" against Muslims, since Islam's followers are making themselves victims of crimes that actually never even happened—and Muslim Brotherhood front groups and the establishment media report on them with predictable outrage. As noted above, this is all to be expected, since totalitarian movements always portray themselves as victims in order to gain power. In the world of the Jihadist Psychopath, therefore, when hate crimes against him and his followers don't exist, *they have to be invented*.

And so we are now witnessing this charade in regards to the myriad hoax "hate crimes" taking place against Muslims—especially since Donald Trump's election victory. Anti-Trump forces are manufacturing victims out of thin air and blaming Trump and/or his supporters. The establishment media, meanwhile, dutifully give credence to the entire hallucination.[20] We provide several typical examples below:

An eighteen-year-old Muslim woman, Yasmin Seweid, inflamed media hysteria by claiming that she had been attacked on a New York City subway on December 1, 2016, by Trump supporters, who she said had called her a terrorist and had attempted to pull her hijab off her head. She was subsequently arrested and charged by the New York City Police Department (NYPD) for fabricating the hate crime and filing a false police report.[21] It turned out that Seweid had made up the hijab hoax in order to avoid having her strict Muslim parents punish her for breaking her curfew by staying out late, drinking with friends. Her parents shaved her head afterwards as punishment.[22] For some reason, CAIR and the establishment media weren't too interested in the abuse Yasmin suffered at her family's hands.

Shortly after Trump was elected president, a Muslim woman at the University of Louisiana at Lafayette (ULL) alleged that her hijab and wallet had been stolen by two white Trump supporters who were shouting racial slurs. The woman's accusation incensed leftists and Muslims across the nation and the world, prompting the ACLU of Louisiana to issue a statement denouncing both the incident and, of course, Donald Trump.[23] The investigation into the incident involved several law-enforcement agencies, including the FBI. The establishment media ate the story up.[24] But under tough police questioning, the ULL student eventually broke down and admitted to police that she had fabricated the entire tale.[25] By that time, of course, the media weren't too interested in such an innocuous little detail and didn't report on it.

Fake hate crimes against Muslims have become legion, and, by no means, do they always involve suggestions that supporters of Donald Trump are the perpetrators. We will now present a few representative examples:

At about 10:00 a.m. on June 22, 2017, local firefighters and police were called to the Islamic Center of Des Moines, where there had been a small fire on the carpet, which the mosque's staff had extinguished by the time firefighters arrived. Islamophobia was in the air, but security cameras in the mosque soon revealed that a member of the congregation, later identified as Aisha Ismail, was the culprit. She had poured lighter fluid on the carpet and then set it aflame. She was charged with first-degree arson. "It seems like she was trying to make a statement," said Des Moines police spokesman Sgt. Paul Parizek.[26] What that statement was, exactly, remained unclear, but CAIR and the media were decidedly uninterested in it.

In February 2016, a Michigan Muslim woman, Said Chatti, was arraigned in Dearborn's Eighteenth District Court for making a false police report about an "Islamophobic" plot to bomb Dearborn Fordson High School, a majority-Muslim institution. She had contacted the Dearborn Police Department and claimed that an "anonymous" friend of hers had overheard a group of individuals plotting to blow up the school as retribution for the November 2015 terrorist attacks in Paris. When the police presented Miss Chatti with evidence of the holes in her story, she admitted it was a false report.[27]

In mid-October, 2016, the *Huffington Post* published a story under the headline "Islamophobia Just Drove This Boy and His Family Out of America."[28] It was all very heartbreaking and unjust. The one little problem with the story, however, was that it never happened.[29] In December 2015, a thirty-seven-year-old Muslim man, Gary Nathaniel Moore of Houston, was charged with first-degree arson for setting a local mosque on fire on Christmas Day—a mosque where he himself had been coming to pray five times per day, seven days per week, for five years. By examining surveillance video from multiple businesses nearby, investigators were able to identify Moore. A warranted search of his home recovered a backpack and clothing similar to that which was seen in surveillance footage, as well as half of a two-pack of charcoal lighter-fluid bottles that seemed to match another lighter fluid bottle found inside the mosque.[30]

In March 2012, a Muslim woman, Shaima Alawadi, was found murdered in her home in El Cajon, California, in Greater San Diego. A note was found by her body that read, "Go back to your country, you terrorist." The Unholy Alliance erupted in outrage at the news of this murder, claiming that the killing was the work of some Islamophobe who hated Shaima Alawadi for wearing a hijab. They even launched a campaign in the dead woman's honor, "One Million Hijabs for Shaima Alawadi."[31] Media darling Reza Aslan entered the fray, pretending that he actually cared about Shaima and sending out a tweet blaming Pamela Geller and Robert Spencer for the murder: "If a 32 year old veiled mother is a terrorist than [sic] so am I you Islamophobic fucks Gellar [sic] Spencer et. [sic] al. Come find me."[32]

But the reality was all a bit different. Shaima Alawadi had told her husband, an Iraqi Muslim named Kassim Alhimidi, that she wanted a divorce, and so he murdered her. In April 2014, he was found guilty of killing Shaima.[33] Meanwhile, the "One Million Hijabs for Shaima Alawadi" campaign fell silent, and none of the activists started another initiative against Islamic honor killings. For some reason, they didn't care about Shaima anymore. Reza Aslan, meanwhile, tweeted no apology to Geller or Spencer, nor did his supposed heartache for Shaima continue. Spencer helped to explain what Aslan's first tweet blaming him and Geller was really all about:

> This tweet indicated how much mileage the "Islamophobia" propaganda machine thought it could get from the Alawadi murder in its efforts to intimidate people into thinking it wrong to oppose jihad terror."[34]

The list of hoax hate crimes against Muslims goes on and on: a Muslim woman in England lies to the police and claims that she was punched in the face for wearing a hijab;[35] a Muslim woman in Dearborn drops a lawsuit against police after video proves she lied when she claimed that they forced her to remove her hijab;[36] a supposed "hit-and-run" on a Muslim woman in Brussels blamed on "far right" anti-Islam demonstrators turns out to have been perpetrated by a Muslim named "Mohamed";[37] a Montreal Muslim man is arrested for a bomb threat against Muslim university students.[38] Robert Spencer has documented ten of some of the most prominent of these hoaxes in his special report, "The Top Anti-Muslim Hate Crime Hoaxes of 2014."[39]

Thus, it becomes quite evident that faking hate crimes is a central tactic of the Jihadist Psychopath, and that Unholy Alliance members are the premier Cry-Bullies of our modern age.[40] While they set fires and break windows,[41] brutally beat young girls for liking Donald Trump,[42] break the faces of those they think look like Trump,[43] and injure police officers,[44] they cry and whine because they are supposedly the *real* victims of *real* hate crimes. But, as the evidence reveals, these are the hate crimes perpetrated by conservative villains *who might have been*—and inflicted on the victims who weren't.[45]

This whole pathology, unsurprisingly, produces more bizarre and surreal pathologies on top of it. The Unholy Alliance has been forced to confront the fact that so many of the "hate crimes" against Muslims have been hoaxes—and it has responded with a variety of imaginary rationales. Indeed, just as the Unholy Alliance has labeled Israeli soldiers as racist *for not* raping Palestinian women,[46] it has now created the argument that Muslims *are victims because they fake anti-Muslim hate crimes.* That's because, it is claimed, *Muslims are driven into mental illness by "Islamophobia"* and so they must be exonerated when they invent fictitious accounts of violence against themselves. CAIR's Ibrahim Hooper has given voice to this intriguing theory, explaining that the "false reports unfortunately give ammunition to the industry of Islamophobes who promote the demonization and dehumanization of Islamic Muslims." He adds that the Muslim community "is under great psychological stress and tension right now, and that that in itself can cause mental health issues that lead to these types of incidents."[47] Robert Spencer explains the reasoning here:

Why is the Muslim community, in Hooper's view, "under great psychological stress and tension"? Because of all the hate crimes against Muslims, you see, which drive Muslims so crazy that they...fake hate crimes against Muslims.[48]

And so, despite the fact that these fake "Islamophobic" hate crimes have become an entirely transparent, phony, and toxic phenomenon, the establishment media remain silent about their significance and what they suggest about Muslim claims of having been victimized. Consequently, the accusations and hoaxes grow in number while Western culture continues its willful blindness regarding this grand deception.

Now that we have demonstrated how crucial it is for Islamic supremacism and its minions to make Muslims the victims in the terror and culture war—even to the point of complete insanity—we move on to explore the other key psychopathic traits of the Islamic supremacist. The next chapter will narrow in on how the Jihadist Psychopath plays the "unappreciated" card while exhibiting a grand sense of entitlement, makes up fake events in his fake past, emphasizes how "we are so much alike" to his victims, and pretends to act in their best interests—all while endlessly making groundless accusations against them and working toward their destruction. We will also establish how the Jihadist Psychopath, like most psychopaths, suffers from *detachment disorder* and a lack of identity that makes it impossible for him to have any genuine self-realization or to engage in any authentic self-expression. This defective trait instills in him the lust to aggressively dominate and annihilate others—which all culminates in the tyranny and violence of jihad and sharia. Our next chapter unveils how this whole psychopathic and pathological formula works, and how it is successfully crippling the foundations of our civilization.

CHAPTER 13

"WE ARE A LOT ALIKE"

Once the Jihadist Psychopath succeeds in getting his victims to blame themselves for the abuse he is inflicting on them, and to apologize to him for the abuse they are receiving, he can more effectively employ the other weapons in his arsenal to tighten the noose around their necks. This chapter will focus in on these particular weapons. As we proceed, we once again encourage our readers to keep Chapter 9 and its key themes at hand, for as we explore the Jihadist Psychopath's other main characteristics, it will become transparently evident how his war is a carbon copy of the psychopath's battle plan, albeit with a jihadist twist.

Throughout his whole *I am the victim* charade, the Jihadist Psychopath also plays his *I am unappreciated* card. This tactic sees him sulking about how all of his supposed accomplishments and acts of generosity have gone unnoticed and have failed to earn him the gratitude and recognition he deserves. We see this clearly in the realm of Islamic supremacists' perpetual complaints about the world's disregard for them and their purported achievements. And yet, when we look more closely at the inventions and discoveries with which Islamic "civilization" has been credited, it quickly becomes clear that they are mostly fabrications. And in those cases when they actually did occur, they occurred *in spite of* Islam, rather than because of it.[1] Author Serge Trifkovic explains,

> Moslems overran societies (Persian, Greek, Egyptian, Byzantine, Syrian, Jewish) that possessed intellectual sophistication in their own right and failed to completely destroy their cultures. To give it the credit for what the remnants of these cultures achieved is like crediting the Red Army for the survival of Chopin in Warsaw in 1970! Islam per se never encouraged science, in the sense of disinterested enquiry, because the only knowledge it accepts is religious knowledge.[2]

Author Robert Spencer amplifies this reality, stating:

> ...there was a time when it was indeed true that Islamic culture was more advanced than that of Europeans, but that superiority corresponds exactly to the period when Muslims were able to draw on and advance the achievements of Byzantine and other civilizations. But when the Muslim overlords had taken what they could from their subject peoples, and the Jewish and Christian communities had been stripped of their material and intellectual wealth and thoroughly subdued, Islam went into a period of intellectual decline from which it has not yet recovered.[3]

What Trifkovic and Spencer are revealing here is that Islamic "inventions" are, in most cases, simply myths. For instance, the Islamic world often boasts that its civilization invented, among other things, the camera, a "flying machine," and rocket-powered flight. But, as writer J. Christian Adams has demonstrated, all of this is simply untrue. In a meticulous deconstruction of a National Geographic Explorers Hall exhibit in February 2013 titled "1001 Inventions: Discover the Golden Age of Muslim Civilization," Adams demonstrates that many of the inventions listed were not "Muslim" at all, and that the supposed "golden age" itself was really about mingling myths with science and transforming rumors into history.[4] Robert Spencer also notes that even where the inventions can authentically be attributed to Muslims, this does not mean that they came about because of Islam. "The Islamic identity of the inventor," he emphasizes, "has nothing to do with the invention."[5]

President Obama routinely jumped on the bandwagon of this myth-making about Islamic inventions. In his Cairo speech in early June 2009, for example, he spoke glowingly about Western civilization's "debt to Islam," claiming that it was Islam "that carried the light of learning through so many centuries, paving the way for Europe's Renaissance and Enlightenment." He alleged:

> It was innovation in Muslim communities that developed the order of algebra; our magnetic compass and tools of navigation; our mastery of pens and printing; our understanding of how disease spreads and how it can be healed.[6]

What the president stated on this score made many of the usual suspects feel good about themselves. But in terms of substance, his assertions were either unmitigated lies or twisted exaggerations. As Robert Spencer noted in his takedown of all of Obama's deceptions in the speech:

> The astrolabe was developed, if not perfected, long before Muhammad was born. The zero, which is often attributed to Muslims, and what we know today as "Arabic numerals" did not originate in Arabia, but in pre-Islamic India. Aristotle's work was preserved in Arabic not initially by Muslims at all, but by Christians such as the fifth century priest Probus of Antioch, who introduced Aristotle to the Arabic-speaking world. Another Christian, Huneyn ibn-Ishaq (809–873), translated many works by Aristotle, Galen, Plato and Hippocrates into Syriac. His son then translated them into Arabic. The Syrian Christian Yahya ibn Adi (893–974) also translated works of philosophy into Arabic, and wrote one of his own, The Reformation of Morals. His student, another Christian named Abu Ali Isa ibn Zur'a (943–1008), also translated Aristotle and others from Syriac into Arabic. The first Arabic-language medical treatise was written by

a Christian priest and translated into Arabic by a Jewish doctor in 683. The first hospital was founded in Baghdad during the Abbasid caliphate—not by a Muslim, but a Nestorian Christian. A pioneering medical school was founded at Gundeshapur in Persia—by Assyrian Christians.[7]

Thus, it was not too surprising that when a Palestinian museum that cost twenty-five million dollars to build opened up in May 2016, it was empty. That's right. *It didn't have one exhibit.* As writer Daniel Greenfield notes, the "exhibit" had "nothing inside for any of the visitors to see except the bare walls."[8]

This whole Muslim charade of taking credit for inventions is a crucial part of the psychopathic trait of *inventing a fictitious and false past.* Many non-Muslims, meanwhile, desperately want to be deceived because they are entirely under the sway of the Control Factor.[9] When presented with tales of supposed Islamic achievements, they dutifully bend over backwards to express their gratitude to, and reverence for, Islam.

Emblematic of this phenomenon were President Obama's frequent statements about how Islam played a fundamental role in building America and how America is a Muslim nation.[10] In reality, these notions are completely absurd and utterly false.[11]

We begin to get a better understanding of the various factors that give Islamic supremacists a grand sense of entitlement. It becomes clearer what lies behind their ever-growing demand to have their "religious" practices accommodated in the West. They insist that their way of life be integrated into the West and that they be given preferential treatment on the West's territory. At the same time, they do not, obviously, reciprocate in the same manner to non-Muslims in Muslim nations. This is because they are well aware that they have already conquered many of the unbelievers psychologically.

At this point, it is important for us to incorporate the term *dhimmi* into our discussion. Mentioned in Chapter 10, dhimmi is the label used to describe the conquered unbeliever. The dhimmi is the non-Muslim in a Muslim-dominated society who accepts a subordinate/inferior legal status in order to receive "protection" from harm. He is also increasingly known today as the unbeliever in a non-Islamic-dominated society who accepts his inferiority and submits to Islamic rule out of fear of Islamic intimidation and terror.[12] Many dhimmis in the West are, as we have described them in our earlier chapters,[13] intoxicated with their own arrogant delusion that, in accepting their inferior status, they can actually change Islamic supremacists. The Jihadist Psychopath knows that this cowardly, narcissistic belief system exists in the dhimmi, and he exploits it. He is well aware that many dhimmis are ruled by the Control Factor and, therefore, have a strong instinct to stay in denial throughout the whole ordeal of their own self-extinction. This sheds light on the reason why Muslim refugees and migrants are, for example, successful in implementing their welfare scam in the West today. While the dhimmis hand out welfare benefits in order to feel good about themselves, the Muslim recipients see this funding as part of their well-deserved *jizya* payment—which is the religiously mandated tax that dhimmis owe to Muslims in Muslim lands under Islamic law.[14]

While this manipulative *I am not appreciated* and *you owe me* charade is in process, the Jihadist Psychopath also focuses in on convincing his victim that *he is acting in the victim's interest* and *wants the best for him*. As we discussed in Chapter 4, this dynamic reflects the story of the Serpent in the Garden of Eden. The Serpent charmed, seduced, and tricked Eve, making her believe that he was looking out for her interests, when in actuality, he was destroying her.

Dinesh D'Souza has used the Serpent in the Garden of Eden story to crystallize the workings of the Left[15]—and to reveal how Obama and Hillary have emulated the deceptive tactics of Saul Alinsky, the Left's Godfather, to foment revolution in America and other free societies. What they learned from Alinsky was the effectiveness of pretending to be part of the middle class—or to like the middle class—and to posture as though they have the middle class's interests in mind. At the same time, they work to destroy the middle class. D'Souza explains that it is no coincidence that Alinsky paid a tribute to Lucifer in his book, *Rules for Radicals*, since the late community organizer clearly appreciated Satan's strategy vis-à-vis Eve. In Lucifer, Alinsky saw a model of how to destroy the country and system that he hated. Indeed, Alinsky treasured the tactic of working to annihilate a system while posing as if he was a part of it and was trying to help it succeed.[16] The key, in all of this, as D'Souza demonstrates, is to "pretend to be like the people you hate" and secretly want to destroy.[17]

Islamic supremacists know this tactic well and practice it brilliantly. It is all part of their strategy of *defeating us by our own hands*.[18] For example, they perpetually sell their supposed "moderation" and peaceful, loving nature to the gullible and desperate dhimmi and explain to him how they are operating in his best interest. They promote the palatable fiction that "jihad" is an internal spiritual, or economic and political, battle that has nothing to do with violence.[19] The stage is then set for the "interfaith dialogue" that will bring everyone together because, as the Islamic supremacists assure the dhimmis, *everyone wants the same thing*. The message is delivered, as it always is by psychopaths, that *"we are a lot alike."*

The seduction process in effect here is obvious. The dhimmis are given myriads of lectures by Islamic supremacists about the great similarities that exist between their respective cultures and religions. The dhimmis are told that Islam is very much like Christianity and Judaism, that it shares so many of the same beliefs and values that are central to those faiths, and that it is actually just a fulfillment of the two religions. In making this argument, Islamic supremacists stress how they respect and also "believe in" Jesus and Mary, and that "we all worship the same God."

But these pronouncements are simply false. Islam cannot possibly "respect" Jesus when it blatantly lies about Him—and lies about what Christianity actually is and what it teaches. Indeed, Islam holds that Jesus *did not* die on the cross, is not divine, and is not part of the Holy Trinity (the existence of which it rejects). *Salvation through Christ's blood is not accepted by Islam.* The Qur'an explicitly rejects Christianity and the Christian notion of God. The Jesus of the Qur'an has been inserted into the Qur'an for the sole purpose of denying the teachings and reality of Jesus of Nazareth.[20] And it is completely evident that the God of the Old and New Testament is definitely not the Allah of the Qur'an.[21] Yet Islamic supremacists still maintain that Islam somehow "respects" Jesus—and gullible Christian dhimmis desperately eat it up. They embrace this argument, grasping at the delusion that Islam wants peace, that Islamic supremacists are just like them and, therefore, that jihad will vanish once all unbelievers just do what they are told and give the Jihadist Psychopath what he wants.[22]

The key in this pathological dynamic is that, just like the victim of the psychopath projects his own values unto the psychopath, so too do many contemporary dhimmis project their illusions unto the Islamic supremacist. As discussed in Chapter 5, this is, on one level, a very self-centered, narcissistic, and egoistic disposition, since the dhimmi who falls for the deceit is ruled by the Control Factor and is engaging in willful blindness rather than in a fight for truth and self-preservation. He is fighting for his own temporary peace of mind and to make sense of the world around him, rather than facing a situation that he himself cannot personally handle.[23]

All the while, just as the psychopath conveys indignation to scare off the accuser and makes groundless accusations,[24] the same is done by the Jihadist Psychopath. This keeps the unbelievers on the defensive and draws attention away from the Jihadist Psychopath's faults. We see this in play 24/7 in our terror and culture war today, as Islamic supremacists perpetually run their grievance industry while the Left supports and fuels them in doing so. The fake hate crimes against Muslims that we discussed earlier exemplify this tactic.[25] The dhimmi culture, meanwhile, desperately caves in and surrenders each time, issuing endless and profuse apologies—instead of calling out the false accusations for what they really are.

The groundless accusations are part of the psychopathic propaganda war. As described in Chapter 9, the psychopath works hard at controlling how people think and see, since he is an expert at molding *the perception of others*.[26] Victims of the psychopath are at a severe disadvantage, because they are not experts, like he is, at this game. The same dynamic transpires between the Jihadist Psychopath and his victims. The former is an expert in shaping the minds of the unbelievers, and many of them simply do not know how, or have the courage, to fight the culture war. The West, therefore, is losing on the battleground of ideas and political war. And that is precisely why truth-telling about Islam is now considered racism and hate speech, since the Jihadist Psychopath has shaped that lie to be a widely accepted article of faith in Western culture. On this realm, our enemy has won a crucial victory.

At this point, it is vital to pinpoint a central foundation of the Jihadist Psychopath's aggression: *detachment disorder*. As discussed in Chapter 9, psychopathy experts Thomas Sheridan and Mary Stout noted that psychopaths suffer from a lack of self, a lack of identity, and a deficient sense of responsibility, emotional attachment, and empathy. It is vital to understand that, as Sheridan and Stout explain, a need to *dominate others* stems from this void.[27] And this is where we begin to better decipher Islamic supremacism's aggression and expansionism. This totalitarian and violent ideology has to subjugate others in order to *nurture a sense of self.* That is because a sense of self is nonexistent in Islamic supremacism.

Islamic supremacism crushes all individuality within itself. Its members cannot have their own identity or beliefs, nor can they explore or nurture their own happiness or talents. They are allowed to do nothing except worship Allah and, in turn, wage jihad. In the world of the Islamic supremacist, the unbeliever must be crushed and dominated so that the Jihadist Psychopath *can temporarily feel something and have an identity of his own.* The root of this reality is, in part, the Jihadist Psychopath's childhood. He grew up in a world of neglect and, very often, severe child abuse and rampant sexual violation.[28] There was such a void of true love and affection in his childhood that there was no true bonding with parents. And it is no surprise that Islamic tradition holds that the prophet himself also had no bonding with his parents. Muhammad's father died soon after Muhammad's birth, and his mother died when he was only six. Before that, Muhammad was in the care of a foster mother and nursemaid.[29] As a result, *detachment disorder is part of the foundation of Islam itself.* Thus, it becomes apparent why many men in Islamic culture find their only avenue to meaning and gratification in the act of dominating and humiliating the foreign "enemy."[30]

The barren world in which the Jihadist Psychopath grew up is connected to the glaring absence of any real interests in Islamic fundamentalist environments—just as in the life of any psychopath. As we demonstrated in Chapter 9, psychopaths have an inability to be interested in the things of life, because they don't feel and appreciate the essence of life the way that normal humans do. There is, for example, no interest in the world of literature, sports, the arts, etc.[31] And the same goes for the Jihadist Psychopath. He is disinterested in most realms of life, be it in movies and books or in music and painting, etc.

Overall, the Jihad Psychopath's belief system sees modernization and creativity as blasphemy. It is a culture and religion that rejects human reason, individual responsibility, and personal achievement as important values. Indeed, in any Islamic fundamentalist environment, the individual must sublimate himself into the collective whole, making it impossible for him to find or express himself as an individual. Sayyid Abul A'la Maududi, a leading twentieth-century Islamic thinker and activist, gave voice to this deep cultural neurosis in Islam:

> No one has the right to become a self-appointed ruler of men and issue orders and prohibitions on his own volition and authority. To acknowledge the personal authority of a human being as the source of commands and prohibitions is tantamount to admitting him as the sharer in the Powers and Authority of God. And this is the root of all evils in the universe.[32]

In contrast, Western civilization is antithetical to this soulless tendency espoused by Maududi. As the literary scholar M. H. Abrams has explained, it was in the eighteenth century that the West developed the concept that the human being is, at his best, an artist whose powers are modeled upon those of the divine creator himself.[33] This concept served as the foundation for the rise of liberal, democratic values in the West. The Western tradition, in other words, sees the individual as possessing within him a divine power, and therefore his creativity is not blasphemous, but is rather a natural and desirable fulfillment of his own nature. This is a crucial distinction between Islam and the Judeo-Christian tradition.[34]

The individual enslaved in an Islamic fundamentalist environment does not have this freedom that is described above. Instead, he must always be subservient to his controlling masters and to the totalitarian collective.[35] Individual self-expression is seen as blasphemy—as is any attempt to change or reform Islam. There is no personal identity or inner self; there is no interest in anything— except in the duty to carry out Allah's mandates. This obvious, gigantic void within the Jihadist Psychopath must be filled by the domination of others and, consequently, the subjugation of the unbeliever.

We begin to understand why there is such a ferocious hatred of music, joy, and laughter in Islamic fundamentalist environments, a hatred that is connected to the shortage or complete nonexistence of toys and games for children in the Muslim-Arab world.[36] Scholar David Pryce-Jones notes,

> There appears never to have been any such thing as an Arab toy or games for children, in the sense that Western children have had a ball or a hoop, a shuttlecock or board games. To this day, toys and games and bicycles are Western imports or imitations. Similarly, there are old and often striking folktales that Arab children may enjoy, but no classic such as Robinson Crusoe or Black Beauty conceived specifically for the imaginative child.[37]

There are, of course, "games" in the Islamic Middle East such as showing Muslim children videos of beheadings,[38] or having the children themselves engage in beheading of either stuffed animals[39] or real people.[40] But it remains debatable whether these activities really belong under the category of anything the civilized world would label a "game."

Consequently, our conclusion becomes clear: psychopathy nurtures a culture of domination over others. The Jihadist Psychopath's control and subjugation of unbelievers, therefore, is his one true priority. With our understanding of this phenomenon now under our belts, our story enters its next stage: unveiling the dhimmi's powerful need to identify with, and to excuse, his jihadist abuser. This dynamic plays a crucial role in the West's contemporary surrender to Islamic supremacism, and we explore it in our next chapter.

PART 3

The Devouring

CHAPTER 14

IDENTIFYING WITH THE JIHADIST PSYCHOPATH

Now that we have outlined the world of the Jihadist Psychopath, we begin to clearly see how and why Islamic supremacism is so successful at charming, deceiving, and devouring the West. At this stage, it is crucial for us to focus in on the codependent relationship between the Jihadist psychopath and his Western dhimmi victim,[1] for this dysfunctional dynamic is a vital factor in the West's current surrender. And to be sure, jihadists are now sealing their victory *by getting their victims to identify with them*.

The best way to begin explaining how Western victims identify with their jihadist abusers is to illuminate how communities and people under chronic siege typically react to their circumstances. This is a subject that Kenneth Levin has masterfully documented in *The Oslo Syndrome: Delusions of a People Under Siege*.[2] Analyzing the tendencies of people in an abused community to cope with their situation, Levin unveils how and why many Israelis and Jews have deluded themselves in the face of a death cult that seeks to annihilate them. He demonstrates how many abused people ignore the reality of the hatred that their abusers have for them, and how they cope with their situation *by embracing the indictments of their abusers* and indulging in *the delusion that self-reform will somehow end their abusers' hatred of them.*

Levin documents how this syndrome of embracing the abuser's indictments has been extremely prominent within Jewish Diaspora communities confronted by chronic anti-Semitism and reflects the overall Jewish experience in the face of Jew hatred. He shows how this Jewish disposition ultimately culminated in what he calls the *Oslo Syndrome*, which saw many Israelis entertain mass delusions that peace could be achieved through the Oslo Peace Accords, when the empirical evidence suggested the very opposite.

Levin unveils the process by which many Jews assume responsibility and guilt for their own victimization. This tendency evolves into the belief that self-reform in conformity with the besiegers' indictments will allay the siege, make the besiegers accept Jews, and ultimately foster peace. Levin points out how the professional literature explaining this tendency has often invoked the psychoanalytic concept of "identification with the aggressor," a dynamic in which the victim engages in to gain a feeling of control. The concept helps explain

> a defense mechanism in which the individual blunts the pain of negative interactions with others, such as criticism or rejection, by embracing the indictment, making it one's own self-criticism. The individual thereby at least attains a sense of being in control of the indictment rather than simply being the passive victim of assault by others, and he or she attains also a sense of shared comprehension and rapport with the attacking other rather than feeling simply the targeted outsider.[3]

Levin explains how the victim often casts the blame for his own abuse onto others in his group, in order to feel better about himself and to ingratiate himself with his abuser. The victim projects the painful indictment onto others, directing at others the same criticism and becoming the victimizer, thereby "mastering" the indictment and further reinforcing the sense of rapport with the subject's own attackers.[4]

In this way, the victim experiences the comfort of perceiving *others* in his besieged community, rather than *himself*, as the possessors of the ugly and hateful characteristics he is accused of having. Levin points to the example of Jews who see other Jews, and not themselves, as fitting anti-Semitic caricatures.[5] This paradigm *applies exactly* to many dhimmis in the West today. And this is no surprise, since, as Levin notes, history records that myriad communities under chronic siege have behaved in exactly the same manner as he documents.[6] He writes,

> The inclination to retreat to delusions of transgression, and of salvation through self-reform and concessions, is common, even endemic, within communities under chronic siege.[7]

We begin to see, therefore, how and why many unbelievers in free societies are responding the way they are to the siege inflicted on them by the Jihadist Psychopath. *They make the truth-tellers about jihad and sharia bear responsibility and guilt.* Their illusion is that *it is our side that has to change.* Through their distorted lens, we are the ones who have to stop being Islamophobic, racist, and imperialistic; we are the ones who need to accommodate the Jihadist Psychopath in all the ways that he demands.

This is why truth-tellers about Islam are now so mercilessly slandered and persecuted by their own political leaders, culture, and media in the West. Indeed, they are castigated and smeared not only by the Jihadist Psychopath, but also by the dhimmis who are preoccupied with *embracing the besiegers' indictments and deflecting them off of themselves and onto the truth-tellers.* In this way, these dhimmis get to feel better about themselves, shift themselves (temporarily) out of harm's way, and delude themselves into thinking that they have somehow forged a sense of rapport and understanding with their accusers and abusers.

This clear manifestation of Stockholm syndrome[8] involves a key ingredient that author Bill Siegel has labeled the *Addiction/ Enabling Dance*.[9] While the jihadist coerces the dhimmi to defend and identify with Islamic supremacism even as he is being abused and conquered by it, a toxic codependency develops between him and his victim. Siegel explains how the West is locked with its Islamic supremacist abuser in an "addiction-enabling dance," whereby the West takes responsibility for its abuser's conduct. In this process, Siegel explains, the West keeps two illusions alive simultaneously: (1) the belief that Islamic terror is something other than what it is, and (2) the belief that it is within our power to change the psychology of Islamic terrorists.[10] We are, therefore, *part of the script*, and that makes us feel good—because it helps us feel in control. This is the role played by the Control Factor, which is the title of Siegel's book and which we have outlined in Chapter 5. "The result," Siegel writes, "resembles a classic addiction/enabling relationship wherein one party's destructive behavior is supported by another's assistance."[11] He explains: "A defining element of addiction is to blame: other people, in essence, have caused the addict's behavior."[12] Thus, the enablers "make endless excuses for the addict and attempt to qualify or redefine the addict's behavior to others."[13]

Siegel also emphasizes how the dhimmi enabler is motivated in this dance by his own grandiosity. He derives tremendous gratification from seeing himself as being part of the script and as having the power to change the addict's behavior.[14] As we discussed earlier, this is directly connected to the narcissism that leads the typical leftist to assume that he can penetrate and soften the heart of the Islamic supremacist.[15] Siegel also explains how the enabler in this whole dynamic has a huge self-interest in keeping the circle of abuse going. This is because *there is pain and agony in sepa-rating from the addict*. To break the cycle would force the enabler to reevaluate his own identity, and he would have to give up his grandiose, fantastical belief in the central role he is playing in the entire drama. Siegel explains:

> Enablers have immense difficulty separating from the addict. This entails not just uprooting the relationship with the addict but re-evaluating much of the thinking and presuppositions that have supported that relationship. This is especially difficult for enablers because it seems to require a reversal of much of what the enabler has previously considered moral, ethical, and even loving in that relationship.[16]

All of this, of course, ultimately leads the enabler into greater danger. As Siegel notes,

> While an alcoholic's enabler believes he is helping the alcoholic, he is actually reinforcing the addiction.... As the enemy obtains more and more powerful weapons, this reinforcement leads us into greater peril.[17]

And so, many dhimmis in the West today are very much respon-sible for the Jihadist Psychopath's behavior, just as the victims of the psychopath are responsible for the psychopath's behavior.[18]

Now that we have illustrated how the West is identifying with the Jihadist Psychopath today, and how this identification is connected to its own surrender, we turn to exposing the key ele-ments of the surrender itself. This entails examining how Islamic supremacists have infiltrated the U.S. government—and the extent to which they are now doing the thinking, and making the deci-sions, for us. And while the Trump administration is, as we have discussed, offering great hope that this catastrophic development can be reversed,[19] the Jihadist Psychopath unfortunately continues to rule over vital realms of our government and culture.

In our next chapter, we build on the tale we began telling in Chapter 1 and continue to unveil the horrifying details of our own willful suicide—conducted at the behest of the Jihadist Psychopath.

CHAPTER 15

LETTING IN THE JIHADIST PSYCHOPATH

The Jihadist Psychopath's war of attrition against the dhimmi unbeliever[1] has clearly resulted in the West's surrender to the Islamic supremacist onslaught. This capitulation has facilitated the enemy's deep penetration of our society—of our government, media, academic institutions, Hollywood, and the culture at large. The more the West surrenders, the more the enemy infiltrates, and the more the enemy infiltrates, the more he molds our minds, instructs us how to think and, in turn, leads us down the road to our own annihilation. In this chapter, we will build on Chapter 1 by continuing the story of how the Jihadist Psychopath has gained his control of us—especially during the Obama years. We begin by demonstrating how our enemy got in through the door in the first place—that vital initial step by which the Jihadist Psychopath gained entry, so that he could begin the process of devouring us.

The Jihadist Psychopath has been working on subjugating us for a long time. It was the 9/11 atrocity, however, that proved to be the major catastrophic turning point, for it was in the crucial post-9/11 moment that this demon gained his entry. When America confronted 9/11, it had a solemn obligation to identify the guilty perpetrator and to be honest about his true character and motives. But at that crucial hour, America dropped the ball. Indeed, President George W. Bush gave in to the self-destructive Jihad Denial agenda,[2] dutifully announcing that Islam was a "religion of peace" and that it had no connection to Islamic terror in general or to 9/11 in particular.[3] Bush gave voice to the utterly unfounded fiction that the Jihadist Psychopath wanted him to tell: that the individuals who perpetrated 9/11 were just a small group of extremists who had misunderstood and hijacked Islam.[4] And so, the foundation for the U.S. war on terror was built on paralytic weakness and toxic denial.

Author Stephen Coughlin has meticulously outlined the catastrophe of the Bush administration's Jihad Denial in the immediate aftermath of 9/11. He crystallizes how, at that dire moment, "a two-tiered" plan of action needed to be implemented. The first tier, says Coughlin, should have been an education campaign that would have properly informed the non-Muslim as well as Muslim population of what Islamic teachings and requirements really were. The second tier ought to have been a thorough analysis of the allegation that Islam was indeed a peaceful faith that had been hijacked by a relative few, so as to ascertain whether or not that was true. But none of this was done, and so, Coughlin observes, "we missed the mark from the beginning."[5] Consequently, it was never actually proven that Islam had been hijacked and that 9/11 was un-Islamic. That false claim was simply embraced as an article of faith.

Because the Bush administration had adopted Jihad Denial in regards to 9/11, the individuals within the administration who didn't embrace the creed that Islam was a Religion of Peace had to go. And go they did. A watershed moment was the termination of Coughlin himself, who had been serving as a U.S. Army Reserve major and Joint Chiefs of Staff intelligence officer. Coughlin was the

Pentagon's lone expert and truth-teller about Islamic law. Yet he was released from the Defense Department in January 2008 because he was sounding the alarm about the Muslim Brotherhood's influence at the highest levels of our government and telling the truth about Islam's doctrines mandating warfare against unbelievers. In his paper, "'To Our Great Detriment': Ignoring What Extremists Say About Jihad," submitted to the National Defense Intelligence College in July 2007, Coughlin warned that the refusal to name the enemy and to be truthful about Islam—a refusal rooted in the fact that the Muslim Brotherhood had gained considerable influence over our government—was jeopardizing U.S. national security. His termination came to pass because Hesham Islam, a Muslim aide to Deputy Defense Secretary Gordon England, urged his firing.[6] The fact that Mr. Islam was an aide to Mr. England revealed the disturbing extent to which the Jihadist Psychopath had already penetrated the U.S. government.

Once Obama took office, things went from bad to worse very quickly. The leftist administration embraced Islamic supremacism's presence in the U.S. government and began to enable it.[7] It was no surprise, for instance, when the new administration forced Egyptian president Hosni Mubarak to accommodate the Muslim Brotherhood and allow its leaders to occupy front-row seats at Obama's famous Cairo speech in June 2009.[8] And when Mubarak's problems escalated in Egypt, the Obama administration, instead of supporting a U.S. ally that was holding jihadists and sharia in check, pressured Mubarak to step down and supported the Muslim Brotherhood takeover instead.[9]

This empowerment of the Brotherhood in Egypt transparently revealed whom the Obama White House was now allied with—and who was also gaining more and more influence within the U.S. government. In this context, it would do well to note that *the Muslim Brotherhood is an enemy of the United States* and that one of its key goals is to destroy America *from within* and to build its caliphate on the ashes of the American Constitution—an objective which the Brotherhood clearly spells out in its own constitution and internal documents.[10] And yet, the Obama administration *allied itself with the Brotherhood* and consistently deceived the American people and the international community about what the Brotherhood actually was.

For instance, on February 10, 2011, Director of National Intelligence James Clapper appeared before the House Select Committee on Intelligence, spewing fictions about how secular and democratically inclined the Muslim Brotherhood had become. The Islamic terrorist organization, he proclaimed,

> is an umbrella term for a variety of movements, in the case of Egypt, a very heterogeneous group, largely secular, which has eschewed violence and has decried al-Qaeda as a perversion of Islam...They have pursued social ends, a betterment of the political order in Egypt, et cetera.... In other countries, there are also chapters or franchises of the Muslim Brotherhood, but there is no overarching agenda, particularly in pursuit of violence, at least internationally.[11]

Writer Daniel Greenfield exposed how utterly fraudulent Clapper's "interpretation" was:

> Clapper was presenting a report from another planet. The one thing that the Muslim Brotherhood was not and could never be was secular. The Brotherhood's motto, "Allah is our objective. The Prophet is our leader. The Qur'an is our law. Jihad is our way. Dying in the way of Allah is our highest hope" could be described in a number of ways. Secular would not be one of them.[12]

Indeed, far from being an "umbrella" group, the Muslim Brotherhood is a genocidal organization originally funded and inspired by Nazi Germany. Every single al-Qaeda leader, including Osama bin Laden, has been a Brotherhood member. And three months after Clapper's testimony, the Brotherhood responded to the assassination of bin Laden by openly endorsing al-Qaeda.[13]

After Muslim Brotherhood leader Mohamed Morsi came to power in June 2012 and made himself an Islamist dictator, the Brotherhood unleashed its rape squads, enabled the burnings of Coptic churches, and tightened the grip of sharia on the reins of political power in Egypt.[14] Expectedly, there were no reprimands for this behavior coming from the White House, the type that Mubarak had consistently heard from Obama. When hundreds of thousands of protesters gathered in Tahrir Square protesting Morsi after his power grab, Obama didn't tell Morsi to step down the way he had done with Mubarak. The Iranian protesters whom Obama had betrayed back in 2009 understood it all too well. As Greenfield observed: "While the ears of Obama were highly attuned to any Islamist protests against non-Islamist regimes, they had a built-in filter that tuned out any outcries against Islamist governments."[15]

This pro-Brotherhood U.S. policy was all facilitated, of course, by the Coughlin purge under Bush. It had been a significant turning point, because from that moment forward, a persistent effort began under Obama to bring jihad-friendly factions into the government. These forces would not question the kinds of policies that had been emblematic of Obama's pro-Morsi disposition. There were many such characters brought in. We now unveil a sampling of some of these dangerous individuals:

The presence of Mohamed Elibiary in the Obama administration really said it all.[16] An admirer of the late Ayatollah Khomeini and a Muslim Brotherhood sympathizer, Elibiary was on Obama's Homeland Security Advisory Council and had access to highly classified intelligence material. During his time with DHS, he was caught misusing classified documents to promote the fabricated notion that "Islamophobia" was widespread in the U.S.; he helped eliminate the training materials that had previously educated DHS and FBI personnel regarding the ideology and tactics of the U.S. Muslim Brotherhood; and he aided the purge of FBI curricula and training materials that drew any connections between Islam and terrorism. Elibiary distinguished himself by signaling his steadfast solidarity with Morsi, a solidarity that included his adding of the "Rabia" symbol, a Brotherhood logo, to his Twitter avatar.[17] In October 2013, while still on the Homeland Security Advisory Council, he declared Islam's victory over the U.S., stating: "I do consider the United States of America an Islamic country with an Islamically compliant constitution."[18]

In August 2014, Elibiary boasted on Twitter of his continued close ties to the Republican Party and to the national security and law-enforcement communities. He assured his followers that the Muslim Brotherhood's infiltration of the U.S. government *had become so deep as to be irreversible*. And the "Rabia" symbol was, again, in his Twitter feed.[19] Elibiary was let go from his position the next month, in September 2014, under mysterious circumstances. He had served the Obama administration for four full years.[20]

John Brennan, the longtime CIA official who served as CIA director for Obama beginning in 2013, was likewise emblematic of the Obama administration's obvious allegiance to the Unholy Alliance.[21] This was an individual who referred to Jerusalem by its Arabic name, "Al-Quds," and who routinely denied that jihad was a problem, arguing that the term meant only "to purify oneself or to wage a holy struggle for a moral goal."[22] Brennan had revealed his true stripes back in September 2010, while he was deputy national security adviser for homeland security and counterterrorism. At that time, under his watch, a high-level Hamas operative in the U.S. and an unindicted coconspirator in the Holy Land Foundation trial—Sheikh Kifah Mustapha—received a guided tour of the top-secret National Counterterrorism Center, one of America's most sensitive counterterrorism facilities, and at the FBI Academy at Quantico, Virginia.[23] Several former intelligence and defense officials, including Center for Security Policy chief and former Reagan administration official Frank Gaffney, called for Brennan to resign; Brennan did not comply.[24]

In 2011, while still serving as deputy national security adviser for homeland security and counterterrorism, Brennan directed U.S. officials to refrain from suggesting that there was any correlation between terror attacks and Islam, and he instructed the FBI to take all references to "jihad" and "radical Islam" out of its curriculum and training manuals.[25] He was also directly involved in crafting the "talking points" that National Security Adviser Susan Rice recited regarding the September 11, 2012, Benghazi terrorist attack, in which U.S. Ambassador Christopher Stevens and three other U.S. nationals were murdered due to Obama's betrayal.[26]

In February 2013, John Guandolo, a former Marine who subsequently worked eight years in the FBI's Counterterrorism Division as a "subject matter expert" regarding the Muslim Brotherhood and the global spread of Islam, stated that Brennan had converted to Islam years earlier in Saudi Arabia while serving in an official capacity on behalf of the U.S. in that country. Guandolo stressed that this conversion represented "the culmination of a counter-intelligence operation against [Brennan] to recruit him." He went on to say:

> The fact that foreign intelligence service operatives recruited Mr. Brennan when he was in a very sensitive and senior U.S. government position in a foreign country means that he is either a traitor ... [or] he has the inability to discern and understand how to walk in those kinds of environments, which makes him completely unfit to be the director of Central Intelligence.... The facts of the matter are confirmed by U.S. government officials who were also in Saudi Arabia at the time that John Brennan was

serving there and have direct knowledge. These are men who work in very trusted positions, they were direct witnesses to his growing relationship with the individuals who worked for the Saudi government and others and they witnessed his conversion to Islam.[27]

Whether the allegation of Brennan's Muslim conversion was true or not, the fact that there had never even been an investigation into the matter, let alone even a single question asked of Brennan on this issue by any major media source, was highly significant. One would think that in a country at war with Islamic supremacism, the possibility of a CIA director being a Muslim would interest the media and the culture, let alone that individual's own government superiors. But that was not the case. What was the case, however, was that Brennan had publicly praised "the goodness and beauty of Islam," which he characterized as "a faith of peace and tolerance."[28]

Other protagonists in this saga included the infamous Huma Abedin, an individual whose entire family is linked to the Muslim Brotherhood and who worked for twelve years as an assistant editor for the *Journal of Muslim Minority Affairs* (*JMMA*), which is run by the Muslim Brotherhood organization, Institute of Muslim Minority Affairs (IMMA). Abedin served on the *JMMA* under her mother, Saleha Mahmood Abedin, who was and still is editor in chief of that journal. While Huma was on board, the *JMMA* published articles that, among other things, blamed the U.S. for 9/11 and blamed women for rape if they dressed provocatively. Huma's mother, a pro-sharia sociologist, edited a book, published in 1999, that justified sharia law and barbaric practices such as female genital mutilation.[29] Huma was the deputy chief of staff for Hillary Clinton while Clinton was secretary of state in the Obama administration; thus, she had access to a great deal of classified information. Curiously enough, Huma was never asked, by even one reporter from the establishment media, what her thoughts were on her mother's views—or on the meaning of her own background at *JMMA*.

The cases of Mohamed Elibiary, John Brennan, and Huma Abedin were just the tip of the iceberg in terms of the Muslim Brotherhood's penetration of the Obama administration. Author Frank Gaffney documented the frightening extent of this phenomenon in his booklet, *The Muslim Brotherhood in the Obama Administration,* which laid bare the catastrophe and named the key players involved.[30]

The lack of any significant questioning in our establishment media and culture about why individuals such as Elibiary, Brennan, and Abedin were serving the U.S. government serves as evidence of the highly influential presence of the enemy in our government and culture. One brave voice did make itself heard, however, that of Republican representative Michele Bachmann, who in 2012 made an effort to initiate a federal investigation of the Muslim Brotherhood's infiltration of the U.S. government. Receiving support *from only four other representatives,* Bachmann became the target of wide-ranging criticism and ridicule—even by members of her own party, including Senator John McCain and House Speaker John Boehner.[31] In the end, the empirical evidence vindicated Bachmann.[32] Even Egypt's *Rose al-Yusuf* magazine confirmed that six highly placed Muslim Brotherhood infiltrators within the Obama administration had transformed the United States "from a position hostile to Islamic groups and organizations in the world to the largest and most important supporter of the Muslim Brotherhood."[33]

Without a doubt, the Muslim Brotherhood heavily penetrated the U.S. government during the Obama years and spread its tentacles across the entirety of U.S. culture. The penetration was actually so extensive that, as Stephen Coughlin notes, Muslim Brotherhood front groups were simply "out of reach of investigators, national security analysts, and even concerned Members of Congress."[34] Coughlin was right. Brotherhood-linked groups and individuals were now clearly above and outside of the law. And from this position of power, the Brotherhood was now able to easily slander and silence the truth-tellers about Islamic supremacism. Indeed, the Brotherhood would just volley the slanders about any idea or individual over to the establishment media, and then that idea or individual would be demonized and silenced. This is a paradigm that Coughlin refers to as a "recurring loop." He writes about what was transpiring under Obama at the time:

> First, government officials or appointees leak allegations of Islamophobic bias in the national security community. A partisan media outlet then amplifies the claim, triggering loud complaints and demands for restitution from Muslim-Brotherhood-linked lobby groups. Next, national security leaders in government, citing the lobby's protests, endeavor to squelch the offending materials, programs, or individuals.[35]

Thus, the Obama administration conducted the terror war in such a way that anything that that might be considered "inflammatory" was simply disallowed. Even if a course of action was legitimate and important, it would not be pursued if it posed the threat of "inflaming." Consequently, as Coughlin points out, all the Muslim Brotherhood front groups had to do to suppress a U.S. anti-terrorism measure was to suggest that the effort was "inflammatory." That course of action would then simply be shut down.[36] It is really no mystery, therefore, why Mohamed Elibiary was so brazen in boasting that the Muslim Brotherhood's infiltration of the U.S. government was irreversible.[37] Because of his own role in, and knowledge about, the infiltration, this reality was wholly evident to him.

The Jihadist Psychopath has, without a doubt, gotten in through the door and acquired significant control of our government, culture, and national discourse. Our next chapter examines the consequences of this control. It is the tragic story of our surrender to Islamic supremacism.

CHAPTER 16

MIND CONTROL UNDER THE JIHADIST PSYCHOPATH

Once the psychopath gains entry into your mind, he begins to frame your thoughts, what you say, and the words that you use. This is exactly what the Jihadist Psychopath has succeeded in doing through his infiltration of our government and culture. To be sure, he is now shaping our mindset, doing the thinking for us and, essentially, framing our disposition toward him.

In the Obama years, once the enemy had infiltrated our government and culture, it was clear that he controlled what words we were permitted to use in describing him. As Stephen Coughlin puts it, the enemy succeeded in establishing *language dominance* over us.[1] Indeed, language codes were embedded into the government under Obama, and anyone who violated those codes (i.e., identifying the Islamic supremacist enemy by his name) was punished. FBI and Homeland Security analysts, for instance, were sanctioned if they referred to the Islamic Movement by name—even if they were citing threat sources that used those very same Islamic terms to articulate their own motives and agendas.[2] In short, the Muslim Brotherhood had effectively succeeded in coercing the

U.S. government to forbid the identification of Islamic law as the ideology terrorizing us. As demonstrated earlier, the Obama administration followed the Brotherhood's directives in 2011–2012 and removed all references to jihad and Islam from its intelligence agencies' lexicon.[3]

To fill in the void of a nonexistent threat assessment in the terror war, the Obama administration incorporated its Countering Violent Extremism (CVE) strategy.[4] One major problem with CVE is that it is vague to the point of meaninglessness. As Coughlin points out, it "displaced any valuable description of the characteristics of the enemy in the War on Terror."[5] And the inherent uselessness of CVE was magnified by the fact that it very clearly encouraged the FBI to *do nothing*. Coughlin explains:

> On closer inspection, the FBI's definition is not randomly wrong, but rather it is precisely incoherent. Indeed, the same Lexicon that demands that FBI personnel use the term "violent extremism" also declares it inappropriate for actual use as a "predication for any investigative actions."[6]

To be sure, CVE injected incoherence into our understanding of who our enemy is. And this pleased the Muslim Brotherhood, whose front groups consistently pressure counterterror analysts to spend their time demonstrating how "terrorists and violent extremists vary in ethnicity, race, gender, and religion." It was no surprise, therefore, that the Muslim Public Affairs Council (MPAC), a Muslim Brotherhood–linked group, gave direction to the government that reflected this effort. Coughlin points out that MPAC

> urges the replacement of the word "Islamic" with abstractions like "radicalized" or "violent extremist." These terms have been used to obscure the discussion in unnecessary and irrelevant discussions on how "terrorists and violent extremists vary in ethnicity, race, gender and religion."[7]

Thus, CVE made the enemy so nebulous and poorly defined that he could not even be seen, nor, in turn, labeled. And it got worse: not only did CVE spawn incoherence and inaction, it also empowered Islamic supremacism by hurting those who were trying to fight it. Brotherhood figures themselves actually framed the CVE construct in such a way that it opposed the counter-jihad agenda and *advanced the Islamist agenda*. Coughlin writes how the Department of Homeland Security had been

> relying on leading members of known Muslim-Brotherhood front groups, including ISNA President Mohamed Imam Magid, to develop policies on Countering Violent Extremism that are demonstrably in line with the underlying requirements envisioned by the OIC's Ten-Year Programme of Action.[8]

The "OIC" Coughlin was referring to is the Organisation of Islamic Cooperation, the Islamic coalition that is made up of all fifty-seven Muslim states worldwide. In 2005, it published its "Ten Year Programme of Action" that identified "Combatting Islamophobia"—which basically meant shutting down truthful speech about Islam across the globe—as a main focus of its plan.[9] The CVE narrative, therefore, clearly empowered the enemy, since it not only followed the enemy's directives, but also targeted the forces trying to protect America and the West. The good guys became the enemy "extremists" who had to be countered.[10]

It becomes clear how the Jihadist Psychopath's penetration of our government led to him actually framing American policy in the Obama era. Individuals with Muslim Brotherhood affiliations dictated who could and could not work for the government on terror issues, and they dictated what could and could not be discussed.[11] When American leaders and strategists tried to formulate any rational policy for dealing with the enemy, they had to do so by consistently ignoring the fact that Islamic law is, in fact, the basis of what inspires and sanctions the actions of jihadists.

Our policy was being framed by people who operated on the assumption that our enemies are waging war on us for reasons *outside of what Islam teaches*, even though the enemies themselves proudly and candidly declare that they are waging war on us *precisely because of what Islam teaches*. It goes without saying that Islamic supremacists undoubtedly found all of this very entertaining in their dealings with the Obama administration. Coughlin notes that Muslim Brotherhood leaders must have had "to work at keeping a straight face when meeting senior government officials."[12]

In essence, under Obama, America was no longer permitted to name the enemy in the terror war. This was a disaster, since the U.S. simply cannot protect itself from an adversary by denying its existence and the ideas that motivate it. As Coughlin stresses, "There are geopolitical consequences to activities sanctioned by Islamic law that need to be recognized before they can be countered."[13] He synthesizes the core problem:

> The enemy in the War on Terror plans to win through subversion in the information battlespace by making it too politically costly to identify the threat. It accomplishes this by manipulating American leadership and media into imposing Islamic defamation standards on the national security and the law enforcement communities and on the American public.[14]

Coughlin continues:

> As long as they keep us from understanding the enemy doctrine, they can keep us from winning the war. There is no knowing the enemy without understanding that doctrine, and there is no victory without knowing the enemy.[15]

Coughlin also points out that Jihad Denial is flawed on a deeper level: it is actually *completely irrelevant* whether the enemy's understanding of Islam is accurate or not, since we must know what motivates the enemy *regardless of whether his motivations are based in legitimate understandings.* In other words, a national security professional's duty

> is not to know true Islam; it is to identify and establish a functional threat doctrine, regardless of whether that doctrine accurately tracks with "true" Islam or not. What matters is that we understand the enemy's doctrines, not whether he is correct about them.[16]

The Obama administration clearly did everything but that. It held firmly that *how we need to see the enemy is more important than how he sees himself.* And so it is no wonder that the administration refused to frame a functional threat doctrine. Coughlin explains,

> The intended effect of manipulating our leaders into undermining doctrinal template development is to destroy a coherent threat assessment. One cannot engage what one is not permitted to define.[17]

Thus, it is clear that, with our language and our freedom to candidly identify the enemy tightly controlled by the forces of political correctness, and with the government penetrated and controlled by the enemy himself, the situation under Obama was catastrophic: *the Jihadist Psychopath was shaping our policies toward himself.*

We now move forward and explore more closely our surrender via the Jihadist Psychopath's control of our minds. In our next chapter, we spell out some of the concrete and catastrophic manifestations of our suicide in his hands.

CHAPTER 17

SUICIDE

With the Jihadist Psychopath having successfully infiltrated our government and culture during the Obama years, it is clear how he took over our minds and set us on the path toward civilizational suicide. In this chapter, we provide a sampling of some of the key examples of our civilization's willful self-destruction in the hands of Islamic supremacism.

In order to fully grasp how our capitulation is taking place, it is vital for us to first crystallize the three primary levels on which our enemy is attacking and defeating the West. On every one of these levels, we are now completely vulnerable and unable to defend ourselves. Author Bill Siegel has outlined these three dimensions in his book, *The Control Factor*, and he identifies them as such: (1) Islamic jihad, (2) stealth jihad, and (3) international institutional jihad.[1]

The first level of attack, Islamic jihad, encompasses violent acts of terror, such as the Halloween Manhattan Massacre on October 31, 2017, the Brussels terror attack in March 2016, the San Bernardino massacre in December 2015, and the Paris Massacre in November 2015. The second level of attack, stealth jihad, is the "Civilization Jihad" that the Muslim Brotherhood has outlined in its documents, such as the *Explanatory Memorandum*.[2] In this realm, the enemy is operating to destroy us from within by *our own hands* through nonviolent tactics of deceit and brainwashing.[3] One form of deadly attack, which clearly involves a combination of levels 1 and 2, is the mass influx of Muslim immigrants and refugees that we now see pouring into Europe and the United States. This is *Hijrah*, jihad by immigration, which is a form of Islamic invasion and takeover that occurs through numbers and demographic occupation rather than by outright violence.[4]

The third level of attack is the "international institutional jihad," where we see Muslim countries pursuing their agenda through international organizations such as the United Nations and the Organisation of Islamic Cooperation (OIC).[5] As international organizations grow in power while America weakens, this agenda becomes ever more lethal and dangerous.

The West is now clearly losing on all of these three levels. In terms of the first level, the West is impotently absorbing the blows of jihadist terror while exhibiting absolutely no clear strategy for preventing such violence. Since America and the West do not have the will to *even name the enemy*, or to connect Islam with Islamic terrorism, they are left completely helpless in the face of Islamic jihad. In terms of the second level, the West is countering with blindness and inaction. The notion that opposing sharia is "racist" now prevails in the culture at large and, therefore, the West is engaged in a perpetual cycle of sharia-compliance.[6]

There has been complete failure in dealing with the third level of attack as well. Most notably, the international agenda is quickly moving to criminalize truth-telling about Islam.[7] For instance, the Obama administration consistently supported the OIC's effort to implement Resolution 16/18 on combating "defamation of religions," whose undeniable objective is, of course, to shut down "Islamophobia."[8]

The OIC is now moving aggressively ahead, with the help of its American Middle East "allies," toward prohibiting any criticism of Islam as a matter of international law.[9] Even though such a law would violate the U.S. First Amendment, prominent figures such as Hillary Clinton have embraced it. While serving as secretary of state, Clinton set an ill-advised precedent in her July 2011 meeting with the general secretary of the OIC and *personally committed the State Department to the effort to outlaw such criticism.* She also affirmed that there would be action—by means of "peer pressure and shaming"—to intimidate Americans who might otherwise be inclined to engage in such speech.[10] Just as troubling was Assistant Attorney General Tom Perez's refusal to answer the chairman of the House Subcommittee on the Constitution when the latter asked him to confirm that the Obama administration would "never entertain or advance a proposal that criminalizes speech against any religion."[11]

All of this is in line with Obama's infamous announcement at the UN General Assembly in October 2012 that "the future must not belong to those that slander the prophet of Islam."[12] And it therefore makes complete sense why Obama strongly supported the "Strong Cities Network," which the administration saw as a new global police effort to fight what it called "violent extremism" in the United States and throughout the world. In reality, this was clearly an effort to silence and stifle truth-telling about Islam.[13]

Thus, on all three of these levels of attack, there is a clear surrender taking place. And as Siegel points out, this surrender entails a mass denial.[14] Most significantly, our leadership and culture are doing everything they can to *not* know the enemy, and to prevent the truth from being told about him. But the key to defeating an enemy is to understand him. Sun Tzu, the Chinese general and military strategist who authored the masterpiece *The Art of War*, which serves as an indispensable guide on military strategy, offers a key insight into the importance of being able to identify one's enemy:

> If you know the enemy and know yourself, you need not fear the result of a hundred battles. If you know yourself but not the enemy, for every victory gained you will also suffer a defeat. If you know neither the enemy nor yourself, you will succumb in every battle.[15]

America and the West are now violating this sacred rule. And while the Jihadist Psychopath is deceiving us in myriad ways, we are practicing absolutely no deception in reverse. And deception is crucial. As Sun Tzu emphasized: "All warfare is based on deception."[16] He warned:

> Hence, when able to attack, we must seem unable; when using our forces, we must seem inactive; when we are near, we must make the enemy believe we are far away; when far away, we must make him believe we are near.[17]

It would also do well to note that one cannot deceive an entity when one is not even able to know, or to be honest about, who or what that entity is. And so, with all of these catastrophes playing themselves out right in front of us, it is no surprise that many of the jihadi massacres taking place on our territory could have easily been prevented. Obama, after all, had crippled the ability of America's intelligence agencies to defend the nation from jihad.[18] For example, how could the FBI have really stopped Tamerlan and Dzhokhar Tsarnaev in the Boston Marathon massacre even when the Russians had warned the bureau about them? The FBI, after all, *was disallowed* to investigate the two brothers on any realms connected to jihad and Islam.[19] And how could the DHS have stopped Sayed Farook and Tashfeen Malik from perpetrating the San Bernardino massacre when former Homeland Security officer Phil Haney's investigation into the migration of Islamists into

America was, as demonstrated earlier, dismantled?[20] How could America have effectively defended itself from jihadists when the Obama DHS secretly scrubbed one thousand names from its U.S. terror watch lists to protect the "civil rights" of suspected individuals?[21]

To fully grasp the potentially catastrophic situation in which Obama had placed America in the terror war, one need only imagine a Cold War scenario in which the FBI was searching for communist spies but was simultaneously not allowed to think about communism. Moreover, when getting its hands on suspicious individuals, imagine if the FBI was not allowed to ask them anything about communism. Even worse, imagine the FBI having to deny the existence of its enemy during the Cold War while *asking the KGB for advice on how to deal with the enemy that supposedly didn't exist.*[22] Let us keep in mind here, as we demonstrated in the last chapter, that American officials under Obama were getting guidance on foreign policy from the Muslim Brotherhood.[23] And let us also keep in mind that, even *after* congressional orders were issued to the FBI to sever its ties with Brotherhood-linked groups, the bureau, to this day, remains CAIR's "partner."[24] The enemy, in other words, is still guiding our intelligence community.

Thus, should it really have been a great surprise when the identity of SEAL Team Six, which killed Osama bin Laden, was *exposed by the Obama administration*—and that the names and locations of that heroic team's members were compromised? This unconscionable development led to the assassination of this whole team by Afghani jihadists affiliated with the Taliban. Internal White House documents obtained by Judicial Watch through a FOIA request revealed that CIA director John Brennan and other White House officials had met twice with Hollywood filmmakers preparing a movie about the killing of bin Laden and had provided them unparalleled access to classified information—which included the identity of a SEAL Team Six operator and commander. These high-level White House meetings between Brennan and the Hollywood filmmakers took place just weeks after the Pentagon and CIA had publicly warned of the dangers posed by leaks surrounding the successful SEAL raid killing bin Laden.[25] And the question, of course, has to be asked: Why would this *not* happen under an administration that was sympathetic to, and had been penetrated by, the Muslim Brotherhood?

Denying the existence of jihad while seeking advice from jihadists has led to myriad other catastrophes as well. For example, many American lives have been lost in vain because of the treacherous rules of military engagement made by our own side. Indeed, under Obama, the rules of engagement in Afghanistan were set to *minimize Afghan casualties* and to *accept greater American casualties*. These rules were part of the Counter Insurgency Strategy (COIN) that was implemented by the Obama administration in 2009. The rules in COIN included the following mindboggling restrictions: forbidding nighttime or surprise searches; requiring that villagers must be warned before searches; requiring that Afghans participate in U.S. searches; disallowing U.S. soldiers from firing at the enemy unless the enemy is preparing to fire first; forbidding U.S. engagement with the enemy if civilians are present; and allowing U.S. troops to fire at a terrorist if he is actively in the process of placing an IED, but not if that same terrorist is walking away from an area where bombs have been placed.[26]

The rules of engagement were set to such a disadvantage to American troops that U.S. causalities skyrocketed under Obama, with over 70 percent of the more than two thousand American deaths in Afghanistan occurring after the rules were implemented.[27] Under Obama, the U.S. was essentially *following Islamic laws* in the war. This basically meant that unbelievers' lives didn't matter—while Muslim lives did. And this fit with the reality that the country is run constitutionally by Islamic law with which *Obama made sure the U.S. military was abiding.* As Stephen Coughlin affirms, the warfighting effort in Afghanistan under Obama was subordinated to what Islamic law permitted U.S. soldiers to do.[28]

Thus, thanks to Obama, the jihadists in Afghanistan knew everything they needed to know about American soldiers, including everything the soldiers planned to do *ahead of time.* This is why surviving families of killed U.S. servicemen in Afghanistan related that their loved ones worried, before their deaths, that it was *the rules* that they had to operate under, and not the terrorists, that would eventually get them killed.[29] Aside from the basic common sense and human decency that this atrocious outrage violated, it was also a mangling of the basic rules of war. Sun Tzu warned, again, that there always had to be deception in war. He emphasized that *plans must never be divulged beforehand*, since the enemy must always be unprepared when attacked.[30] But Obama, being one of the leaders of the Unholy Alliance,[31] made sure that the opposite was the case.

It is vital to state, at this juncture, that there is hope of these rules of engagement being abolished—thanks to the Trump administration, which has taken measures to reverse them in Afghanistan and in other areas where lives are in danger.[32]

The tragedy of our surrender to the Jihadist Psychopath is evident not only on the battlefield, but also in the realm of religious faith. One can't help but reflect on the symbolic gesture offered up by the Church of Sweden's new, and first female, archbishop, Antje Jackelén, who stepped into that role of leadership in 2013. On its website, the Church of Sweden reported in that year that it had approximately 6.5 million members and that the organization was divided into thirteen dioceses. Every diocese was led by a bishop, and above the bishops was the archbishop. All the bishops have their own motto, and Jackelén's choice for her *Christian* diocese was quite intriguing: "God is greater." It is important to note that the Arabic translation renders it as "Allahu Akbar"—the term that means "Allah is greater" than the other gods of other religions, and that is why Islam's followers are commanded to subjugate and/or kill the followers of other religions.[33]

During a question-and-answer period in Uppsala on October 1, 2013, the candidates for the highest position in the Swedish Church were asked if they thought Jesus presented a truer picture of God than Muhammad. Jackelén found that question to be a really tough one. She agonized over it and then finally stated that *she couldn't choose between Jesus and Muhammad*. Interestingly enough, on other occasions she has opined that the Church of Sweden has more in common with other religions than with other Christian denominations, that the Virgin Birth must be understood metaphorically, that hell doesn't exist, and that the Biblical texts should not be taken as truth.[34]

Jackelén is, of course, just a tiny microcosm of a much bigger problem in the religious realm, seeing that Pope Francis, the head of the Catholic Church, is a serial apologist for Islam who perpetually seeks to emphasize the notion that there is nothing inherently violent about Islam.[35]

Another indicator of the dire and bizarre situation we now find ourselves in is found in the fact that leading truth-tellers about Islam such as Robert Spencer and Pamela Geller have actually been banned from UK territory, while Islamists like Muhammad al-Arifi, who advocate Jew hatred, wife beating, and Islamic texts that promote jihad, are allowed into the UK with no problem.[36] Spencer comments on this surreal absurdity:

> Britain has not actually banned the truth about Islam. You can get into Britain if you believe that Islam mandates warfare against unbelievers. You just have to think warfare against unbelievers is a fine thing to pursue.[37]

SUICIDE

Our willful blindness is now, without doubt, deeply embedded into our psyches, and it is, in turn, spawning our capitulation to the Jihadist Psychopath. As we have stressed, President Trump offers us tremendous hope that the catastrophic cycle of our defeat can be reversed, but he faces a robust Unholy Alliance that rules the media and culture, remains entrenched within government, and has even penetrated his own administration and inner circle. Trump's hands, therefore, have been tied on many levels. In our next and final chapter, we outline these major obstacles that Trump is facing—with the Jihadist Psychopath and his minions trying to block him at every turn.

CHAPTER 18

JIHADIST PSYCHOPATH BLOCKS TRUMP

As this work has demonstrated, President Trump has been a godsend to those who wish to protect themselves and Western civilization from the Jihadist Psychopath. He offers tremendous hope that the tide can be turned against Islamic supremacism. At the same time, the new president faces great challenges, since he is essentially an island of candor and courage surrounded by a swamp of Jihad Denial—and that swamp is growing bigger and deeper with each passing day. This is the case because the Jihadist Psychopath and his minions are not only entrenched in many realms of the U.S. government, but have also managed to penetrate the Trump administration's inner circle itself. This chapter explores this disturbing development.

President Trump has, without doubt, convincingly demonstrated that he understands the threat we face—and he has shown many signs of truly intending to do something about it. He got off to a great start, initially bringing aboard many good people who understood the nature of the jihadist threat. He not only emphasized the importance of openly and explicitly naming the enemy, but also did so himself on numerous occasions, such as during his first speech to a joint session of Congress on February 28, 2017, where he stated that his administration was "taking steps to protect our nation from radical Islamic terrorism."[1] Other positive signs included Trump's efforts to enact a temporary ban on travel from terrorism hot spots,[2] as well as his request to Congress to end the diversity visa lottery, which in 2010 helped jihadist Sayfullo Saipov get to the United States, where he would eventually perpetrate the Halloween massacre that killed eight people in New York City on October 31, 2017.[3]

Notwithstanding these positive aspects of the new administration, some very troubling developments have also unfortunately transpired. First, the enemy camp has succeeded in getting rid of some of the best people around the president. These were the individuals who wanted to truly assess the security threats America faces. Now, tragically, they have been replaced with Jihad Deniers. For instance, Trump started off strong by bringing in Gen. Michael Flynn, Steve Bannon, and Sebastian Gorka—individuals who sought to make a coherent threat assessment of the aims and agendas of Islamic supremacism.[4] Flynn became national security adviser, Bannon was appointed as White House chief strategist, and Gorka assumed the role of deputy assistant to Trump. But despite this promising start, it soon became apparent that the Muslim Brotherhood's penetration of the U.S. government was as powerful as Mohamed Elibiary had boasted it was.[5] Sadly, strange things began to happen:

Before Trump even took his oath of office, Obama officials were busy spying on Americans in an effort to actually *protect the interests of Iran and the Muslim Brotherhood.*[6] A number of these Americans were close to Trump and, as in the case of Michael Flynn, they ended up serving in his administration. Obama's spying operation had monitored certain Americans, including Flynn, who had contact with foreigners prior to Trump's inauguration. Because Flynn had become NSC adviser, his meeting with Russia's ambassador to the U.S., Sergey Kislyak, during the transition period became controversial and he consequently had to resign from his position.[7] But this begs a very significant question: How exactly did it become publicly known that Flynn had met with Kislyak? The answer is quite simple: because the Obama administration had found out about the meeting during its "surveillance" activity, and then administration loyalists, in turn, leaked the matter to the media and the public. Former national security adviser Susan Rice, after all, *had admitted unmasking the identities of Trump officials to Congress*. And the evidence suggested that the targets of the Obama administration's spying and leaks included Rice's own successor, General Flynn.[8]

These disturbing affairs are central to the narrative of our own story, since Flynn ended up being temporarily replaced by Lt. Gen. H. R. McMaster, *a longtime apologist for Islam*. McMaster was opposed to using the label "radical Islamic terrorism" because, from his Jihad Denial perspective, Islamic terrorists are "un-Islamic" and operate according to "an ideology that uses a perverted interpretation of religion to justify crimes against all humanity."[9] This man, with this pathetically myopic vision, became Trump's national security adviser. Sebastian Gorka commented on this disaster, noting how the new national security adviser "sees the threat of Islam through an Obama administration lens, meaning that religion has nothing to do with the war we are in." Gorka continued: "He believes—and he told me in his office—that all of these people are just criminals. That is simply wrong."[10]

It was clear what side McMaster was on. And so it only made sense that he soon began protecting Susan Rice and the Obama holdovers at the NSC—while purging Trump loyalists. In other words, *he began safeguarding the Muslim Brotherhood's interests*.

It turns out that, because Flynn and his people gained temporary access to classified information, they discovered that Susan Rice had been spying on Americans *for the Brotherhood*, and this was leaked.[11] So it became quite evident that the Brotherhood and its Obama minions made sure that Flynn got pushed out and was replaced by McMaster, who, in turn, quickly began getting rid of the people whom the Unholy Alliance[12] wanted gone. In this way, McMaster stopped the leaks and was able to push for a policy that embraced Jihad Denial and avoided any real threat assessment.[13] Daniel Greenfield has documented these disturbing dynamics[14] that no establishment media have dared to touch. He explains:

> Susan Rice's eavesdropping would have remained hidden if Flynn and his appointees hadn't temporarily obtained the keys to the kingdom. And the network quickly worked to have Flynn forced out and replaced with McMaster. And McMaster has steadily forced out Flynn's appointees so that there are no more leaks like the one that exposed the Rice eavesdropping. The swamp looks after its own.[15]

And so, the best people in Trump's National Security Council were pushed out. One of them was Richard T. Higgins, an outspoken critic of the faulty strategic assessment that is the basis for current U.S. security. Higgins told the truth about the catastrophe in American strategic policy in a memo that stressed how the Unholy Alliance is controlling not just the national and cultural discourse, but also the framework of U.S. government. He detailed a plot between globalists, the Left, and Islamists to sabotage Trump's nationalist agenda and unveiled how American officials are not allowed to frame a true threat assessment, which includes a factual understanding of Islamic threat doctrines. Instead, Higgins demonstrated, U.S. officials are depending upon fifth column Muslim Brotherhood cultural advisers.[16] Arguing that the whole problem constituted a national-security priority, his report outlined a set of recommendations.[17] For the thought-crime of writing this memo, Higgins was fired by McMaster, who also purged other supporters of the foreign policy priorities on which Trump had based his presidential campaign, such as Ezra Cohen-Watnick and Derek Harvey. All the while, McMaster not only retained and promoted Obama holdovers, but also *brought in* high-ranking officials from the Obama administration to serve in senior National Security Council roles.[18]

Soon after these troubling developments, in the month of August 2017, two other truth-tellers about Islamic suprema-cism were pushed out of the administration: Bannon and Gorka. Bannon returned to whence he initially had come, to Breitbart News, vowing to continue helping Trump, albeit from outside of the White House.[19] Gorka, meanwhile, the author of *Defeat-ing Jihad*,[20] a book that outlines the strategy needed to defeat the global jihadist threat, wrote a telling resignation letter that stressed the dire mistake the administration was making by aban-doning honesty about jihad. He mentioned, for instance, the text of Trump's speech on Afghanistan at that time, pointing to how drafters of the text had removed any mention of radical Islam, and how the speech listed operational objectives without ever clearly defining what the U.S. is fighting for.[21]

Another worrisome sign followed Gorka's letter when then-Secretary of State Rex Tillerson told Chris Wallace on *Fox News Sunday* that Gorka was "completely wrong" to have criticized Trump for not identifying "radical Islam" by name.[22] So now it was not just the national security adviser, *but also the secretary of state* who was opposed to making a coherent threat assessment. As if that were not enough, Defense Secretary Jim Mattis was like-wise on board with McMaster and Tillerson's view that Islam has no substantive connection to Islamic jihad. Indeed, Mattis had previously made various statements echoing that theme, which included his belief that al-Qaeda terrorists "defame Islam."[23] Even worse, he had announced that the U.S. was killing al-Qaeda terrorists *for defaming Islam*, implying that the U.S. was acting for the sake of enforcing Islamic blasphemy laws and, therefore, acting as a mercenary for Islam.[24]

Meanwhile, it was highly significant that the Council on American-Islamic Relations (CAIR), a Muslim-Brotherhood front group, *praised Gorka's departure from the administration*. Responding to CAIR's announcement, Gorka affirmed: "I'll have to add this to my resume. Given that CAIR was an unindicted coconspirator in the largest terrorist finance trial in US history."[25] Gorka was right: this Brotherhood front group was an unindicted coconspirator in the Holy Land Foundation terrorism-financing trial in 2007–2008. It has also been declared a terrorist organization by the United Arab Emirates, and many of its leaders and members have been jailed for terror-related offenses. In 2009, a federal judge concluded that the U.S. government had found "ample evidence" to link CAIR with Hamas.[26]

With all of these disturbing developments, it became tragically evident that the Unholy Alliance had succeeded in infiltrating Trump's inner circle. And there were serious consequences to this penetration. Surrounded by Jihad Denial forces, Trump suddenly started mentioning "radical Islam" with much less frequency. In his Afghanistan speech, for instance, as Gorka pointed out, the president did not even utter those words. Nor did he use them in his September 11, 2017, speech marking the sixteenth anniversary of 9/11. Something truly ominous was taking place, ominous enough for author Brigitte Gabriel to observe that in Trump's and other administration officials' speeches commemorating the 9/11 anniversary:

> it was obvious that something has happened in the Trump presidency that has changed and changed dramatically. When

I listened to the speeches yesterday...by all the leaders in the administration—by Trump, by Mattis, by Pence—it was literally a speech that could have been uttered by President Obama himself.[27]

Gabriel was onto something. To be sure, not only was the Trump administration increasingly reluctant to make a genuine threat assessment, but it had also abandoned its initial efforts to designate the Muslim Brotherhood a terrorist organization. In its first few months, the administration seemed to make this a new and important goal,[28] but as more time went by, all talk about it was dropped. And with people like Gorka, Bannon, and Higgins gone, and Jihad Denial characters left in charge of foreign policy, such an objective clearly had little chance to succeed.

Telling also was the fact that by the end of his first year in office, Trump had shown no interest in going after CAIR and other Brotherhood front groups that were unindicted coconspirators in the Holy Land Foundation Trial of 2007–2008.[29] Mountains of evidence had been obtained through that trial for follow-up trials of these terror-linked groups. Obama's Department of Justice (DOJ), naturally, shut down the investigations and prosecutions of these organizations.[30] More was expected of Trump's DOJ—which has, unfortunately, made zero moves on this score.

Despite all of these setbacks under Trump, there is still much to be hopeful about, since the enemy camp has by no means achieved a final victory within Trump's administration. Indeed, there are strong signs that the president is himself fighting back on the matter of a threat assessment. On several occasions, for instance, such as in his speech to the UN on September 19, 2017, the president has noticeably been pushing back against the Jihad Deniers around him and insisting on still articulating the words "radical Islam."[31] Then, on March 13, 2018, Trump removed Jihad Denier Secretary of State Tillerson and replaced him with CIA boss Mike Pompeo.[32] This was a major positive move by the president, seeing that Pompeo is known to view Islamic terrorism as one of the nation's top national security challenges.[33] Nine days later, on March 22, 2018, Trump made another highly important step, replacing Jihad Denier McMaster as his national security adviser with John Bolton, a former U.S. ambassador to the United Nations.[34] The appointment of Bolton is a huge statement about the direction the president is now taking in terms of confronting Islamic supremacism, since Bolton is far from a Jihad Denier and extremely focused on making a real threat assessment and confronting America's enemies.[35] The prospect of Bolton cleaning house at the NSC is also a real and positive one.[36]

A tug-of-war, therefore, is clearly taking place within the White House on how to deal with Islamic supremacism—and Trump's most recent moves give great grounds for optimism that American can still push the Jihadist Psychopath back.

The United States, without doubt, has reached a watershed moment in its history. This work makes it no secret that it is cheering for Trump and for the people around him who seek to truly understand the threat we are facing in the terror war—for it is only by knowing and clearly identifying the Jihadist Psychopath that we stand a chance of defeating him.

* * * * *

And so, we come to the end of our story. As we reflect on the troublesome and sometimes frightening events and details that we have described in these pages, it is fitting to turn to the profound words of author Alexander Maistrovoy to help bring closure to our chilling tale. In his article, "The Hypnotic Dance of Death," published at JihadWatch.org on January 28, 2016, Maistrovoy reflected on how the culture of postmodernism has achieved what even communism failed to do: it has incapacitated men from defending their own women and young girls.[37] Writing about the case of Cologne, Germany, on New Year's Eve, December 31, 2015, where Muslim migrants perpetrated mass sexual assaults on German women,[38] he notes:

> In my correspondence regarding the events in Cologne, an editor of a Russian newspaper asked a natural but discouraging question. Perplexed, he asked me: "Where were the German men?"
>
> Indeed, for those of us who grew up in Soviet Russia, it would be inconceivable that some drunk young people could publicly mock and harass girls on New Year's Eve in the very center of Moscow or Saint Petersburg. If they dared to do this, they wouldn't survive until the morning; they would become "martyrs" and would have their way with 72 virgins in a completely different realm.
>
> ...As it turned out, in Germany, Sweden, Austria and elsewhere, these codes were fatally violated. A great number of strong healthy men, having heard the girls screaming and crying, and having seen the crimes being committed, didn't do anything to save the victims. In rare cases, the girls were defended by migrants from Eastern Europe or Third World countries.

Maistrovoy reminds us that if "'refugees' ever dared to do the same at home—in Algeria, Iraq, Afghanistan and Somalia—with Muslim girls, they would be buried alive." He continues,

> What has happened to the world when men, women, politicians, and the elite betray their daughters and children in order to please newcomers with their baser instincts and a cult of male power?
>
> The answer is sad: the culture of postmodernism has managed to do what couldn't be achieved even by the Communist propaganda machine. It has degraded the instinct of self-preservation, a natural reaction embedded in humans on a genetic level, the ability to feel compassion and protect a victim—a woman, a girl, a child. An abstract ideology has suppressed the mind and

senses.... It changed the very nature of man, and indeed, it was a unique experiment on their own people.

...There is a small carnivorous animal in Siberia—a stoat. It hunts rabbits and hares, which are significantly heavier, faster and stronger than the stoat itself. It doesn't creep, doesn't sit in ambush and doesn't catch its prey on the run. It performs a hypnotic dance of death in front of it—with wriggles, acrobatic leaps and somersaults. The stoat dazzles the prey and, gradually approaching it, then grabs its throat. The rabbit dies from shock. Why does the prey allow the stoat to dazzle and kill it without resisting? Biologists are unable to solve the riddle of the stoat's hypnotic dance.

Maistrovoy concludes that "the hypnotic dance of death is gaining momentum." That it is. The Jihadist Psychopath is indeed wriggling, performing acrobatic leaps and somersaults, biding his time to grab our throats—as we sit impotently in awe and denial, watching his conniving and sinister performance, as our own death in his merciless claws draws near.

We still have a small window of opportunity in which we might resist the Jihadist Psychopath—and liberate ourselves from his deadly and ruthless grasp.

The key is for us to recognize and label him for who he truly is—and to then suffer all the short-term pain that we need to endure in order to cut the ties that bind us to our approaching obliteration.

We have to do this now.

For there is not much time.

CONCLUSION

Our story has unveiled the dark, conniving, and murderous world of the Jihadist Psychopath and the remarkable success he has had in charming, seducing, and devouring us. While laying bare all of the elements of this catastrophic tale, we have also gauged the tragic weakness and willful illusions inside of ourselves that enable the Jihadist Psychopath to exercise power over us.

Author Shelby Steele delivered a profound warning to America about the only way it could overcome its racial strife—a warning that proved to be extremely relevant to our present-day conflict with the Jihadist Psychopath. Steele explained that America had to move beyond the "victim-focused black identity" charade and had to make "a difficult but crucial distinction: between actual victimization, which we must resist with every resource, and iden-tification with the victim's status."[1] If we apply this wise and piercing counsel to the circumstances surrounding our present-day sur-render to Islamic supremacism, we begin to gauge the urgency of overcoming our own desperate need to embrace the Jihadist Psy-chopath's sinister "I am the victim" ploy. Indeed, if we have learned anything from our story, it is that we urgently have to stop seeing ourselves as the perpetrators and Islam as the victim. Once we can break our addiction to that pathological perspective—which the Unholy Alliance has forced on us—the Jihadist Psychopath's most effective weapon will be dismantled.

CONCLUSION

Author Alexander Maistrovoy has given much thought to the voluntary suicide that the West is now engaging in at the hands of our deadly enemy. He reminds us that surrender often occurs before the "conquered" party is even defeated:

> When Alaric entered Rome, he was amazed by a great number of Romans who like Germans wore skins and worshiped German idols. Rome had submitted to barbarians long before it fell to their hands.[2]

It is now our challenge to confront the reality of the skins that many of those around us are increasingly wearing—and the idols that they are increasingly worshiping. The harrowing question lies before us: Have we already submitted to the Jihadist Psychopath before he even has to unleash his final reign of terror?

Psychopathy expert Thomas Sheridan gives crucial advice to those who have somehow managed to survive the abuses and torments meted out by psychopaths, and to untangle themselves from their victimizers' web. He counsels that, after one's escape, "you must then take a good look at what you may have felt was lacking in your own life that they sniffed out and zeroed-in-on."[3] He continues: "[I]n order to defeat this evil you must be able to recognize it for what it is—you must be able to *truly know it*, and to know it, a part of you must die."[4]

As we look into the Jihadist Psychopath's charming and killer eyes, we are confronted with what is perhaps the most critical decision in the history of Western civilization: to let him get close enough so he can grab our throats and suffocate us—or to allow our illusions about him, and about ourselves, to die the death they deserve.

The choice, at this precarious stage, is still in our hands.

But not for long.

ENDNOTES

Preface

1 Martha Stout, *The Sociopath Next Door* (New York: Three Rivers Press, 2005).
2 Alexander Maistrovoy, *Agony of Hercules or a Farewell to Democracy (Notes of a Stranger)* (Xlbiris, 2016), p. 157.

Introduction

1 Tina Moore, Larry Celona and Danika Fears, "8 Killed As Truck Plows Into Pedestrians in Downtown NYC Terror Attack," NYPost.com, October 31, 2017. https://nypost.com/2017/10/31/8-killed-truck-pedestrians-downtown-nyc -terror-attack/.
2 Matthew Vadum, "America's Terrorist Lottery," Frontpagemag.com, November 2, 2017. http://www.frontpagemag.com/fpm/268299/americas-terrorist -lottery-matthew-vadum.
3 Patrick Poole, "New York City Terror Attack Is Confirmed as 'Known Wolf' Terrorism...Again," PJMedia.com, November 1, 2017. https://pjmedia.com/ homeland-security/new-york-city-terror-attack-confirmed-known-wolf-terror- ism/; Rich Schapiro, "FBI tracks down second Muslim in connection with NYC truck jihad massacre," NyDailyNews.com, November 1, 2017. http:// www.nydailynews.com/new-york/. fbi-tracks-man-nyc-terror-attack-article-1.3604765.
4 Stefan Becket, "Feds Reveal What They Found in NYC Terror Suspect Sayfullo Saipov's Truck," CBSNews.com, November 2, 2017. https://www.cbsnews.com/ news/new-york-attack-suspect-sayfullo-saipov-what-feds-found-truck -cellphones/.
5 Vadum, "America's Terrorist Lottery."
6 Ibid.
7 Danusha V. Goska, "Did New Jersey Muslims Celebrate on 9/11?," Frontpage- mag.com, November 30, 2015. http://www.frontpagemag.com/fpm/260952/ did-new-jersey-muslims-celebrate-911-danusha-v-goska.
8 Robert Spencer, "NYC Jihad Mass Murderer Saipov a 'Devout' Muslim, Wife Wears a Niqab," JihadWatch.org, November 2, 2017. https://www.jihadwatch

.org/2017/11/nyc-jihad-mass-murderer-saipov-a-devout-muslim-wife-wears
-a-niqab.

9   *New York Times* tweet: https://twitter.com/nytimes/status/9269449271535
77985.

10 John Nolte, "Very Jake News: Tapper Melts Down over Criticism of Inaccurate
'Allahu Akbar',"Breitbart.com, November 2, 2017. http://www.breitbart.com/
big-journalism/2017/11/02/tapper-melts-criticism-inaccurate-allahu-akbar/.

11 Katie Reilly and Alana Abramson, "8 People Were Killed in New York's
Deadliest Terror Attack Since 9/11. Here's What to Know," Time.com,
November 1, 2017. http://time.com/5004500/new-york-city-lower-manhat-
tan-attack/; Matthew Vadum, "America's Terrorist Lottery."

12 Nicole Chavez, Holly Yan, Eric Levenson, and Steve Almasy, "New York Attack
Suspect Charged with Federal Terrorism Offenses," CNN.com, November 2,
2017. http://www.cnn.com/2017/11/01/us/new-york-attack/index.html.

13 Robert Spencer, "NY Deputy Police Commissioner: 'This isn't about Islam, this
isn't about the mosque he attends'," JihadWatch.org, November 1, 2017. https://
www.jihadwatch.org/2017/11/
ny-deputy-police-commissioner-this-isnt-about-islam-this-isnt-about-the-
mosque-he-attends.

14 Aaron Klein, "H. R. McMaster Avoids Islamic Terrorist Label Again, Calls
Manhattan Jihadist a 'Mass Murderer'," Breitbart.com, November 3, 2017.
http://www.breitbart.com/
jerusalem/2017/11/03/h-r-mcmaster-avoids-islamic-terrorist-label-again-calls-
manhattan-jihadist-a-mass-murderer/.

15 Wayne Parry, "In Aftermath of Bike Path Killings, Mosques Near NYC Face
Hostility Again," PressHerald.com, November 2, 2017. www.pressherald.com
/2017/11/02/in-aftermath-of-bike-path-killings-mosques-near-nyc-face
-hostility-again/.

16 Ibid.

17 Anna Russell and Ben Taub, "A Terrorist Attack in Lower Manhattan,"
NewYorker.com, October 31, 2017. https://www.newyorker.com/news/
news-desk/terror-in-lower-manhattan?mbid=social_twitter.

18 Robert Spencer, "FP 'journalist' Isaac Stone Fish: 'The most Trumpian thing
most people do is overreact to a small terrorist attack'," JihadWatch.org,
November 2, 2017, 12:57. https://www.jihadwatch.org/2017/11/fp-journalist
-isaac-stone-fish-the-most-trumpian-thing-most-people-do-is-overreact-to-a-
small-terrorist-attack.

19 Robert Spencer, "Indictment of NYC Truck Jihadi Treats ISIS As If It Were a
Mafia Family, Charges Jihadi with 'Racketeering'," JihadWatch.org, November
22, 2017. https://www.jihadwatch.org/2017/11/
indictment-of-nyc-truck-jihadi-treats-isis-as-if-it-were-a-mafia-family-
charges-jihadi-with-racketeering.

20 Daniel Greenfield, "'Allahu Akbar' Is the Motive for Islamic Terror," Frontpage-
mag.com, November 8, 2017. http://www.frontpagemag.com/fpm/268309/

allahu-akbar-motive-islamic-terror-daniel-greenfield; see also: Glazov Gang video, "Daniel Greenfield on the Real Meaning of 'Allahu Akbar,'" JamieGlazov. com, March 27, 2015. http://jamieglazov.com/2015/03/27/daniel-greenfield -on-the-real-meaning-of-allahu-akbar-on-the-glazov-gang/.

21 Bukhari 64.238.4198.

22 Greenfield, "'Allahu Akbar' Is the Motive for Islamic Terror." See also: Glazov Gang video, "Daniel Greenfield on the Real Meaning of 'Allahu Akbar.'"

23 Greenfield, "'Allahu Akbar' Is the Motive for Islamic Terror."

24 TheGuardian.com, "Last Words of a Terrorist," September 30, 2001. https:// www.theguardian.com/world/2001/sep/30/terrorism.september113.

25 Scholar Bill Warner estimates that 270 million non-Muslims have been murdered by the jihad since the foundation of Islam. See: Bill Warner, "Tears of Jihad," PoliticalIslam.com, May 3, 2008. https://www.politicalislam.com/ tears-of-jihad/.

26 Cheryl K. Chumley, "Jake Tapper, CNN's Finest, Defends 'Allahu akbar' as 'beautiful,'" WashingtonTimes.com, November 1, 2017. https://www.washing-tontimes.com/news/2017/nov/1/jake-tapper-cnns-finest-defends-allahu -akbar-beaut/.

27 Robert Spencer, "Vehicular Jihad Comes to Barcelona," Frontpagemag.com, August 18, 2017. http://www.frontpagemag.com/fpm/267619/vehicular-jihad -comes-barcelona-robert-spencer.

28 Ibid.

29 Robert Spencer, "Indictment of NYC Truck Jihadi Treats ISIS As If It Were a Mafia Family, Charges Jihadi with 'Racketeering,'" JihadWatch.org, November 22, 2017. https://www.jihadwatch.org/2017/11/ indictment-of-nyc-truck-jihadi-treats-isis-as-if-it-were-a-mafia-family-charges-jihadi-with-racketeering.

30 Robert Spencer, "NYPD Monitored Jihad Murderer Saipov's Mosque Until Linda Sarsour Convinced Them to Stop," JihadWatch.org, November 1, 2017. https://www.jihadwatch.org/2017/11/nypd-monitored-jihad-murderer-saipovs-mosque-until-linda-sarsour-convinced-them-to-stop; Daniel Greenfield, "The Left Has Blood on its Hands in Manhattan," Frontpagemag. com, November 1, 2017. http://www.frontpagemag.com/fpm/268286/ left-has-blood-its-hands-manhattan-daniel-greenfield.

31 David Horowitz, *Unholy Alliance: Radical Islam and the American Left* (Washington, DC: Regnery, 2004). The site DiscovertheNetworks.org identifies the constituents of the Islamist jihad and describes the radical leftist networks that aid and abet it—especially the networks that surrounded the Obama administration and the Democratic Party leadership up till this moment. For more discussion and analysis on the Left's romance with Islamic supremacism and how this romance is an extension of the Left's alliance with communism during the Cold War, see Jamie Glazov, *United in Hate: The Left's Romance with Tyranny and Terror* (Los Angeles: WND, 2009).

ENDNOTES

32 For the resistance of the courts see Associated Press, "Appeals Court Denies Request to Immediately Reinstate Travel Ban," February 5, 2017. http://nypost. com/2017/02/05/appeals-court-denies-request-to-immediately-reinstate-travel-ban/?utm_source=maropost&utm_medium=email&utm_campaign=nypdaily&utm_content=20170205 and Joseph Klein, "Judicial Overreach on National Security," Frontpagemag.com, February 6, 2017. http://www.frontpagemag.com/fpm/265711/judicial-overreach-national-security-joseph-klein. For State Department resistance see Jeffrey Gettlemanjan, "State Dept. Dissent Cable on Trump's Ban Draws 1,000 Signatures," NYTimes.com, January 31, 2017. https://www.nytimes.com/2017/01/31/world/americas/state-dept-dissent-cable-trump-immigration-order.html?_r=0.

33 See Soeren Kern, "White House Officials Divided on Islam, ISIS, Israel and Iran," GatestoneInstitute.org, April 5, 2017. https://www.gatestoneinstitute.org/10158/white-house-islam-isis-israel-iran. For a discussion on the war within Trump's inner circle on how to deal with Islamic supremacism, see Chapter 18.

34 For a discussion on Trump's strengthening of his inner circle with strong people ready to confront Islamic supremacism, see Chapter 18.

Chapter 1

1 Stephen Dinan, "Holder Balks at Blaming 'Radical Islam'," *Washington Times*, May 14, 2010. http://www.washingtontimes.com/news/2010/may/14/holder-balks-at-blaming-radical-islam/#ixzz30MluWyrS.

2 Robert Spencer, "Platitudes and Naivete: Obama's Cairo Speech," JihadWatch.org, June 4, 2009. https://www.jihadwatch.org/2009/06/platitudes-and-naivete-obamas-cairo-speech.

3 "Obama Gave Front-Row Seats to Muslim Brotherhood in 2009 Cairo Speech," *American Thinker*, September 16, 2012. http://www.americanthinker.com/video/2012/09/obama_gave_front-row_seats_to_muslim_brotherhood_in_2009_cairo_speech.html.

4 Robert Spencer, "The Muslim Brotherhood's Man in the White House," Frontpagemag.com, October 22, 2013. http://www.frontpagemag.com/fpm/208267/muslim-brotherhoods-man-white-house-robert-spencer.

5 Robert Spencer, "Hillary Lets the Jihadist Cat Out of the Bag," Frontpagemag.com, January 24, 2013. http://www.frontpagemag.com/2013/robert-spencer/hillary-lets-the-jihadist-cat-out-of-bag/print/.

6 Stephen Coughlin, *Catastrophic Failure: Blindfolding America in the Face of Jihad* (Center for Security Policy Press: Washington DC, 2015), p. 21.

7 Robert Spencer, *Arab Winter Comes to America: The Truth About the War We're In* (Washington, DC: Regnery, 2015), pp. xiii–xvi; Frank Gaffney, *The Muslim Brotherhood in the Obama Administration* (Sherman Oaks, CA: David Horowitz Freedom Center, 2012).

8 Leo Hohmann, "Exploding Muslim Immigration Overwhelms FBI," WorldNet-Daily.com, July 17, 2015. http://www.wnd.com/2015/07/exploding-muslim-immigration-overwhelms-fbi/#vJezltXyYmuQXXOj.99.

9 Daniel Greenfield, "Counterterrorism Gov Guide: Keeping Out Muslims for Sharia Law Violates First Amendment," The Point, Frontpagemag.com, December 16, 2015. http://www.frontpagemag.com/point/261149/counterterrorism-gov-guide-keeping-out-muslims-daniel-greenfield.

10 Ibid.

11 "Secretary Napolitano Swears in Homeland Security Advisory Council Members," DHS.gov, October 18, 2010. https://www.dhs.gov/news/2010/10/18/secretary-napolitano-swears-homeland-security-advisory-council-members; Ryan Mauro, "Pro-Brotherhood DHS Advisor Creates Lawfare Blind Spot," CenterforSecurityPolicy.org, October 28, 2013. http://www.centerforsecurity-policy.org/2013/10/28/pro-brotherhood-dhs-advisor-creates-lawfare-blind-spot/.

12 John Rossomando, "Elibiary: America Is an Islamic Country," Investigative Project.org, June 23, 2014. https://www.investigativeproject.org/4435/elibiary-america-is-an-islamic-country.

13 Robert Spencer, "Muslim DHS Adviser Mohamed Elibiary, Open Supporter of Muslim Brotherhood, Resigns," JihadWatch.org, September 8, 2014. http://www.jihadwatch.org/2014/09/muslim-dhs-adviser-mohamed-elibiary-open-supporter-of-muslim-brotherhood-resigns.

14 The media outlet found no substance to the claim and decided against running the story. Patrick Poole, "Homeland Security Adviser Allegedly Leaked Intel to Attack Rick Perry," PJMedia.com, October 26, 2011. http://pjmedia.com/blog/breaking-homeland-security-adviser-allegedly-leaked-intel-to-attack-rick-perry/?print=1; Robert Spencer, "Mohamed Elibiary Declares Victory Over the Constitution," Frontpagemag.com, October 31, 2013. http://frontpagemag.com/2013/robert-spencer/mohamed-elibiary-declares-victory-over-constitution/.

15 Kerry Picket, "Fireworks at Napolitano Hearing-DHS Sec Unaware Of Classified Doc Leak And WH Terror Group Visit," WashingtonTimes.com, July 19, 2012. http://www.washingtontimes.com/blog/watercooler/2012/jul/19/picket-video-fireworks-napolitano-hearing-dhs-sec-/.

16 Ibid.

17 The video of the exchange between Gohmert and Napolitano is embedded in Picket, "Fireworks at Napolitano hearing—DHS Sec unaware of classified doc leak and WH terror group visit."

18 Ibid.

19 Robert Spencer, "Muslim DHS Adviser Mohamed Elibiary, Open Supporter of Muslim Brotherhood, Resigns," JihadWatch.org, September 8, 2014. http://www.jihadwatch.org/2014/09/muslim-dhs-adviser-mohamed-elibiary-open-supporter-of-muslim-brother-hood-resigns.

ENDNOTES

20 See DiscovertheNetworks.org's Mohamed Elibiary profile: http://www. discoverthenetworks.org/individualProfile.asp?indid=2560.

21 Robert Spencer, "Former Obama DHS official on Islamic State slaughtering Egyptian Christians: 'how what goes around comes around,'" JihadWatch.org, May 8, 2017. https://www.jihadwatch.org/2017/05/former-obama-dhs-official -on-islamic-state-slaughtering-egyptian-christians-how-what-goes-around -comes-around.

22 For the best work on Islam's war on Christianity, including the Muslim Brotherhood's persecution of Copts in Egypt, see Raymond Ibrahim, *Crucified Again: Exposing Islam's New War on Christians* (Washington, DC: Regnery Publishing, 2013).

23 For an authoritative account of the CVE strategy, see Stephen Coughlin interview, "The Hoax of 'Countering Violent Extremism'" on The Glazov Gang, JamieGlazov.com, April 12, 2016. http://jamieglazov.com/2016/04/12/the-hoax -of-countering-violent-extremism-on-the-glazov-gang/.

24 Ibid.

25 Coughlin, p. 12.

26 Ibid.

27 Ibid.

28 Ibid., p. 13.

29 Ibid., p. 17.

30 Ibid., p. 14.

31 Ibid., p. 17.

32 John R. Schindler, "The Intelligence Lessons of San Bernardino," Observer.com, December 14, 2015. http://observer.com/2015/12/the-intelligence-lessons-of -san-bernardino/.

33 Ibid.

34 Robert Spencer, "House Democrats Move to Criminalize Criticism of Islam," Frontpagemag.com, December 29, 2015. http://www.frontpagemag.com/ fpm/261268/house-democrats-move-criminalize-criticism-islam-robert -spencer.

35 Ibid.

36 Deborah Weiss, "Democrats Castigate 'Anti-Muslim' Speech in Proposed Legislation," Frontpagemag.com, January 26, 2016. http://www.frontpagemag. com/fpm/261550/democrats-castigate-anti-muslim-speech-proposed-debo- rah-weiss; Robert Spencer, "Secretary of State Clinton Says State Department Will Coordinate with OIC on Legal Ways to Implement UN's Resolution Criminalizing 'Defamation of Religion,'" JihadWatch.org, August 3, 2011. http://www.jihadwatch.org/2011/08/ secretary-of-state-clinton-says-state-department-will-coordinate-with-oic-on- legal-ways-to-implement.

37 Melanie Arter, "DOJ Official Won't Say Whether Justice Department Would 'Criminalize Speech against Any Religion,'" CNSNews.com, July 26, 2012.

http://www.cnsnews.com/news/article/doj-official-won-t-say-whether-justice
-department-would-criminalize-speech-against-any. See also Coughlin, p. 22.

38 John Perazzo, "The MSA Defeats New York," Frontpagemag.com, January 12, 2016. http://www.frontpagemag.com/fpm/261427/msa-defeats-new-york-john-perazzo; for documentation of the MSA being a Muslim Brotherhood front group, see the profile on the MSA at DiscovertheNetworks.org: http://www.discoverthenetworks.org/groupProfile.asp?grpid=6175.

39 Ibid.

40 Paul Sperry, "The Purge of a Report On Radical Islam Has Put NYC at Risk," NYPost.com, April 15, 2017. http://nypost.com/2017/04/15/the-purge-of-a-report-on-radical-islam-has-put-nyc-at-risk/; Patrick Dunleavy, "NYPD Caves to Political Correctness," InvestigativeProject.org, January 8, 2016. http://www.investigativeproject.org/5121/nypd-caves-to-political-correctness.

41 See the website thereligionofpeace.com, which keeps track of the number of Islamic terrorist attacks since 9/11.

42 Kevin Johnson, "Comey: Feds Have Roughly 900 Domestic Probes About Islamic State Operatives, Other Extremists," USAToday.com, October 23, 2015. http://www.usatoday.com/story/news/politics/2015/10/23/fbi-comey-isil-domestic-probes/74455460/.

43 Daniel Greenfield, "Bill de Blasio Cripples NYPD Surveillance of Muslim Terrorism," The Point at Frontpagemag.com, January 7, 2016. http://www.frontpagemag.com/point/261384/bill-de-blasio-cripples-nypd-surveillance-muslim-daniel-greenfield.

44 Robert Spencer, "The Hijrah Into Europe," Frontpagemag.com, September 4, 2015. http://www.frontpagemag.com/fpm/260019/hijrah-europe-robert-spencer.

45 Robert Spencer, "Cologne Mayor to Victims of Migrant Sex Assaults: You Asked For It," Frontpagemag.com, January 8, 2016. http://www.frontpagemag.com/fpm/261380/cologne-mayor-victims-migrant-sex-assaults-you-robert-spencer.

46 Ibid.

47 Jamie Glazov, "No Naomi Wolf, You Apologize," Frontpagemag.com, September 03, 2009. http://archive.frontpagemag.com/readArticle.aspx?ARTID=36177.

48 Fjordman, "Norwegian Authorities Still Covering Up Muslim Rapes," Gates of Vienna, Thursday, July 27, 2006. http://gatesofvienna.blogspot.ca/2006/07/norwegian-authorities-still-covering.html.

49 Robert Spencer, "German Police Fire Water Cannons at Anti-'Rapefugee' Protesters in Cologne," JihadWatch.org, January 9, 2016. http://www.jihadwatch.org/2016/01/german-police-fire-water-cannons-at-anti-rapefugee-protesters-in-cologne.

50 Oliver JJ Lane, "Cologne Police Attacked for 'Racial Profiling' During New Year's Eve Security Operation," Breitbart.com, January 2, 2017. http://www.breitbart

.com/london/2017/01/02/cologne-police-attacked-racial-profiling-new
-years-eve-security-operation/.

51 Jamie Glazov, "Avoiding Rape is White Privilege—on The Glazov Gang,"
JamieGlazov.com, April 21, 2016. http://jamieglazov.com/2016/04/21/
avoiding-rape-is-white-privilege-on-the-glazov-gang/; Oliver JJ Lane, "After
Anal Rape, Left Wing Activist Felt 'Guilt And Responsibility' His Migrant
Attacker Was Deported," Breitbart.com, April 7, 2016. http://www.breitbart
.com/london/2016/04/07/
after-anal-rape-leftist-felt-despair-that-his-somalian-attacker-was-deported/.

52 Peter McLoughlin report "'Easy Meat': Multiculturalism, Islam and Child Sex
Slavery" published by the Law and Freedom Foundation in 2014. http://l
awandfreedomfoundation.org/wp-content/uploads/2014/03/Easy-Meat
-Multiculturalism-Islam-and-Child-Sex-Slavery-05-03-2014.pdf.

53 Nima Gholam Ali Pour, "Islam's Sexual Abuses in Sweden and the 'Cultural
Challenge,'" Frontpagemag.com, January 22, 2016. http://www.frontpagemag
.com/fpm/261555/islams-sexual-abuses-sweden-and-cultural-challenge
-nima-gholam-ali-pour.

54 Joe Johns, Barbara Starr, Gloria Borger, and Carol Cratty, "Russia Asked U.S.
Twice to Investigate Tamerlan Tsarnaev," CNN.com, April 24, 2013. http://
security.blogs.cnn.com/2013/04/24/russia-asked-u-s-twice-to-investigate-ta-
merlan-tsarnaev-official-says/; Robert Spencer, "Russia Told FBI in 2011 That
Tsarnaev Was 'Follower of Radical Islam and a Strong Believer,'" JihadWatch.
org, April 10, 2014. https://www.jihadwatch.org/2014/04/
russia-told-fbi-in-2011-that-tsarnaev-was-follower-of-radical-islam-and-a-
strong-believer.

Chapter 2

1 John Milton, *Paradise Lost* (Mineola, New York: Dover Publications, 2005).
For a profound discussion of the serpent's strategy vis-à-vis Eve, see Dinesh
D'Souza's summary of his interview with Stanley Fish, one of the world's
leading John Milton scholars. Fish elaborates on how Lucifer is portrayed in
Paradise Lost and in the Western tradition, explaining Lucifer's strategy
against God as well as his tactics and motives with Eve in the Garden. Dinesh
D'Souza, *America: Imagine a World Without Her* (Washington, DC: Regnery
Publishing, 2014), pp. 83–84.

2 The term *utopian virus* is used in this work to depict man's yearning to build
utopia on earth, a yearning that presumes the perfectibility of human
institutions and of the human race. The term is by no means original to this
work. See, for instance, Joe White, "Engels, Owen and Utopianism" in Casey
Harison (ed.), *A New Social Question: Capitalism, Socialism, and Utopia* (UK:
Cambridge Scholars Publishing, 2015), p. 192.

3 While a large focus of this work is on the spiritual dimension of the human
struggle against, as well as its embrace of, the utopian virus, there are,

obviously, also many atheists who, as a result of their own keen insights and bravery, reject the virus.

4 Dietrich von Hildebrand, *The New Tower of Babel: Modern Man's Flight from God* (Manchester, New Hampshire: Sophia Institute Press, 1994), p. 10.

5 Hildebrand, pp. 19–21 and 27.

6 Scholars such as Eric Hoffer have described members of mass and utopian movements as "believers." See Eric Hoffer, *The True Believer: Thoughts on the Nature of Mass Movements* (New York: Harper & Row, 1951). For a description of the believer in the context of the Marxist/leftist vision, see Chapter 1, "The Believer's Diagnosis" in Jamie Glazov, *United in Hate: The Left's Romance with Tyranny and Terror* (Los Angeles: WND, 2009), pp. 5–21.

7 David Horowitz, *Left Illusions: An Intellectual Odyssey* (Dallas: Spence, 2003). Horowitz's ideas and writings on this theme are capsulized in Jamie Glazov, "The Life and Work of David Horowitz," Frontpagemag.com, November 13, 2015. http://www.frontpagemag.com/fpm/260760/life-and-work-david-horowitz-jamie-glazov.

8 Hildebrand, p. 21.

9 Rev. Livio Fanzaga, *The Deceiver: Our Daily Struggle with Satan* (Fort Collins, CO: Roman Catholic Books, 2000), p. 36.

10 Hildebrand, p. 47.

11 Anonymous, *Meditations on the Tarot: A Journey into Christian Hermeticism*, translated by Robert Powell (TarcherPerigee: 2002), pp. 14–15.

12 David Horowitz, *The End of Time* (San Francisco: Encounter Books, 2005), p. 90.

13 Ibid., pp. 105–106.

14 For an extended discussion of the believer's death wish, which emanates from his needs to rid himself of his own unwanted self and to dissolve his individuality into a collective totalitarian whole, see Jamie Glazov, "The Believer's Diagnosis."

15 See Horowitz's essay, "The Religious Roots of Radicalism" in *The Politics of Bad Faith: The Radical Assault on America's Future* (New York: Free Press, 2000).

16 George Orwell, *1984* (online copy: New York: Plume Printing, 1983), p. 234. http://www.thirdworldtraveler.com/Authors/Part_Three_1984.html.

17 Author's interview with Daniel Greenfield, May 25, 2017.

18 Hildebrand, p. 19.

19 For a discussion of the fellow travelers and their death wish, see Glazov, *United in Hate*. For the two definitive masterpieces on the fellow travelers, see Paul Hollander's books, *Political Pilgrims: Travels of Western Intellectuals to the Soviet Union, China, & Cuba 1928–1978* (New York: Oxford University Press, 1981) and *Anti-Americanism: Critiques at Home and Abroad, 1965–1990* (New York: Oxford University Press, 1992).

20 See Glazov, "The Believer's Diagnosis."

21 To see how leftists celebrated 9/11, see Glazov, *United in Hate*, pp. xxvii–xxviii.

22 Jamie Glazov's *United in Hate* tells the story of how the fellow travelers have continued their romance with the totalitarian adversaries of America, replacing their former allegiance to communism with a newfound sympathy for Islamic jihad.

23 As already referred to in our Introduction, the *Unholy Alliance* is the term this work uses to label the Left-Islamic supremacist alliance, a phenomenon documented by David Horowitz in his work, *Unholy Alliance: Radical Islam and the American Left* (Washington, DC: Regnery, 2004), and on his online database, DiscovertheNetworks.org. For more discussion and analysis on the Left's romance with Islamic supremacism and how this romance is an extension of the Left's alliance with communism during the Cold War, see Glazov, *United in Hate*.

Chapter 3

1 See Introduction, p. 17, and Chapter 18.

2 The *Unholy Alliance* is the term this work uses to label the Left-Islamic supremacist alliance, a phenomenon documented by David Horowitz in his work, *Unholy Alliance: Radical Islam and the American Left* (Washington, DC: Regnery, 2004), and on his website/database, DiscovertheNetworks.org. See the description of the alliance in our Introduction, pp. xxxiii–xxxiv. For more discussion and analysis on the Left's romance with Islamic supremacism and how this romance is an extension of the Left's alliance with communism during the Cold War, see Jamie Glazov, *United in Hate: The Left's Romance with Tyranny and Terror* (Los Angeles: WND, 2009).

3 See Chapter 1, "The Case." The damage caused by the Obama administration will also be solidified in subsequent chapters, especially in Chapters 15–17.

4 For two strong works that demonstrate how and why the Left controls our media, see: Tim Groseclose, *Left Turn: How Liberal Media Bias Distorts the American Mind* (New York: St. Martin's Press: 2011) and Ben Shapiro, *Bullies: How the Left's Culture of Fear and Intimidation Silences Americans* (New York: Threshold Editions, 2014).

5 Bradford Richardson, "Liberal Professors Outnumber Conservatives Nearly 12 to 1, Study Finds," *Washington Times*, October 6, 2016. http://www.washingtontimes.com/news/2016/oct/6/liberal-professors-outnumber-conservatives-12-1/.

6 For the riots blocking Yiannopoulos' talk, see Matthew Vadum, "Berkeley Riots Provoked by Freedom Center Campaign," Frontpagemag.com, February 2, 2017. http://www.frontpagemag.com/fpm/265678/berkeley-riots-provoked-freedom-center-campaign-matthew-vadum. For the cancellations of Coulter's and Horowitz's appearances, see Thomas Fuller, "Conservative Groups Sue Berkeley Over Ann Coulter Cancellation," NYTimes.com, April 24, 2017. https://www.nytimes.com/2017/04/24/us/ann-coulter-university-of-california-berkeley.html?_r=0 and David Horowitz, "My Free Speech at Berkeley,

Not," Frontpagemag.com, April 12, 2017, http://www.frontpagemag.com/fpm/266394/my-free-speech-berkeley-not-david-horowitz.

7 Daniel Mael, "Yale Students 'Disrespected' That Ayaan Hirsi Ali Is Speaking On Campus," TruthRevolt.org, September 11, 2014. http://www.truthrevolt.org/news/yale-students-disrespected-ayaan-hirsi-ali-speaking-campus; Natalie Johnson, "Campus Protesters Try to Silence Conservative Speaker, Demand College President's Resignation," DailySignal.com, February 26, 2016. http://dailysignal.com/2016/02/26/campus-protesters-try-to-silence-conservative-speaker-demand-college-presidents-resignation/.

8 See David Horowitz's four works on the Left's Stalinist control of American campuses: *The Professors: The 101 Most Dangerous Academics in America* (Washington, DC: Regnery 2006), *Indoctrination U.: The Left's War on Academic Freedom* (New York: Encounter, 2009), *One-Party Classroom*—coauthored with Jacob Laksin—(New York: Crown, 2009), and *Reforming Our Universities: The Campaign for an Academic Bill of Rights* (Washington, DC: Regnery, 2010).

9 Denis MacEoin, "Western Universities: The Best Indoctrination Money Can Buy," GatestoneInstitute.org, June 26, 2016. https://www.gatestoneinstitute.org/8331/universities-indoctrination; "Saudi & Arab Influence on American Education," DiscoverTheNetworks.org, http://www.discoverthenetworks.org/viewSubCategory.asp?id=213; Gitika Ahuja, "Saudi Prince Donates $40 Million to Harvard, Georgetown Universities," abcnews.go.com, http://abcnews.go.com/International/story?id=1402008.

10 For a powerful discussion on how the Left controls Hollywood's boundaries of discourse on the terror war, see: Oliver Williams, "Hollywood, Islam, and Political Correctness," GatestoneInstitute.org, July 10, 2014. http://www.gatestoneinstitute.org/4397/hollywood-islam-political-correctness.

11 Georg Szalai, "Hollywood Primes the Pump for Mideast Money," Hollywood Reporter.com, June 12, 2007. http://www.hollywoodreporter.com/news/hollywood-primes-pump-mideast-money-156661.

12 Andrew C. McCarthy, "The History of MPAC," NationalReview.com, August 7, 2012. http://www.nationalreview.com/article/313257/history-mpac-andrew-c-mccarthy.

13 Deborah Weiss, "Islamist Influence in Hollywood," HumanEvents.com, August 8, 2015. http://humanevents.com/2015/08/08/islamist-influence-in-hollywood/. For a thorough documentation on this issue, see Deborah Weiss's book, *Islamist Influence in Hollywood* (Washington, DC: The Center for Security Policy, 2018).

14 Ben Shapiro provides a strong work documenting the Left's control of Hollywood in his book, *Primetime Propaganda: The True Hollywood Story of How the Left Took Over Your TV* (New York: Broadside Books, 2011).

15 See previous chapter, Chapter 2, "The Utopian Virus."

ENDNOTES

16 For the most comprehensive reading on the Left's nature, ability to accumulate power, and how it wields that power, see David Horowitz's nine-volume series *The Black Book of the American Left*, which is the most complete, first-hand portrait of the Left as it has evolved from the inception of the Cold War through the era of Barack Obama. Visit: blackbookoftheamericanleft.com.

17 David Horowitz, *Take No Prisoners: The Battle Plan for Defeating the Left* (Washington, DC: Regnery, 2014).

18 For an excellent account of how the Left sees culture as the main vehicle through which to achieve power, how Gramsci molded this vision, and how the Left captured power through its culture wars, see Horowitz, *The Black Book of the American Left, Volume V: Culture Wars* (Los Angeles: Second Thought Books, 2015).

19 Ibid. and Barry Rubin, *Silent Revolution: How the Left Rose to Political Power and Cultural Dominance* (New York: HarperCollins, 2014).

20 David Horowitz and Richard Poe, *The Shadow Party: How George Soros, Hillary Clinton, and Sixties Radicals Seized Control of the Democratic Party* (Nashville, Tennessee: Thomas Nelson, 2006).

21 Ibid.

22 David Horowtz and Jacob Laksin, Chapter 2, "The Making of a President" in *The New Leviathan: How the Left-Wing Money Machine Shapes American Politics and Threatens America's Future* (New York: Crown Forum, 2012).

23 Horowtz and Laksin, *The New Leviathan*.

24 Ibid.

25 Horowitz, *Take No Prisoners*.

26 To learn more about the necessity and rationale for DiscovertheNetworks.org, which went online in February 2005, and the uproar surrounding its publication, see volume 2, *Progressives*, of *The Black Book of the American Left*.

Chapter 4

1 *Unholy Alliance* is the term this work uses to label the Left-Islamic supremacist alliance, a phenomenon documented by David Horowitz in *Unholy Alliance: Radical Islam and the American Left* (Washington, DC: Regnery, 2006) and on his website/database, DiscovertheNetworks.org. See the description of the alliance in our Introduction, pp. xxxiii–xxxiv. For more discussion and analysis on how the Left aided and abetted communism during the Cold War, and how the Left's romance with Islamic supremacism as an extension of its alliance with communism, see Jamie Glazov, *United in Hate: The Left's Romance with Tyranny and Terror* (Los Angeles: WND, 2009).

2 To see how the Left rooted for the Soviet Union in the Cold War and how it denied the Soviet regime's barbarities, see John Earl Haynes and Harvey Klehr, *In Denial: Historians, Communism, and Espionage* (San Francisco: Encounter Books, 2005). See also Horowitz, *Unholy Alliance*; Glazov, *United in Hate*; and

Horowitz, *The Politics of Bad Faith: The Radical Assault on America's Future* (New York: Free Press, 2000).

3 For the Left's plan to build the Tower of Babel, see Chapter 2.

4 The efforts to demonize and criminalize truth-telling about Islam in the United States and worldwide are well under way and are discussed in Chapter 1, p. 1.

5 For a typical leftist attack on Pamela Geller, see the Southern Poverty Law Center's slanderous profile of her: "Pamela Geller: Pamela Geller Is the Anti-Muslim Movement's Most Visible and Flamboyant Figurehead," https://www.splcenter.org/fighting-hate/extremist-files/individual/pamela-geller.

6 Pamela Geller, "Aqsa in Israel," PamelaGeller.com, August 25, 2011. http://pamelageller.com/2011/08/it-was-a-glorious-day-and-the-dedication-to-aqsa-parvez-and-all-of-the-brave-and-courageous-young-honor-killing-victims-who.html/. See also: Robert Spencer, "The Lonesome Death of Aqsa Parvez," JihadWatch.org, June 21, 2010. https://www.jihadwatch.org/2010/06/spencer-the-lonesome-death-of-aqsa-parvez.

7 Pamela Geller, "Honor Killings Grow in the West: Islam's Gruesome Gallery," PamelaGeller.com, March 31, 2009. http://pamelageller.com/2009/03/honor-killing-islams-gruesome-gallery.html/#sthash.lm9vStk6.dpuf.

8 For a powerful discussion of how leftists inferiorize Muslims by holding them to lesser moral standards, see The Glazov Gang, "Christine Williams Moment: The Heart-Wrenching Screams of Dina Ali Lasloom," JamieGlazov.com, April 23, 2017. http://jamieglazov.com/2017/04/23/christine-williams-moment-the-heart-wrenching-screams-of-dina-ali-lasloom/. For the masterpiece that delineates why and how leftists in the West hold their own societies up to a higher moral accountability than the totalitarian regimes they worship, see Paul Hollander, *Political Pilgrims: Travels of Western Intellectuals to the Soviet Union, China, and Cuba* (New York: Oxford University Press, 1981).

9 For an authoritative account of how the Left worshipped and made victims and martyrs out of communists, communist spies, and sympathizers who were damaging America during the Cold War, see Haynes and Klehr.

10 See Chapter 1, p. 13, and Robert Spencer, "The Hijrah Into Europe," Frontpage-mag.com, September 4, 2015. http://www.frontpagemag.com/fpm/260019/hijrah-europe-robert-spencer.

11 Leo Hohmann, "Refugees Secretly Flooding Into These States," WorldNetDaily .com, July 19, 2016. http://www.wnd.com/2016/07/refugees-secretly -flooding-into-these-states/.

12 Joseph Klein, "Judicial Overreach on National Security," Frontpagemag.com, February 6, 2017. http://www.frontpagemag.com/fpm/265711/judicial -overreach-national-security-joseph-klein.

13 For a clear example of how people are now not only shunned, but also criminalized, for the crime of telling the truth about Islam, see the ordeal experienced by Dutch Freedom Party leader Geert Wilders, who was charged and then found guilty by a Dutch court for his truthful comments about the

inordinate number of crimes committed by Muslim migrants. See Gordon Darroch in The Hague, "Geert Wilders Found Guilty of Inciting Discrimina- tion," TheGuardian.com, December 9, 2016. https://www.theguardian.com/ world/2016/dec/09/geert-wilders-found-guilty-in-hate-speech-trial-but-no-sentence-imposed. For a solid background on the case, see: Hugh Fitzgerald, "Geert Wilders, Or, A Daniel Come to Judgment 'More In Sorrow,'" Jihad-Watch.org, November 6, 2016. https://www.jihadwatch.org/2016/11/ hugh-fitzgerald-geert-wilders-or-a-daniel-come-to-judgment-more-in-sorrow.

Chapter 5

1 Robert Spencer, *The Truth About Muhammad: Founder of the World's Most Intolerant Religion* (Washington, DC: Regnery, 2006). For a powerful takedown of the *It's Just the Extremists!* argument, see The Glazov Gang, "Anne Marie Waters Moment: Easy Guide to Debating the Useful Infidel, Part III: Nothing to Do with Islam," JamieGlazov.com, May 18, 2017. http:// jamieglazov.com/2017/05/18/ anne-marie-waters-moment-easy-guide-to-debating-the-useful-infidel-part-iii-nothing-to-do-with-islam/.

2 "By The Numbers—The Untold Story of Muslim Opinions & Demographics," Clarion Project—Challenging Extremism/Promoting Dialogue, December 10, 2015, https://www.youtube.com/watch?v=pSPvnFDDQHk; See also: "Ben Shapiro: The Myth of the Tiny Radical Muslim Minority," TruthRevoltOrigi-nals, October 15, 2014, https://www.youtube.com/watch?v=g7TAAw3oQvg.

3 *Unholy Alliance* is the term this work uses to refer to the alliance between the Left and Islamic Supremacism, a phenomenon documented by David Horowitz in his work, *Unholy Alliance: Radical Islam and the American Left* (Washington, DC: Regnery, 2004). For more discussion and analysis on the Left's romance with Islamic supremacism, and how this romance is an extension of the Left's alliance with communism during the Cold War, see Jamie Glazov, *United in Hate: The Left's Romance with Tyranny and Terror* (Los Angeles: WND, 2009).

4 For a powerful takedown of the *But Not All Muslims Do That!* argument, see The Glazov Gang, "Anne Marie Waters Moment: Easy Guide to Debating the Useful Infidel, Part I: 'Not All,'" JamieGlazov.com, April 16, 2017. http:// jamieglazov.com/2017/04/16/ anne-marie-waters-moment-easy-guide-to-debating-the-useful-infidel-part-i-not-all/.

5 Interview with Daniel Greenfield, July 1, 2017.

6 Raymond Ibrahim, "But ISIS Kills More Muslims Than Non-Muslims!," Frontpagemag.com, December 18, 2015. http://www.frontpagemag.com/ fpm/261156/isis-kills-more-muslims-non-muslims-raymond-ibrahim.

7 Ibid.; see also Daniel Greenfield on The Glazov Gang episode, "But ISIS Kills Muslims Too," JamieGlazov.com, February 5, 2016. http://jamieglazov. com/2016/02/05/but-isis-kills-muslims-too-on-the-glazov-gang/.

8 Interview with Daniel Greenfield, July 1, 2017.

9 Raymond Ibrahim, "Ben Affleck: Portrait of Islam's Clueless Apologists," PJMedia, October 6, 2014, http://pjmedia.com/blog/ben-affleck-clueless-islam-apologist/?print=1.

10 For the best work on Islam itself and how it inspires tyranny and violence, see Robert Spencer, *The Truth About Muhammed* and Spencer, *Religion of Peace? Why Christianity Is and Islam Isn't* (Washington, DC: Regnery, 2007).

11 Ibrahim, "Ben Affleck: Portrait of Islam's Clueless Apologists."

12 Robert Spencer, "Watch What Happens When 3 Muslim Spokesmen Are Asked About Islam's Death Penalty for Apostasy," PJMedia.com, March 24, 2015. https://pjmedia.com/lifestyle/2015/03/24/watch-what-happens-when-3-muslim-spokesmen-are-asked-about-islams-death-penalty-for-apostasy/.

13 Ibrahim, "Ben Affleck: Portrait of Islam's Clueless Apologists."

14 Robert Spencer, "He Said That Raping Me Is His Prayer to God," PJMedia.com, August 14, 2015. https://pjmedia.com/blog/he-said-that-raping-me-is-his-prayer-to-god/.

15 Robert Spencer, "Canada: Muslim Beats His Wife In Front of Cops, Says She Is His 'Property'," JihadWatch.org, August 16, 2015. http://www.jihadwatch.org/2015/08/canada-muslim-beats-his-wife-in-front-of-cops-says-she-is-his-property.

16 For an outline of the Islamic nature of female genital mutilation, see Jamie Glazov, "Why 17-Year-Old Mayar Mohamed Mousa Had to Die," Frontpagemag.com, June 15, 2016. http://www.frontpagemag.com/fpm/263192/why-17-year-old-mayar-mohamed-mousa-had-die-jamie-glazov.

17 For a strong work documenting how Islamic texts inspire and sanction violence against unbelievers, see: Spencer, *Religion of Peace? Why Christianity Is and Islam Isn't*. For documentation on how Islamic texts sanction Muslims to take non-Muslim girls and women as sex slaves, see Spencer, "He Said That Raping Me Is His Prayer to God."

18 See Spencer, *Religion of Peace? Why Christianity Is and Islam Isn't*.

19 Robert Spencer, "The Diversity of Islam?" Frontpagemag.com, October 13, 2014. http://www.frontpagemag.com/2014/robert-spencer/the-diversity-of-islam/.

20 Robert Spencer, "What We Have Learned Since 9/11," Frontpagemag.com, September 11, 2015. https://www.jihadwatch.org/2015/09/what-we-have-learned-since-911. For a powerful takedown of the *Others Do It Too!* argument, see The Glazov Gang, "Anne Marie Waters Moment: Easy Guide to Debating the Useful Infidel, Part II: 'But the Bible...'" JamieGlazov.com, April 27, 2017. http://jamieglazov.com/2017/04/27/anne-marie-waters-moment-easy-guide-to-debating-the-useful-infidel-part-ii-but-the-bible/.

21 Fox News, "State Department Spokeswoman Floats Jobs as Answer to ISIS," Fox News, February 17, 2015. http://www.foxnews.com/politics/2015/02/17/state-department-spokeswoman-floats-jobs-as-answer-to-isis.html.

22 See Chapter 5, "Does Poverty Cause Militant Islam?" in Daniel Pipes, *Militant Islam Reaches America* (New York: W. W. Norton, 2002), pp. 52–63.

23 Rebecca Kimitch, "What We Know About San Bernardino Mass Shooting Killers Syed Farook and Tashfeen Malik," *San Bernardino County Sun*, December 3, 2015. http://www.sbsun.com/general-news/20151203/what-we-know-about-san-bernardino-mass-shooting-killers-syed-farook-and-tashfeen-malik.

24 Yasmin Khorram, Ben Brumfield, and Scott Zamos, "Chattanooga Shooter Changed After Mideast Visit, Friend Says," CNN.com, September 15, 2015. http://www.cnn.com/2015/07/17/us/tennessee-shooter-mohammad-youssuf-abdulazeez/.

25 Pipes, *Militant Islam Reaches America*, p. x.

26 Ibid., p. 56.

27 Robert Spencer, "New Report: Islamic State Recruits Not Driven By Poverty, and Above Average in Education," JihadWatch.org, October 6, 2016. https://www.jihadwatch.org/2016/10/new-report-islamic-state-recruits-not-driven-by-poverty-and-above-average-in-education.

28 Chapter 1, pp. 7–9.

29 Robert Spencer, "John Kerry's Jobs Program for Would-Be Jihadists," Frontpagemag.com, October 4, 2013, http://frontpagemag.com/2013/robert-spencer/john-kerrys-jobs-for-potential-jihadists-program/.

30 Ibid.

31 Bruce Thornton, "Still Getting Jihadism Wrong," Frontpagemag.com, October 14, 2014, http://www.frontpagemag.com/2014/bruce-thornton/still-getting-jihadism-wrong/print/.

32 Ibid.

33 Nonie Darwish, *The Devil We Don't Know* (New Jersey: John Wiley & Sons Inc., 2012), p. 16.

34 "Chapter 1: Beliefs About Sharia," Polling and Analysis, PewForum.org, April 30, 2013. http://www.pewforum.org/2013/04/30/the-worlds-muslims-religion-politics-society-beliefs-about-sharia/. See also Jamie Glazov, "200 Million Women Victimized by Female Genital Mutilation—on The Glazov Gang," JihadWatch.org, February 7, 2016. http://www.jihadwatch.org/2016/02/200-million-women-victimized-by-female-genital-mutilation-on-the-glazov-gang.

35 Raymond Ibrahim, "How Obama's Arab Spring Created the Islamic State," Frontpagemag.com, October 5, 2014. http://www.frontpagemag.com/fpm/242422/how-obamas-arab-spring-created-islamic-state-raymond-ibrahim.

36 Daniel Greenfield, "How Islam in America Became a Privileged Religion," Frontpagemag.com, June 2, 2015. http://www.frontpagemag.com/fpm/257819/how-islam-america-became-privileged-religion-daniel-greenfield.

37 Robert Spencer, "Islam Is Not a Race? Obama White House Wants to Change That," JihadWatch.org, October 1, 2016. https://www.jihadwatch.org/2016/10/islam-is-not-a-race-obama-white-house-wants-to-change-that.

38 Ibid.

39 Daniel Greenfield, "Obama to Add Muslims as a Race," The Point at Frontpagemag.com, October 4, 2016. http://www.frontpagemag.com/point/264383/obama-add-muslims-race-daniel-greenfield.

40 Shelby Steele, *The Content of Our Character* (New York, NY: HarperPerennial, 1991). See Chapter 1: "I'm Black, You're White, Who's Innocent?" pp. 1–20.

41 Steele, pp. 79–82.

42 Robert Spencer, "CNN Guest Says 'White People' Don't Understand Islamic Culture—Ibrahim Hooper Hardest Hit," JihadWatch.org, March 25, 2016. https://www.jihadwatch.org/2016/03/cnn-guest-says-white-people-dont-understand-islamic-culture-ibrahim-hooper-hardest-hit.

43 Ibid.

44 Daniel Greenfield, "White People Can't Understand Islam," The Point at Frontpagemag.com, March 25, 2016. http://www.frontpagemag.com/point/262285/white-people-cant-understand-islam-daniel-greenfield.

45 Ibid.

46 Ibid.

47 Robert Spencer, "The Diversity of Islam?" Frontpagemag.com, October 13, 2014. http://www.frontpagemag.com/2014/robert-spencer/the-diversity-of-islam/.

48 Robert Spencer, "Obama: 'There's No Religious Rationale That Would Justify In Any Way Any of the Things' Jihad Terrorists Do," JihadWatch.org, September 29, 2016. https://www.jihadwatch.org/2016/09/obama-theres-no-religious-rationale-that-would-justify-in-any-way-any-of-the-things-jihad-terrorists-do.

49 For how Islam is more of a political ideology than a religion, see "Political Islam Has Subjugated Civilizations for 1,400 years," PoliticalIslam.com, https://www.politicalislam.com/about/.

50 For how the FBI can no longer surveil mosques, see Jessica Chasmar, "Mosques Off-Limits by Government Snooping Since 2011, IBD Editorial Claims," *Washington Times*, June 13, 2013. http://www.washingtontimes.com/news/2013/jun/13/mosques-limits-government-snooping-2011-ibd-editor/.

51 For how mosques are used as a cover for jihad, see Jamie Glazov, "Shari'a and Violence in American Mosques," Frontpagemag.com, June 9, 2011. http://www.frontpagemag.com/fpm/95567/sharia-and-violence-american-mosques-jamie-glazov.

52 For a discussion and documentation of Islamic theological teachings that inspire and sanction misogyny and crimes against women, such as honor killings, see Chapter 10 (pp. 115–131), "To Hate a Woman" in Jamie Glazov, *United in Hate: The Left's Romance with Tyranny and Terror* (Los Angeles: WND, 2009).

ENDNOTES

Chapter 6

1 April Glover and Max Margan, "'This is for Allah, stop living this life': What London Terror Knifemen Screamed As They Slit Australian Victim's Throat in Scenes 'Like A Horror Movie' in Packed Restaurant During Rampage That Killed Eight," DailyMail.co.uk, June 11, 2017. http://www.dailymail.co.uk/news/article-4593188/London-terror-survivor-relives-moment-throat-slashed.html#ixzz4k9yDjnwN; Daniel Greenfield, "Run, Hide and Deny in London," Frontpagemag.com, June 5, 2017. http://www.frontpagemag.com/fpm/266896/run-hide-and-deny-london-daniel-greenfield.

2 Jay Croft and Hilary Whiteman, "London Terror Attacks: What We Know," CNN.com, June 4, 2017. http://www.cnn.com/2017/06/03/europe/london-terror-attacks-what-we-know/index.html.

3 Greenfield, "Run, Hide, and Deny in London."

4 Ibid.

5 Stephen Wright, Chris Greenwood, Inderdeep Bains, Emily Kent Smith, Sam Greenhill, Gareth Davies, and Martin Robinson, "Killer Who Was Filmed in Regent's Park with an ISIS Flag and Tried to Radicalize Children with Sweets Was Shopped to Police TWICE As It Emerges One of His Fellow Terrorists lived in DUBLIN," DailyMail.co.uk, June 5, 2017. http://www.dailymail.co.uk/news/article-4571902/London-Bridge-killer-slipped-police-s-net.html#ixzz4k4bl4ic2.

6 Robert Spencer, "'Robert Spencer and Pamela Geller Are Still Fighting Back against Their Ban' from the UK." JihadWatch.org, January 22, 2014. https://www.jihadwatch.org/2014/01/robert-spencer-and-pamela-geller-are-still-fighting-back-against-their-ban-from-the-uk.

7 Robert Spencer, "Theresa May's New Approach: More of the Same," Frontpagemag.com, June 5, 2017. http://www.frontpagemag.com/fpm/266895/theresa-mays-new-approach-more-same-robert-spencer.

8 Robert Spencer, "MSNBC Host Asks If There Is Risk of 'Overreaction' to London Jihad Murders," JihadWatch.org, June 4, 2017. https://www.jihadwatch.org/2017/06/msnbc-host-asks-if-there-is-risk-of-overreaction-to-london-jihad-murders.

9 Robert Spencer, "Reza Aslan: Trump 'Piece Of S**T' for Calling for Travel Ban In Wake of London Jihad Attacks," JihadWatch.org, June 3, 2017. https://www.jihadwatch.org/2017/06/reza-aslan-trump-piece-of-st-for-calling-for-travel-ban-in-wake-of-london-jihad-attacks.

10 Ibid.

11 Ibid. CNN cut ties with Aslan after these tweets. See Dave Nemetz, "CNN Drops Host Reza Aslan After Vulgar Anti-Trump Tweets," TVLine.com, June 9, 2017. http://tvline.com/2017/06/09/reza-aslan-fired-cnn-donald-trump-tweets-believer-cancelled/.

12 Kim Hjelmgaard , Jane Onyanga-Omara and John Bacon, "Manchester bombing vigil draws thousands as attack investigation intensifies," USAToday.

com, May 23, 2017. https://www.usatoday.com/story/news/world/2017/05/23/manchester-arena-terror-attack/102044682/.

13 CNN Library, "July 7, 2005 London Bombings Fast Facts," CNN.com, June 29, 2016. http://www.cnn.com/2013/11/06/world/europe/july-7-2005-london-bombings-fast-facts/index.html.

14 Simon Osborne, "'What comes next will be more severe' ISIS boasts about Manchester terror in vile message ISIS has posted a sick message of support for the cowardly suicide bomber who targeted children and teenagers in the Manchester bombing," Express.co.uk, May 23, 2017. http://www.express.co.uk/news/uk/808397/Manchester-terror-bombing-explosion-attack-ISIS-threats-vile-message-social-media.

15 Robert Spencer, "Robert Spencer's Open Letter to the University at Buffalo," UBSpectrum, May 25, 2017. http://www.ubspectrum.com/article/2017/05/robert-spencer-open-letter-to-the-university-at-buffalo.

16 Pamela Geller, "Manchester jihadi & Didsbury mosque: Salman Abedi was 'devout Muslim' 'learned the Qur'an by heart' 'would do the five and call the adhan' Didsbury mosque," PamelaGeller.com, May 23, 2017. http://pamelageller.com/2017/05/manchester-jihadi-didsbury-mosque-salman-abedi-devout-muslim-learned-quran-heart-five-call-adhan-didsbury-mosque.html/; Robert Spencer, "New York Times on Manchester jihad mass murderer: 'No one yet knows what motivated him to commit such a horrific deed,'" JihadWatch.org, May 24, 2017. https://www.jihadwatch.org/2017/05/new-york-times-on-manchester-jihad-mass-murderer-no-one-yet-knows-what-motivated-him-to-commit-such-a-horrific-deed.

17 Melanie Phillips, "Denial Still Flows Over Londonistan," MelaniePhillips.com, May 25, 2017. http://www.melaniephillips.com/denial-still-flows-londonistan/.

18 Ibid.

19 Glazov Gang Video, "Jamie Glazov Moment: Why Islamic Terror Targeted Children in Manchester," JamieGlazov.com, May 28, 2017. http://jamieglazov.com/2017/05/28/jamie-glazov-moment-why-islamic-terror-targeted-children-in-manchester/; Anna Geifman, "Why Terrorism Strikes at Children," Frontpagemag.com, July 1, 2014. http://www.frontpagemag.com/fpm/235431/why-terrorism-strikes-children-anna-geifman.

20 The Editorial Board, "When Terrorists Target Children," NYTimes.com. May 23, 2017. https://www.nytimes.com/2017/05/23/opinion/manchester-attack-isis.html?_r=1; Spencer, "New York Times on Manchester Jihad Mass Murderer: 'No one yet knows what motivated him to commit such a horrific deed.'"

21 Andrew Buncombe, "There's Only One Way Britain Should Respond to Attacks Such As Manchester. That Is By Carrying On Exactly As Before," Independent.co.uk, May 23, 2017. http://www.independent.co.uk/voices/manchester-arena-ariana-grande-terror-carry-on-teenagers-respond-a7750486.html.

22 Robert Spencer, "UK's Independent Pleads That Nothing Be Done to Stop Jihad Terror After Manchester Massacre," JihadWatch.org, May 23, 2017. https://www.jihadwatch.org/2017/05/uks-independent-pleads-that-nothing-be-done-to-stop-jihad-terror-after-manchester-massacre.

23 Nick Ferrari, "Manchester Mayor: Bomber Was a Terrorist, Not a Muslim," IBC. co.uk, May 24, 2017, 10:17. http://www.lbc.co.uk/radio/presenters/nick-ferrari/manchester-mayor-bomber-was-a-terrorist-not-muslim/; Narjas Zatat, "Manchester Bomber Salman Abedi No More Represents Muslims Than Jo Cox's Killer Represents White People, Says Andy Burnham," Independent. co.uk, May 24, 2017. http://www.independent.co.uk/news/uk/home-news/manchester-bomber-salman-abedi-andy-burnham-muslims-jo-cox-killer-white-people-greater-mayor-arena-a7752466.html.

24 Robert Spencer, "UK: Manchester Jihad Mass Murderer 'Devout' Muslim Who Learned Qur'an by Heart," JihadWatch.org, May 23, 2017. https://www.jihadwatch.org/2017/05/uk-manchester-jihad-mass-murderer-devout-muslim-who-learned-quran-by-heart.

25 Conor Gaffey, "Muslims in Manchester Fear Reprisals as ISIS Claims Responsibility for Concert Attack," Newsweek.com, May 23, 2017. http://www.newsweek.com/muslims-manchester-fear-reprisals-isis-claims-responsibility-concert-attack-614159?spMailingID=1890836; Andrew Kugle, "ABC News Worried About Potential 'Anti-Islamic Backlash' After Manchester Terror Attack," FreeBeacon.com, May 23, 2017. http://freebeacon.com/national-security/abc-news-worried-potential-anti-islamic-backlash-manchester-terror-attack/.

26 Daniel Greenfield, "Manchester Top Cop Emphasizes 'Diversity', Warns Against 'Hate'," Frontpagemag.com, May 23, 2017. http://www.frontpagemag.com/point/266789/manchester-top-cop-emphasizes-diversity-warns-daniel-greenfield.

27 For a strong work documenting how Islam inspires terror against unbelievers, see Robert Spencer, *The Truth About Muhammed* and Spencer, *Religion of Peace? Why Christianity Is and Islam Isn't* (Washington, DC: Regnery, 2007).

28 Greenfield, "Manchester Top Cop Emphasizes 'Diversity'," Frontpagemag.com, May 23, 2017. http://www.frontpagemag.com/point/266789/manchester-top-cop-emphasizes-diversity-warns-daniel-greenfield.

29 Robert Spencer, "Muslim Refugee Brings Jihad Terror to Ohio State," Frontpagemag.com, November 29, 2016. http://www.frontpagemag.com/fpm/264981/muslim-refugee-brings-jihad-terror-ohio-state-robert-spencer.

30 Robert Spencer, "OSU Jihadi: 'By Allah, I am willing to kill a billion infidels,'" JihadWatch.org, November 28, 2016. https://www.jihadwatch.org/2016/11/osu-jihadi-by-allah-i-am-willing-to-kill-a-billion-infidels; Robert Spencer, "Muslim Refugee Brings Jihad Terror to Ohio State."

31 Robert Spencer, "We Will Conquer Your Rome, Break Your Crosses, and Enslave Your Women, by the Permission of Allah," JihadWatch.org, September 21, 2014. https://www.jihadwatch.org/2014/09/islamic-state-we-will-conquer

-your-rome-break-your-crosses-and-enslave-your-women-by-the-permission-of-allah.

32 Robert Spencer, "Muslim Refugee Brings Jihad Terror to Ohio State."

33 Robert Spencer, "OSU Group Says Jihadi Was Wrongly Killed: Justice Can't 'Come from a Cop's Bullet,'" JihadWatch.org, December 11, 2016. https://www.jihadwatch.org/2016/12/osu-group-says-jihadi-wrongly-killed-justice-cant-come-from-a-cops-bullet.

34 Ibid.

35 Aubrey Whelan, Mari A. Schaefer, Jeremy Roebuck, and Stephanie Farr, "Police: Gunman Who Shot Cop Pledged Allegiance to the Islamic State," Philly.com., January 8, 2016. http://mobile.philly.com/beta?wss=/philly/news&id=364624321.

36 Jordan Schachtel, "Imam Lied About Philly Islamic State Shooter's Connection to His Mosque," Breitbart.com, January 11, 2016. http://www.breitbart.com/national-security/2016/01/11/imam-lied-about-philly-islamic-state-shooters-connection-to-his-mosque/.

37 Robert Spencer, "Philly Shooter: I Did It For Allah. Philly Mayor: No, You Didn't." Frontpagemag.com, January 11, 2016. http://www.frontpagemag.com/fpm/261414/philly-shooter-i-did-it-allah-philly-mayor-no-you-robert-spencer.

38 Robert Spencer, "Meet the Farooks: The Modern Jihad Family," Frontpagemag.com, December 9, 2015. http://www.frontpagemag.com/fpm/261066/meet-farooks-modern-jihad-family-robert-spencer.

39 Matthew Vadum, "Suppress Shooters' Islamist Ties, Obama Ordered," Frontpagemag.com, December 14, 2015. http://www.frontpagemag.com/fpm/261116/suppress-shooters-islamist-ties-obama-ordered-matthew-vadum#.Vm77M810Pi4.gmail.

40 Spencer, "Meet the Farooks: The Modern Jihad Family."

41 Islamic Circle of North America, profile in DiscovertheNetworks.org: http://www.discoverthenetworks.org/groupProfile.asp?grpid=6380.

42 Ibid.

43 Ibid.

44 Ibid.

45 Ben Ashford, "EXCLUSIVE: Shooting Targets, GoPro Packaging, Hammer and 'Vise Grips' Found by FBI In Car Belonging to San Bernardino Shooter's MOTHER," DailyMail.co.uk, December 8, 2015. http://www.dailymail.co.uk/news/article-3350280/Shooting-targets-GoPro-packaging-hammer-Syed-Farook-s-mother-s-car.html#ixzz49tdr29X2.

46 Pamela Geller, "San Bernardino Jihadis Strapped GoPros to Their Body Armor," PamelaGeller.com, December 3, 2015. http://pamelageller.com/2015/12/san-bernardino-jihadis-strapped-gopros-to-their-body-armor.html/#sthash.NN2UEc6P.dpuf.

47 Ibid.

48 Spencer, "Meet the Farooks: The Modern Jihad Family."

ENDNOTES

49 *Unholy Alliance* is the term this work uses to label the Left-Islamic supremacist alliance, a phenomenon documented by David Horowitz in *Unholy Alliance: Radical Islam and the American Left* (Washington, DC: Regnery, 2006) and on his website/database, DiscovertheNetorks.org. See the description of the alliance in our Introduction, pp. xxxiii–xxxiv. For more discussion and analysis on how the Left aided and abetted communism during the Cold War, and how the Left's romance with Islamic supremacism as an extension of its alliance with communism, see Jamie Glazov, *United in Hate: The Left's Romance with Tyranny and Terror* (Los Angeles: WND, 2009).

50 Vadum, "Suppress Shooters' Islamist Ties, Obama Ordered."

51 Ibid.

52 Ibid.

53 For the complete myth of the "self-radicalized" terrorist and "lone-wolf" see: The Glazov Gang: "Ex-CIA Station Chief Exposes 'Lone-Wolf' Myth," JamieGlazov.com, June 27, 2017. http://jamieglazov.com/2017/06/27/ex-cia -station-chief-exposes-lone-wolf-myth-glazov-gang/.

54 Daniel Greenfield, "Obama's ISIS Cover-Up Gets Its Own Speech," Frontpage-mag.com, December 7, 2015. http://www.frontpagemag.com/fpm/261048/ obamas-isis-cover-gets-its-own-speech-daniel-greenfield.

55 Trey Sanchez, "Fear of Islamophobia Caused DHS to Pull Program That Might Have Prevented California Massacre," TruthRevolt.org, December 14, 2015. http://www.truthrevolt.org/news/fear-islamophobia-caused-dhs-pull -program-might-have-prevented-california-massacre.

56 Ibid.

57 Ibid.

58 Katie Pavlich, "Neighbor Didn't Report Suspicious Activity of San Bernardino Killers for Fear of Being Called Racist," Townhall.com, December 3, 2015. http://townhall.com/tipsheet/katiepavlich/2015/12/03/ neighbor-didnt-report-suspicious-activity-of-san-bernardino-killers-for-fear-of-being-called-racist-n2088543.

59 Robert Spencer, *Arab Winter Comes to America: The Truth About the War We're In* (Washington, DC: Regnery, 2014).

60 See Chapter 4, "Jihad Denial."

61 Spencer, "Meet the Farooks: The Modern Jihad Family."

62 Daniel Greenfield, "Homeland Security Banned from Checking Social Media of Visa Applicants," Frontpagemag.com, December 14, 2015. http://www. frontpagemag.com/point/261120/ homeland-security-banned-checking-social-media-daniel-greenfield.

63 Daniel Greenfield, "San Bernardino Jihadist's Visa was Improperly Approved," Frontpagemag.com, December 19, 2015. http://www.frontpagemag.com/ point/261178/san-bernardino-jihadists-visa-was-improperly-daniel-greenfield.

64 Robert Spencer, "Chattanooga Jihad Murderer Texted Islamic Verse to Friend Before Attack," JihadWatch.org, July 18, 2015. http://www.jihadwatch.org /2015/07/chattanooga-jihad-murderer-texted-islamic-verse-to-friend-before

-attack; Robert Spencer, "Reza Aslan Comes Out Strong for Hamas," Jihad-Watch.org, August 5, 2014. http://www.jihadwatch.org/2014/08/reza-aslan-comes-out-strong-for-hamas; Winfield Myers, "No Jihad Here: Middle East Studies Profs on Chattanooga Shooting," Frontpagemag.com, July 23, 2015. http://www.frontpagemag.com/fpm/259555/no-jihad-here-middle-east-studies-profs-winfield-myers.

65 Robert Spencer, "Dzhokhar Tsarnaev's Insincere Apology," Frontpagemag.com, June 24, 2015. http://www.frontpagemag.com/fpm/259092/dzhokhar-tsarnaevs-insincere-apology-robert-spencer; "Russia Warned U.S. About Boston Marathon Bomb Suspect Tsarnaev: Report," Reuters.com, http://www.reuters.com/article/us-usa-explosions-boston-congress-idUSBREA2P02Q20140326; For a discussion on the denial of the Tsarnaevs' Islamic inspirations, see Daniel Greenfield, "Is Islamic Terrorism a Motive?" Frontpagemag.com, April 21, 2013. http://www.frontpagemag.com/point/186563/islamic-terrorism-motive-daniel-greenfield. For a typical effort in the media to blame anything but Islam for the Tsarnaevs' terrorism, see Dave Herrera, "Boston Marathon Bombing Suspect Was a Rap Fan: Ten Song Lyrics Dzhokhar Tsarnaev Tweeted," Westword.com, April 25, 2013. http://www.westword.com/music/boston-marathon-bombing-suspect-was-a-rap-fan-ten-song-lyrics-dzhokhar-tsarnaev-tweeted-5680793.

66 "A Ticking Time Bomb: Counterterrorism Lessons from the U.S. Government's Failure to Prevent the Fort Hood Attack," *A Special Report by Joseph I. Lieberman, Chairman, Susan M. Collins, Ranking Member, U.S. Senate Committee on Homeland Security and Governmental Affairs*, Washington DC 20510, February 2011. http://www.globalsecurity.org/military/library/report/2011/ft-hood_hsga_special-report.htm; Patrick Goodenough, "Six Years Later: Obama Finally Calls Fort Hood a Terrorist Attack," *cnsnews.com*, December 7, 2015. http://www.cnsnews.com/news/article/patrick-goodenough/obama-six-years-later-calls-fort-hood-terrorist-attack.

67 Robert Spencer, "Philly Shooter: I Did It For Allah. Philly Mayor: No, You Didn't." Frontpagemag.com, January 11, 2016. http://www.frontpagemag.com/fpm/261414/philly-shooter-i-did-it-allah-philly-mayor-no-you-robert-spencer.

68 When "March Against Sharia" rallies were held in North America in early June, 2017, there were actually counter-protests that were equally sized or even larger in number. The pro-sharia activists called the anti-sharia protestors "racist" and "Islamophobic." The magazine *Teen Vogue*, meanwhile, represented many leftist outlets in calling the rallies "hate speech." See James Doubek, "'Anti-Sharia' Marchers Met with Counter-Protests Around the Country," NPR.org, June 11, 2017. http://www.npr.org/sections/thetwo-way/2017/06/11/532454216/anti-sharia-marchers-met-with-counter-protests-around-the-country and Mordechai Sones, "Teen Vogue calls March Against Sharia 'hate speech'," IsraelNationalNews.com, June 14, 2017. http://www.israelnationalnews.com/News/News.aspx/231020.

ENDNOTES

Chapter 7

1 Daniel Greenfield, "Should Ben Carson Endorse Sharia Slavery in Islamic Law?" The Point in Frontpagemag.com, September 21, 2015. http://www.frontpage-mag.com/point/260200/should-ben-carson-endorse-sharia-slavery-islamic-daniel-greenfield.

2 For one of the most authoritative works on sharia law, see Nonie Darwish, *Cruel and Usual Punishment: The Terrifying Global Implications of Islamic Law* (Nashville, Tennessee: Thomas Nelson, 2009).

3 *Unholy Alliance* is the term this work uses to label the Left-Islamic supremacist alliance, a phenomenon documented by David Horowitz in his work, *Unholy Alliance: Radical Islam and the American Left* (Washington, DC: Regnery, 2006) and on his website/database, DiscovertheNetorks.org. See the description of the alliance in our Introduction, pp. xxxiii–xxxiv. For more discussion and analysis on the Left's romance with Islamic supremacism and communism, see Jamie Glazov, *United in Hate: The Left's Romance with Tyranny and Terror* (Los Angeles: WND, 2009).

4 For a discussion on how the Unholy Alliance has gained control of the boundaries of discourse, see Chapter 3, "The Virus in Power."

5 To learn why Jihad Denial is so crucial in the Unholy Alliance's agenda, see Chapters 3–5.

6 For a strong discussion on how sharia and jihad are interlinked, see: "What Is the Relationship between Jihad and Sharia?", citizensagainstsharia.wordpress.com. https://citizensagainstsharia.wordpress.com/2007/12/28/what-is-the-relationship-between-jihad-and-sharia/.

7 Paul Waldman, "Ben Carson's Anti-Muslim Comments Are at Odds with Traditional American Principles," *Washington Post*, September 21, 2015. https://www.washingtonpost.com/blogs/plum-line/wp/2015/09/21/ben-carsons-anti-muslim-comments-are-at-odds-with-traditional-american-principles/.

8 Sara Dogan, "Reza Aslan Accuses Republicans of Rewarding 'Xenophobia,' 'Muslim-Bashing,'" TruthRevolt.org, September 22, 2015. http://www.truthrevolt.org/news/reza-aslan-accuses-republicans-rewarding-xenophobia-muslim-bashing. For an expose on who Reza Aslan really is, see Robert Spencer, "Reza Aslan: Trump Is Popular Because of 'Islamophobia,'" Frontpagemag.com, April 12, 2016. http://www.frontpagemag.com/fpm/262476/reza-aslan-trump-popular-because-islamophobia-robert-spencer.

9 Robert Spencer, "Washington Post Quotes Islamic Apologists' Taqiyya to 'Prove' Ben Carson Wrong About Taqiyya," JihadWatch.org, September 22, 2015. http://www.jihadwatch.org/2015/09/washington-posts-fact-checker-quotes-dishonest-islamic-apologists-taqiyya-to-prove-ben-carson-wrong-about-taqiyya.

10 Ibid. For an excellent discussion about *taqiyya* in general, see Raymond Ibrahim, "Taqiyya about Taqiyya," RaymondIbrahim.com, April 12, 2014. http://raymondibrahim.com/2014/04/12/taqiyya-about-taqiyya/.

11 See Chapter 5, "Not All Muslims Do That."

12 Pamela Geller, "Ben Carson Zooms to Top of Media's Kill List," Breitbart.com, September 22, 2015. http://www.breitbart.com/big-government/2015/09/22/ben-carson-zooms-to-top-of-medias-kill-list/.

13 Leo Hohmann, "'Muslim President' Issue Scorching Republicans," WorldNetDaily.com, September 23, 2015. http://www.wnd.com/2015/09/muslim-president-issue-scorching-republicans/#M5Vtd5OyjLIUsh2l.99.

14 "Carson: 'Absolutely I stand by the comments' about Muslim president," FoxNews.com, September 22, 2015. http://www.foxnews.com/politics/2015/09/22/ben-carson-muslim-president-absolutely-stand-by-comments/?intcmp=hpbtl; Jeff Poor, "Fiorina: Carson Muslim President Remarks 'Wrong,'" Breitbart.com, September 21, 2015. http://www.breitbart.com/video/2015/09/21/fiorina-carson-muslim-president-remarks-wrong/.

15 "Carson stands by Muslim president remarks, Trump weighs in," FoxNews.com, September 22, 2015. http://www.foxnews.com/politics/2015/09/21/trump-it-not-my-job-to-defend-president.html.

16 Breitbart TV, "Levin: Media Should Receive 'Backlash' For Carson Coverage," Breitbart.com, September 21, 2015. http://www.breitbart.com/video/2015/09/21/levin-media-should-receive-backlash-for-carson-coverage/.

17 See Darwish. *Cruel and Usual Punishment.*

18 William Kilpatrick, "One Nation Under Allah?" Frontpagemag.com, September 21, 2015. http://www.frontpagemag.com/fpm/260192/one-nation-under-allah-william-kilpatrick.

19 Ibid.

20 Stephen Brown, "The Obama Administration's Slavery Disgrace," Frontpagemag.com, March 31, 2015. http://www.frontpagemag.com/fpm/254297/obama-administrations-slavery-disgrace-stephen-brown.

21 Robert Spencer, "Ben Carson in CAIR's Crosshairs," Frontpagemag.com, September 21, 2015. http://www.frontpagemag.com/fpm/260190/ben-carson-cairs-crosshairs-robert-spencer.

22 Ibid.

23 CAIR profile, DiscoverTheNetworks.org. http://www.discoverthenetworks.org/Articles/cairprofilestand.html.

24 Daniel Greenfield, "CAIR Muslim Who Wants US Under Islamic Law Condemns Ben Carson," The Point in Frontpagemag.com, September 20, 2015. http://www.frontpagemag.com/point/260189/cair-muslim-who-wants-us-under-islamic-law-daniel-greenfield.

25 Ibid.

26 Ibrahim Hooper profile, DiscoverTheNetworks.org. http://www.discoverthenetworks.org/individualProfile.asp?indid=2136.

27 Jordan Schachtel, "Huma Abedin Debuts on Twitter, Rips Ben Carson," Breitbart.com, September 21, 2015. http://www.breitbart.com/big-government/2015/09/21/huma-abedin-debuts-twitter-rips-ben-carson/.

28 Huma Abedin profile, DiscoverThe Networks.org. http://www.discoverthenet-works.org/individualProfile.asp?indid=2556.

29 Saleha Mahmood Abedin profile, DiscoverThe Networks.org. http://www.discoverthenetworks.org/individualProfile.asp?indid=2557.

30 James Doubek, "'Anti-Sharia' Marchers Met with Counter-Protests Around the Country," NPR.org, June 11, 2017. http://www.npr.org/sections/thetwo-way/2017/06/11/532454216/anti-sharia-marchers-met-with-counter-protests-around-the-country.

31 Mordechai Sones, "Teen Vogue Calls March Against Sharia 'Hate Speech,'" IsraelNationalNews.com, June 14, 2017. http://www.israelnationalnews.com/News/News.aspx/231020.

32 Bill Siegel, *The Control Factor: Our Struggle to See the True Threat* (New York: Hamilton Books, 2012).

Chapter 8

1 Bill Siegel, *The Control Factor: Our Struggle to See the True Threat* (New York: Hamilton Books, 2012).

2 Charles Montaldo, "The Definition and Examples of Stockholm Syndrome," thoughtco.com, March 6, 2017. https://www.thoughtco.com/what-is-stockholm-syndrome-973324.

3 *Unholy Alliance* is the term this work uses to label the Left-Islamic supremacist alliance, a phenomenon documented by David Horowitz in his work, *Unholy Alliance: Radical Islam and the American Left* (Washington, DC: Regnery, 2006) and on his website/database, DiscovertheNetworks.org. See the description of the alliance in our Introduction, pp. xxxiii–xxxiv. For more discussion and analysis on the Left's romance with Islamic supremacism and communism, see Jamie Glazov, *United in Hate: The Left's Romance with Tyranny and Terror* (Los Angeles: WND, 2009).

4 The Left's goals within the Unholy Alliance is spelled out in the Introduction and Chapter 2, "The Utopian Virus."

5 See Chapter 1, p. 13.

6 See Chapter 2, "The Utopian Virus."

7 Siegel, p. xx.

8 Siegel, p. xvii.

9 Maria Konnikova, *The Confidence Game: Why We Fall for It...Every Time* (New York: Penguin Random House, 2016).

10 Ibid., p. 5.

11 Ibid.

12 Ibid., p. 6.

13 Potemkin villages were the literally fabricated villages built in the communist world to create the illusion that communism was achieving social and economic perfection. In reality, nothing in these villages was real; even the "villagers" were actors who had been told what to say. The charade continues in present-day North Korea. See: Alastair Bonnett, "North Korea's Creepy Fake

Civilian Village Fools No One," boingboing.net, July 8, 2014. http://boingboing
.net/2014/07/08/north-koreas-creepy-fake-civ.html.

14 Jamie Glazov, *United in Hate: The Left's Romance with Tyranny and Terror*
(Los Angeles: WND, 2009), Chapter 2: "The Believer's Diagnosis," pp. 5–21.

15 Konnikova, p. 321.

16 Konnikova, p. 52.

17 The *Explanatory Memorandum* is an internal document of the Muslim
Brotherhood captured by the FBI in 2005 that outlines the Brotherhood's
design to destroy America by America's own hands as part of its overall goal of
"eliminating and destroying Western civilization from within, and sabotaging
its miserable house." See Discover the Network's profile, "The Muslim
Brotherhood's General Strategic Goal' for North America." http://www.
discoverthenetworks.org/viewSubCategory.asp?id=1235.

18 Steele, p. 91.

19 For how the Left has taken control of U.S. culture and how it maintains power,
see Chapter 3, "Utopian Virus in Power." For how Jihad Denial slanders
truth-tellers about Islam as racist, see Chapter 5, "Not All Muslims Do That!",
pp. 50–51.

20 This leftist mindset is documented in the chapter "The Believer" and
throughout the text in *United in Hate: The Left's Romance with Tyranny and
Terror*. See also Chapter 4, "Jihad Denial."

21 Daniel Greenfield, "The Leftist Jihad Has Nothing to Do with Liberalism,"
Frontpagemag.com, October 9, 2014, http://www.frontpagemag.com/2014/
dgreenfield/the-leftist-jihad-has-nothing-to-do-with-liberalism/print/.

22 See Chapter 4, "Jihad Denial" and Chapter 5, "Not All Muslims Do That!"

Chapter 9

1 Thomas Sheridan, *Puzzling People: The Labyrinth of the Psychopath* (Vellumi-
nous Press, 2011), p. 3.

2 Ibid., pp. 1–2. See also Robert D. Hare, *Without Conscience: The Disturbing
World of the Psychopaths Among Us* (New York: The Guilford Press, 1999), pp.
40–44.

3 Hare, pp. 62–66. Kevin Dutton, *The Wisdom of Psychopaths: What Saints,
Spies, and Serial Killers Can Teach Us About Success* (New York: Scientific
American/Farrar, Straus and Giroux, 2013), p. 42.

4 Martha Stout, *The Sociopath Next Door* (New York: Three Rivers Press, 2005),
p. 90.

5 Ibid., p. 89.

6 Jason MacKenzie delineates this dynamic of "we have so much in common"
within the dynamic of how the psychopath tricks his victims into romance in
*Psychopath Free: Recovering from Emotionally Abusive Relationships with
Narcissists, Sociopaths, and Other Toxic People* (New York: Berkley Books,
2015), pp. 23–28.

7 Stout, p. 90.

8 Dutton, p. 112. See also Hare, pp. 46–52.

9 Dutton, p. 113.

10 Ibid., p. 1.

11 Stout, p. 91.

12 Ibid., p. 108.

13 Ibid., p. 108.

14 See Preface, p. 1.

15 Sandra L. Brown, *Women Who Love Psychopaths: Inside the Relationships of Inevitable Harm with Psychopaths, Sociopaths, and Narcissists* (Penrose, N.S.: Mask Publishing, 2009), p. 118.

16 Stout, p. 91.

17 Sheridan, p. 69.

18 Stout, p. 29.

19 Sheridan, p. 17.

20 See Chapter 8, "The Control Factor" and Chapter 4, "Jihad Denial."

21 Stout, p. 87.

22 Sheridan, p. x.

23 For how people want to be seen as innocent in the context of the Left's accusations in the culture war, see Chapter 5, "Not All Muslims Do That!", p. 51.

24 Stout, p. 131.

25 Sheridan, p. 96.

26 Stout, pp. 128–135 and 210–211.

27 Ibid., p. 110.

28 Quoted in Sutton, pp. 47–48.

29 Dutton, p. 48.

Chapter 10

1 Suras 3:54, 7:99, and 8:30. See Nonie Darwish, *Wholly Different: Why I Chose Biblical Values Over Islamic Values* (Washington, DC: Regnery, 2017), pp. 48–49.

2 Raymond Ibrahim, "Taqiyya about Taqiyya," RaymondIbrahim.com, April 12, 2014. http://raymondibrahim.com/2014/04/12/taqiyya-about-taqiyya/.

3 Darwish, pp. 47–52.

4 Robert Spencer, *The Truth About Muhammad* (Washington, DC: Regnery, 2006), pp. 8–10.

5 Raymond Ibrahim, "Islam's Celestial Concubines—Muslim Men Die for Them, Muslim Women Envy Them," JihadWatch.org, November 25, 2016. https:// www.jihadwatch.org/2016/11/raymond-ibrahim-islams-celestial-concubines-muslim-men-die-for-them-muslim-women-envy-them; For the Qur'an's descriptions of paradise see Robert Spencer, *The Truth About Muhammad*, pp. 57–58.

6 A typical example of Muslims' *taqiyya* about the meaning of jihad is Linda Sarsour's calling for jihad against Trump and then, after being called out on it,

explaining that she was really talking about fighting for racial and economic justice—when it was completely clear what she meant. A masterpiece takedown of Sarsour's *taqiyya* on this matter is Robert Spencer, "Yes, Linda Sarsour Did Incite Violence Against President Trump," PJMedia.com, July 10, 2017. https://pjmedia.com/homeland-security/2017/07/10/yes-linda-sarsour -did-incite-violence-against-president-trump/.

7   A teaching outlined in the *Reliance of the Traveler*, a classical manual of sharia law, quoted in Darwish, p. 50.

8   For why apostates have to be killed in Islam, see Spencer, *The Truth About Muhammad*, pp. 147–148.

9   Darwish, pp. 136–141.

10 Darwish, p. 32. See also Bosch Fawstin's article on how Muslims are the victims of Islam: "The Muslim World Is a World Where the Bad Guy Won," Frontpage-mag.com, May 2, 2013. http://www.frontpagemag.com/fpm/188241/muslim -world-world-where-bad-guy-won-bosch-fawstin.

11 See Pamela Geller, "Kuwait: Muslim Kills His Own Brother for Not Fasting During Ramadan," PamelaGeller.com, June 30, 2016. http://pamelageller.com /2016/06/kuwait-muslim-kills-his-own-brother-for-not-fasting-during -ramadan.html/.

12 Interview with Daniel Greenfield, September 18, 2018.

13 Darwish, p. 137.

14 The rigid rules that Christians under the Islamic State have to abide if they take dhimmi status ("protected" non-Muslim people living in inferior status) is a clear example of this one cruel loophole non-Muslims have to survive under Islam, and it is rooted in Islamic teachings. See Robert Spencer, "11 Dhimma rules that Christians must obey in the Islamic State," JihadWatch.org, September 7, 2015. https://www.jihadwatch.org/2015/09/11-dhimma-rules -that-christians-must-obey-in-the-islamic-state.

15 Darwish, pp. 42–43.

16 Darwish outlines these differences in the God of the Bible as a loving and forgiving God in whom there is grace, and Islam's Allah, who is a sadistic controller who wants submission. See especially her chapter, "Healing, Salvation, and the Holy Spirit," in *Wholly Different*, pp. 29–46, and for the phenomenon of submission to Allah, see pp. 62–63.

17 Darwish, p. 137.

18 Interview with Daniel Greenfield, September 18, 2018.

19 Ibid., pp. 14–15. See also: Robert Spencer, "Does the Qur'an Teach Hate?" Frontpagemag.com, September 17, 2013. http://www.frontpagemag.com/fpm /204505/does-quran-teach-hate-robert-spencer.

20 Darwish, pp. 14–15.

21 Darwish, p. 16–18; Spencer, "Does the Qur'an Teach Hate?" See Qur'an 3:110.

22 Darwish, p. 22.

23 Ibid., pp. 26–27.

ENDNOTES

24 See Chapter 9, "Yearnings for Death and Suicide," pp. 101–115 and Chapter 12, "Killing and Dying for Purity," pp. 145–151 in Jamie Glazov, *United in Hate: The Left's Romance with Tyranny and Terror* (Los Angeles, CA: WND Books, 2009).

25 Paul Berman, *Terror and Liberalism* (New York: W. W. Norton, 2003), p. 120.

26 Darwish, p. 19.

27 Surah 2:191–193.

28 Darwish, p. 85.

29 For Kasem's long list of the many ways Islam views itself as a victim when an unbeliever somewhere on the planet does not abide by Islamic laws, see: Abul Kasem, "When Is Islam Oppressed?" Islam-Watch.org, November 20, 2005. http://www.islam-watch.org/AbulKasem/IslamOppressed.htm.

30 Author's interview with Ali Sina, February 28, 2016.

31 Surah 22:39–40.

32 Qur'an 2:193, 8:39. See Mark Durie, *Liberty to the Captives: Freedom from Islam and Dhimmitude Through the Cross*, section 4.

33 Robert Spencer, *The Truth About Muhammad*, pp. 128–133.

34 David Wood, "Three Stages of Jihad," AnsweringMuslims.com, http://www.answeringmuslims.com/p/jihad.html.

35 Ibid.

36 For a discussion on the nature and roots of Muhammad's war against Jewish tribes, see Robert Spencer, Chapter 7, "War Is Deceit, pp. 103–123, in *The Truth About Muhammad*.

37 Mark Durie, *The Third Choice: Islam, Dhimmitude, and Freedom* (Australia: Deror Books, 2010), p. 113.

38 Ibid.

39 This story is told by the first biographer of Muhammad, Ibn Ishaq. Retold and quoted by Spencer, *The Truth About Muhammad*, pp. 162–163. See also Robert Spencer, "Malala: Muhammad Never Advised His Followers to 'Go Around Killing People…We Are Not Representing the True Islam,'" JihadWatch.org, April 16, 2017. https://www.jihadwatch.org/2017/04/malala-muhammad-never-advised-his-followers-to-go-around-killing-people-we-are-not-repre-senting-the-true-islam.

40 Mark Durie discusses Islam's attack on the human conscience on "The Glazov Gang: Mark Durie on 'Our Fear of Islam,'" Glazov Gang YouTube Channel, June 13, 2014. https://www.youtube.com/watch?v=xn0km52dCIg.

41 Darwish, p. 23.

42 To learn about the agendas of CAIR, ISNA, and the MSA, read the profiles of each group at DiscovertheNetworks.org: CAIR: http://www.discoverthenetworks.org/Articles/cairprofilestand.html; ISNA: http://www.discoverthenetworks.org/groupProfile.asp?grpid=6178; MSA: http://www.discoverthenetworks.org/groupProfile.asp?grpid=6175.

43 See Chapter 2, "The Utopian Virus."

44 Nonie Darwish, "The Islamic Terror Orchestra," Frontpagemag.com, August 25, 2014. http://www.frontpagemag.com/fpm/239437/islamic-terror -orchestra-nonie-darwish.

45 Ibid.

46 Christine Douglass-Williams, *The Challenge of Modernizing Islam: Reformers Speak Out and the Obstacles They Face* (New York: Encounter Books, 2017).

47 Stephen M. Kirby, "Muslim Reform Group Reached Out to 3,000 US Mosques, Got Only 40 Responses," JihadWatch.org, February 24, 2017. https:// www.jihadwatch.org/2017/02/muslim-reform-group-reached-out-to-3000 -us-mosques-got-only-40-responses.

48 See Chapter 5, "Not All Muslims Do That!"

49 *Unholy Alliance* is the term this work uses to refer to the alliance between the Left and Islamic supremacism, a phenomenon documented by David Horowitz in his work, *Unholy Alliance: Radical Islam and the American Left* (Washington, DC: Regnery, 2004). For more discussion and analysis on the Left's romance with Islamic supremacism, and how this romance is an extension of the Left's alliance with communism during the Cold War, see Jamie Glazov, *United in Hate: The Left's Romance with Tyranny and Terror* (Los Angeles: WND, 2009).

50 See Chapter 12, pp. 133–134, 139–140.

51 Robert Spencer, "Obama to Visit Muslim Brotherhood-Aligned Mosque," PJMedia.com, February 3, 2016. https://pjmedia.com/homeland-security /2016/02/03/obama-to-visit-muslim-brotherhood-aligned-mosque/.

52 Interview with Daniel Greenfield, September 18, 2018. We expand on this codependent relationship between the Jihadist Psychopath and his willing surrendering victims in Chapter 14, "Identifying with the Abuser."

53 This dynamic is explained in Chapter 5: "Not All Muslims Do That!"

54 The *Explanatory Memorandum* is an internal document of the Muslim Brotherhood captured by the FBI in 2005 that outlines the Brotherhood's design to destroy America by America's own hands as part of its overall goal of "eliminating and destroying Western civilization from within, and sabotaging its miserable house." The memorandum named the front groups doing this dirty work, and revealed what they are doing: destroying the house from within with many different tactics, including Jihad Denial propaganda, interfaith tricks, etc. For more information see the Discover the Network's profile on "The Muslim Brotherhood's General Strategic Goal' for North America." http://www.discoverthenetworks.org/viewSubCategory.asp?id=1235.

55 David M. Swindle, "Oops: Islamist Leader Boasts 'Thank God for Islamophobia' at Conference," Islamist-Watch.org, June 6, 2016. http://www.islamist-watch. org/blog/2016/06/oops-islamist-leader-boasts-thank-god-for#continued.

56 Ibid.

57 Robert Spencer, "Did the Muslim Brotherhood invent the term 'Islamophobia'?," JihadWatch.org, August 27, 2012. http://www.jihadwatch.org/2012/08/ did-the-muslim-brotherhood-invent-the-term-islamophobia.

ENDNOTES

58 See Chapter 1, "The Case," pp. 11–12.

59 Stephen Coughlin, *Catastrophic Failure: Blindfolding America in the Face of Jihad* (Washington DC: Center for Security Policy Press, 2015), pp. 269.

60 Coughlin, p. 269.

61 Ali Sina, "The Search of the Moderate Muslim," FaithFreedom.org. http://www.faithfreedom.org/oped/sina31107.htm.

62 Author's interview with Ali Sina, February 28, 2016.

63 Trey Sanchez, "TIME Makes Omar Mateen the Victim," TruthRevolt.org, July 18, 2016. http://www.truthrevolt.org/news/time-makes-omar-mateen-victim.

64 James Delingpole, "Muslims Were the Real Victims of the Nice Terror Attack, the BBC Explains," Breitbart.com, July 18, 2016. http://www.breitbart.com/london/2016/07/18/muslims-were-the-real-victims-of-the-nice-terror-attack-the-bbc-explains/.

Chapter 11

1 Robert Spencer, "Obama Proselytizes for Islam at UN Summit for 'Countering Violent Extremism,'" PamelaGeller.com, September 29, 2015. http://pamelageller.com/2015/09/obama-serves-up-cliches-and-falsehoods-as-his-anti-isis-strategy.html/#sthash.2sjoXyTx.dpuf.

2 Some analysts saw Obama's reference to ISIS as "ISIL" as a way to separate Islam from the Islamic State, as well as to insult Israel. See Amil Imani, "Why Does Obama Call ISIS 'ISIL'?", AmericanThinker.com, December 10, 2015. http://www.americanthinker.com/articles/2015/12/why_does_obama_call_isis_isil.html#ixzz4r2o9MphD.

3 Ibid.

4 *Unholy Alliance* is the term this work uses to refer to the alliance between the Left and Islamic supremacism, a phenomenon documented by David Horowitz in his work, *Unholy Alliance: Radical Islam and the American Left* (Washington, DC: Regnery, 2004). For more discussion and analysis on the Left's romance with Islamic supremacism, and how this romance is an extension of the Left's alliance with communism during the Cold War, see Jamie Glazov, *United in Hate: The Left's Romance with Tyranny and Terror* (Los Angeles: WND, 2009).

5 Chapter 5, "Not All Muslims Do That!", p. 42.

6 Robert Spencer, "Obama Proselytizes for Islam at UN Summit for 'Countering Violent Extremism.'" See also Joseph Klein, "Obama's Foreign Policy of Fantasies 'Anti-Immigrant bigotry' and Lack of Jobs Are Causing the Rise of ISIS?" Frontpagemag.com, October 1, 2015. http://www.frontpagemag.com/fpm/260296/obamas-foreign-policy-fantasies-joseph-klein.

7 For a strong work on Islam's war on Christianity, see Raymond Ibrahim, *Crucified Again: Exposing Islam's New War on Christians* (Washington, DC: Regnery Publishing, 2013).

8 For information on how the Muslim Brotherhood paid for Ellison's hajj and his other many links to the Brotherhood, see DiscoverTheNetwork's profile on him: http://www.discoverthenetworks.org/individualProfile.asp?indid=2158.

9 Quoted in Pamela Geller, "Grotesque Liar Keith Ellison's Crocodile Tears Over Made-Up Tale," PamelaGeller.com, March 10, 2011. http://pamelageller. com/2011/03/grotesque-liar-keith-ellisons-crocodile-tears-over-made-up-tale. html/#sthash.ZuhAWOF2.lZdT6v7v.dpuf. See video of speech on YouTube. com posted by The Blaze, "Rep. Keith Ellison Testimony," March 10, 2011. https://www.youtube.com/watch?t=131&v=BHq3ndwZNyA.

10 Geller, "Grotesque Liar Keith Ellison's Crocodile Tears Over Made-Up Tale."

11 Ibid.

12 DiscoverTheNetwork's Keith Ellison's profile: http://www.discoverthenetworks.org/individualProfile.asp?indid=2158.

13 Quoted in Mark Durie, The Third Choice: Islam, Dhimmitude, and Freedom.

14 Quoted in Durie. https://www.memri.org/tv/la-psychologist-wafa-sultan-clashes-algerian-islamist-ahmad-bin-muhammad-over-islamic-teachings/transcript.

15 Raymond Ibrahim, "Exposed: Egypt's Institutionalized Persecution of Coptic Christians," Frontpagemag.com, May 5, 2015. http://www.frontpagemag.com/fpm/256430/exposed-egypts-institutionalized-persecution-raymond-ibrahim. See also Raymond Ibrahim, Crucified Again: Exposing Islam's New War on Christians (Washington, DC: Regnery, 2013).

16 John Rossomando, "Muslim Brotherhood Memo Blesses Egyptian Church Burnings," TheInvestigativeProject.org, August 19, 2013. http://www.investigativeproject.org/4127/muslim-brotherhood-memo-blesses-egyptian-church.

17 See Chapter 1, "The Case," pp. 5–7.

18 John Rossomando, "Coptic Leaders Condemn Obama Adviser's Anti-Coptic Tweets," InvestigativeProject.org, October 11, 2013. https://www.investigativeproject.org/4184/coptic-leaders-condemn-obama-adviser-anti-coptic.

19 Raymond Ibrahim, "Surreal and Suicidal: Modern Western Histories of Islam," Frontpagemag.com, October 4, 2013. http://frontpagemag.com/2013/raymond-ibrahim/surreal-and-suicidal-modern-western-histories-of-islam/.

20 Robert Spencer, "Iran Threatens to End Nuclear Deal, Demands That US Apologize," JihadWatch.org, November 13, 2015. http://www.jihadwatch.org/2015/11/iran-threatens-to-end-nuclear-deal-demands-that-us-apologize.

21 Jeffrey Goldberg, "Iran Killing American Troops in Iraq and Afghanistan," TheAtlantic.com, July 6, 2011. http://www.theatlantic.com/international/archive/2011/07/iran-killing-american-troops-in-iraq-and-afghanistan/241486/.

22 Daniel Greenfield, "Obama Blames America for Iran Feeling 'Defensive' and 'Vulnerable'," The Point at Frontpagemag.com, April 5, 2015. http://www.frontpagemag.com/point/254582/obama-blames-america-iran-feeling-defensive-and-daniel-greenfield.

23 Hen Mazzig, "An Israeli Soldier to American Jews: Wake up!" Blogs.TimesofIs-
    rael.com, October 10, 2013. http://blogs.timesofisrael.com/
    an-israeli-soldiers-call-to-american-jews.
24 Lee Kaplan, "The Raping of Israeli Academia-Tal Nitzan, Zali Gurevitch and
    Hebrew U.," Israpundit, January 3, 2008. http://www.israpundit.org/archives
    /6972.
25 Ibid.
26 Daniel Greenfield, "Ex-Israeli Soldier Denounced on US Campus for Not
    Raping Palestinian Women," The Point, Frontpagemag.com, October 14, 2013.
    http://frontpagemag.com/2013/dgreenfield/ex-israeli-soldier-denounced-on
    -us-campus-for-not-raping-palestinian-women/.
27 Chapter 1, "The Case," pp. 13–15.
28 Robert Spencer, "Cologne Mayor to Victims of Migrant Sex Assaults: You
    Asked For It," Frontpagemag.com, January 8, 2016. http://www.frontpagemag.
    com/fpm/261380/cologne-mayor-victims-migrant-sex-assaults-you-robert
    -spencer.
29 Jamie Glazov, "No Naomi Wolf, You Apologize," Frontpagemag.com, Septem-
    ber 3, 2009. http://archive.frontpagemag.com/readArticle.aspx?ARTID=36177.
    Naomi Wolf writes about her political pilgrimage to the Islamic Middle East in
    her article "Behind the Veil Lives a Thriving Muslim Sexuality," for the *Sydney
    Morning Herald* on August 30, 2008, so we are assuming her travels occurred
    in the earlier part of that year. They may have been earlier. http://www.smh.
    com.au/news/opinion/behind-the-veil-lives-a-thriving-muslim-sexual-
    ity/2008/08/29/1219516734637.html?page=fullpage#contentSwap1.
30 Fjordman, "Norwegian Authorities Still Covering Up Muslim Rapes," *Gates of
    Vienna*, July 27, 2006. http://gatesofvienna.blogspot.ca/2006/07/norwegian
    -authorities-still-covering.html.
31 Robert Spencer, "German Police Fire Water Cannons at Anti-'Rapefugee'
    Protesters in Cologne," JihadWatch.org, January 9, 2016. http://
    www.jihadwatch.org/2016/01/german-police-fire-water-cannons-at-anti
    -rapefugee-protesters-in-cologne.
32 Gaby Hinsliff, "Let's Not Shy Away from Asking Hard Questions About the
    Cologne Attacks," TheGuardian.com, January 8, 2016. http://www.theguardian
    .com/commentisfree/2016/jan/08/
    cologne-attacks-hard-questions-new-years-eve.
33 Daniel Greenfield, "Guardian Feminist: Muslim Rapists are the Real Victims in
    Cologne," The Point, Frontpagemag.com, January 19, 2016. http://www.
    frontpagemag.com/point/261522/guardian-feminist-muslim-rapists-are
    -real-victims-daniel-greenfield.
34 Oliver JJ Lane, "After Anal Rape, Left Wing Activist Felt 'Guilt and Responsibil-
    ity' His Migrant Attacker Was Deported," Breitbart.com, April 7, 2016. http://
    www.breitbart.com/london/2016/04/07/after-anal-rape-leftist-felt-despair
    -that-his-somalian-attacker-was-deported/.

35 Liam Deacon "CLAIM: 'No Borders' Activist Gang Raped By Migrants, Pressured Into Silence To Not 'Damage Cause,'" Breitbart.com, October 6, 2015. http://www.breitbart.com/london/2015/10/06/no-borders-activist -gang-raped-migrants-pressured-silence-not-damage-cause/.

36 Daniel Greenfield, "Aftermath of Muslim Terror Attacks Always a 'Difficult Time for Muslims,'" Frontpagemag.com, March 24, 2016. http:// www.frontpagemag.com/point/262270/aftermath-muslim-terror-attacks -always-difficult-daniel-greenfield.

37 A teaching outlined in the *Reliance of the Traveler*, a classical manual of sharia law, quoted in Darwish, p. 50.

38 A masterpiece takedown of Sarsour's *taqiyya* on this matter is Robert Spencer, "Yes, Linda Sarsour Did Incite Violence Against President Trump," PJMedia. com, July 10, 2017. https://pjmedia.com/homeland-security/2017/07/10/ yes-linda-sarsour-did-incite-violence-against-president-trump/.

39 Ibid.

40 Robert Spencer, "Linda Sarsour Warns Critics After Calling for 'Jihad' Against Trump: 'I Am Taking Names,'" JihadWatch.org, July 13, 2017. https:// www.jihadwatch.org/2017/07/linda-sarsour-warns-critics-after-calling -for-jihad-against-trump-i-am-taking-names.

41 Ibid.

42 Robert Spencer, "Justine Damond: Killed by 'Islamophobia'", Frontpagemag. com, July 21, 2017. http://www.frontpagemag.com/fpm/267340/ justine-damond-killed-islamophobia-robert-spencer.

43 Robert Spencer, "After Muslim Cop Kills Unarmed Woman, Minneapolis Mayor Reassures Muslims, Warns Against 'Islamophobia'", JihadWatch.org, July 20, 2017. https://www.jihadwatch.org/2017/07/after-muslim-cop-kills -unarmed-woman-minneapolis-mayor-reassures-muslims-warns-against -islamophobia.

44 Yuliya Talmazan, "Vancouver Lawyers Launch Free, Confidential Islamophobia Hotline," GlobalNews.ca. http://globalnews.ca/news/2567393/vancouver -lawyers-launch-free-confidential-islamophobia-hotline/?sf22259178=1.

45 Robert Spencer, "Boston to Hang 50 Posters Addressing Public Harassment, 'Islamophobia' Around City," JihadWatch.org, July 19, 2017. https:// www.jihadwatch.org/2017/07/boston-to-hang-50-posters-addressing-public -harassment-islamophobia-around-city.

46 Dinesh D'Souza, *The Big Lie: Exposing the Nazi Roots of the America Left* (Washington, DC: Regnery, 2017), pp. 1–3.

47 Ibid., p. 3.

48 Hen Mazzig, "An Israeli Soldier to American Jews: Wake up!" Blogs.Timesof Israel.com, October 10, 2013. http://blogs.timesofisrael.com/an-israeli -soldiers-call-to-american-jews.

49 Yori Yanover, "Has The American Jewish Left Gone Bunkers or Is It Only Rob Eshman?" JewishPress.com, October 16th, 2013. http://www.jewishpress.com/

indepth/opinions/has-the-american-jewish-left-gone-bunkers-or-is-it-only
-rob-eshman/2013/10/16/.

50 Bob Unruh, "Dems Call GOP Jihadists, Arsonists, Terrorists," WND.com, October 3, 2013. http://www.wnd.com/2013/10/ dems-call-gop-jihadists-arsonists-terrorists/#E1OQ6M3o8IKeRD1r.99.

51 Carl Campanile, "Obama Adviser 'Architect' of Showdown: Author," NYPost. com, October 15, 2013. http://nypost.com/2013/10/15/obama-adviser -orchestrated-shutdown-showdown-author/.

Chapter 12

1 The *Unholy Alliance* is the term this work uses to refer to the alliance between the Left and Islamic supremacism, a phenomenon documented by David Horowitz in his work, *Unholy Alliance: Radical Islam and the American Left* (Washington, DC: Regnery, 2004). For more discussion and analysis on the Left's romance with Islamic supremacism and how this romance is an extension of the Left's alliance with communism during the Cold War, see Jamie Glazov, *United in Hate: The Left's Romance with Tyranny and Terror* (Los Angeles: WND, 2009).

2 Julie Burchill, "Meet the Cry-Bully: A Hideous Hybrid of Victim and Victor," blogs.spectator.co.uk, April 21, 2015. https://blogs.spectator.co.uk/2015/04/ meet-the-cry-bully-a-hideous-hybrid-of-victim-and-victor/.

3 Writer Daniel Greenfield uses this powerful term "Cry-Bully" in his work to demonstrate how the Left/Islam alliance weaves its victimhood card. See, for example, Daniel Greenfield, "Islam, Social Justice Warriors and the Cry-Bully," The Point, Frontpagemag.com, November 7, 2015. http://www.frontpagemag. com/point/260687/islam-social-justice-warriors-and-cry-bully-daniel-green-field; and Daniel Greenfield, "Crymobs, Crybullying and the Left's Whiny War on Speech," The Point, Frontpagemag.com, November 12, 2015. http:// www.frontpagemag.com/fpm/260744/ crymobs-crybullying-and-lefts-whiny-war-speech-daniel-greenfield.

4 For a profound read on the growing leftist totalitarian impulse on U.S. campus to carve out a "safe space" as a camouflage to drown out dissent and intellectual freedom, see Judith Shulevitz, "In College and Hiding from Scary Ideas," Sunday Review, NYTimes.com, March 2015. http://www.nytimes.com/2015/03 /22/opinion/sunday/judith-shulevitz-hiding-from-scary-ideas.html?smid=fb-.

5 For the riots blocking Yiannopoulos' talk, see Matthew Vadum, "Berkeley Riots Provoked by Freedom Center Campaign," Frontpagemag.com, February 2, 2017. http://www.frontpagemag.com/fpm/265678/berkeley-riots-provoked-freedom -center-campaign-matthew-vadum. For the cancellations of Coulter's and Horowitz's appearances, see, Thomas Fuller, "Conservative Groups Sue Berkeley Over Ann Coulter Cancellation," NYTimes.com, April 24, 2017. https://www.nytimes.com/2017/04/24/us/ann-coulter-university-of-califor-nia-berkeley.html?_r=0, and David Horowitz, "My Free Speech at Berkeley,

Not," Frontpagemag.com, April 12, 2017. http://www.frontpagemag.com/
fpm/266394/my-free-speech-berkeley-not-david-horowitz.
6 Daniel Mael, "Yale Students 'Disrespected' That Ayaan Hirsi Ali Is Speaking
On Campus," TruthRevolt.org, Sept. 11, 2014. http://www.truthrevolt.org/
news/yale-students-disrespected-ayaan-hirsi-ali-speaking-campus; Natalie
Johnson, "Campus Protesters Try to Silence Conservative Speaker, Demand
College President's Resignation," *DailySignal.com*, February 26, 2016. http://
dailysignal.com/2016/02/26/campus-protesters-try-to-silence-conservative
-speaker-demand-college-presidents-resignation/.
7 See David Horowitz's four works on the Left's Stalinist control of American
campuses: *The Professors: The 101 Most Dangerous Academics in America*
(Washington, DC: Regnery 2006), *Indoctrination U.: The Left's War on
Academic Freedom* (New York: Encounter, 2009), *One-Party Classroom*—
coauthored with Jacob Laksin—(New York: Crown, 2009), and *Reforming Our
Universities: The Campaign for an Academic Bill of Rights* (Washington, DC:
Regnery, 2010).
8 Denis MacEoin, "Western Universities: The Best Indoctrination Money Can
Buy," GatestoneInstitute.org, June 26, 2016. https://www.gatestoneinstitute.
org/8331/universities-indoctrination; "Saudi & Arab Influence on American
Education," DiscoverTheNetworks.org, http://www.discoverthenetworks.org/
viewSubCategory.asp?id=213; Gitika Ahuja, "Saudi Prince Donates $40 Million
to Harvard, Georgetown Universities," abcnews.go.com, http://abcnews.
go.com/International/story?id=1402008.
9 Greenfield, "Crymobs, Crybullying, and the Left's Whiny War on Speech."
10 Greenfield, "Islam, Social Justice Warriors, and the Cry-Bully."
11 Greenfield, "Crymobs, Crybullying, and the Left's Whiny War on Speech."
12 Ibid.
13 Ibid.
14 Greenfield, "Islam, Social Justice Warriors, and the Cry-Bully."
15 Shelby Steele, *The Content of Our Character* (New York, NY: HarperPerennial,
1991). See especially Chapter 1: "I'm Black, You're White, Who's Innocent?",
pp. 47–48.
16 Chapter 10, "Jihadist Psychopath," pp. 106–107.
17 Greenfield, "Islam, Social Justice Warriors, and the Cry-Bully."
18 Greenfield, "Crymobs, Crybullying, and the Left's Whiny War on Speech."
19 Robert Spencer, "Michigan Muslima fabricated 'Islamophobic' plot to bomb
majority-Muslim high school," JihadWatch.org, February 23, 2016. http://
www.jihadwatch.org/2016/02/michigan-muslima-fabricated-islamopho-
bic-plot-to-bomb-majority-muslim-high-school; See the profile by
DiscovertheNetworks.org on CAIR: http://www.discoverthenetworks.org/
Articles/cairprofilestand.html.
20 Robert Spencer, "CNN Pushes False Narrative of Trump-Inspired Anti-Muslim
Crimewave," JihadWatch.org, November 13, 2016. https://www.jihadwatch.

org/2016/11/cnn-pushes-false-narrative-of-trump-inspired-anti-muslim
-crimewave.

21 John Binder, "Hate Hoax: NYC Muslim Arrested After Claiming Attack by
Trump Fans," Breitbart.com, December 14, 2016. http://www.breitbart.com/
texas/2016/12/14/
hate-hoax-nyc-muslim-arrested-claiming-attack-trump-fans/.

22 Trey Sanchez, "Teen Made Up Hijab Hoax to Avoid Punishment from 'Strict
Muslim Parents,'" TruthRevolt.org, December 16, 2016. http://www.truthrevolt.
org/news/teen-made-hijab-hoax-avoid-punishment-strict-muslim-parents.

23 "Louisiana Woman Faces Charges After Falsely Accusing Trump Supporters of
Robbing Her," Milo.Yiannopoulos.Net, November 12, 2016. https://milo.
yiannopoulos.net/2016/11/louisiana-woman-falsely-accuse-trump/.

24 Ibid. See also John Binder, "Police: Muslim Student 'Fabricated' Hijab-Grab by
Trump Supporters," Breitbart.com, November 10, 2016. http://www.breitbart.
com/texas/2016/11/10/
police-muslim-student-fabricated-hijab-grab-trump-supporters/.

25 Binder, "Police: Muslim Student 'Fabricated' Hijab-Grab by Trump
Supporters."

26 Charly Haley, "Woman Suspected of Setting Iowa Mosque On Fire," *Des Moines
Register*, June 24, 2017. https://www.usatoday.com/story/news/nation-now/2017
/06/24/woman-suspected-setting-iowa-mosque-fire/426050001/; Pamela
Geller, "Muslima Arrested for Setting Iowa Mosque On Fire," JihadWatch.org,
June 25, 2017. https://www.jihadwatch.org/2017/06/pamela-geller-muslima
-arrested-for-setting-iowa-mosque-on-fire.

27 Ibid.

28 Gabe Ortiz, "Must-Read from Huffington Post: 'Islamophobia Just Drove This
Boy and His Family Out of America,'" AmericasVoice.org, October 14, 2016.
http://americasvoice.org/blog/must-read-huffington-post-islamophobia
-just-drove-boy-family-america/.

29 Robert Spencer, "Video: Robert Spencer On Yet Another 'Islamophobic Hate
Crime' Hoax," JihadWatch.org, November 15, 2016. https://www.jihadwatch.
org/2016/11/video-robert-spencer-on-yet-another-islamophobic-hate
-crime-hoax.

30 Carol Christian and Leah Binkovitz, "Man Charged with Setting Houston
Mosque Fire Says He Was a Devout Attendee," Chron.com, December 30, 2015.
http://www.chron.com/houston/article/Federal-officials-arrest-man-in-c
onnection-with-6727623.php.

31 Robert Spencer, "The Top Anti-Muslim Hate Crime Hoaxes of 2014,"
Frontpagemag.com, December 28, 2014. http://www.frontpagemag.com/
fpm/248313/top-anti-muslim-hate-crime-hoaxes-2014-robert-spencer.

32 Ibid.

33 Ibid.

34 Ibid.

35 Michael Qazvini, "Teen Who Claimed She Was Assaulted for Wearing Hijab Just Got Charged for Lying to Police," DailyWire.com, March 19, 2016. http://www.dailywire.com/news/4235/teen-who-claimed-she-was-assaulted-wearing-hijab-michael-qazvini.

36 Pamela Geller, "Faked Hate in Dearborn: Muslima Drops Lawsuit Against Police After Video Proves She Was Lying When Claiming They Forced Her to Remove Hijab," PamelaGeller.com, March 23, 2016. http://pamelageller.com/2016/03/faked-hate-in-dearborn-muslima-drops-lawsuit-against-police-after-video-proves-she-was-lying-when-claiming-they-forced-her-to-remove-hijab.html/.

37 Robert Spencer, "Perps of 'Far-Right' Hit-and-Run on Muslim Woman Were Muslims," Frontpagemag.com, April 6, 2016. http://www.frontpagemag.com/fpm/262408/perps-far-right-hit-and-run-muslim-woman-were-robert-spencer.

38 Robert Spencer, "Fake anti-Muslim Hate Crime in Montreal: Muslim Arrested for Bomb Threat Against Muslim University Students," JihadWatch.org, March 2, 2017. https://www.jihadwatch.org/2017/03/fake-anti-muslim-hate-crime-in-montreal-muslim-arrested-for-bomb-threat-against-muslim-university-students.

39 Robert Spencer, "The Top Anti-Muslim Hate Crime Hoaxes of 2014." See also Hugh Fitzgerald, "Muslim Hate Crimes 'Soaring to Their Highest Levels' Since 2001," JihadWatch.org, September 28, 2016. https://www.jihadwatch.org/2016/09/hugh-fitzgerald-those-anti-muslim-hate-crimes-soaring-to-their-highest-levels-since-2001 and Daniel Greenfield, "The Fake Hijab Hate Crimes Witch Hunt," Frontpagemag.com, December 16, 2016. http://www.frontpagemag.com/fpm/265155/fake-hijab-hate-crimes-witch-hunt-daniel-greenfield.

40 Michelle Malkin, "Never Forget: Muslim Hate Crime Hoaxes," Frontpagemag.com, September 14, 2017. http://www.frontpagemag.com/fpm/267867/never-forget-muslim-hate-crime-hoaxes-michelle-malkin. See also: Ann Coulter, "Why the Media are in a Never-Ending Hunt for Right-Wing Violence," Frontpagemag.com, August 31, 2017. http://www.frontpagemag.com/fpm/267746/why-media-are-never-ending-hunt-right-wing-ann-coulter.

41 "Anti-Trump demonstrators Set Fires, Break Windows in California," AOL.com, November 9, 2016. https://www.aol.com/article/news/2016/11/09/anti-trump-demonstrators-set-fires-break-windows-in-california/21602381/.

42 Alex Christoforou, "Shocking: California High School Girl Is Brutally Beaten for Liking Donald Trump, Caught on Video," TheDuran.com, November 11, 2016. http://theduran.com/shocking-california-high-school-girl-is-brutally-beaten-for-liking-donald-trump-caught-on-video/.

43 Publicerad, "Swedish TV Chef Brutally Beaten by 'Muslim Men' Because He 'Looked Like Mr. Trump'", Friatider.se, November 12, 2016. http://www.friatider.se/swedish-tv-star-chef-brutally-beaten-muslim-men-because-he-looked-mr-trump.

ENDNOTES

44 "Officers Injured During Anti-Trump Protests in Oakland," CNN.com. http://www.cnn.com/videos/us/2016/11/10/oakland-trump-protests-officers-in-jured-watson-bpr.cnn.

45 Jamie Glazov, "The 'Hate-Crime' Victims of Trump Who Weren't," DailyCaller.com, November 18, 2016. http://dailycaller.com/2016/11/18/the-hate-crime-victims-of-trump-who-werent/.

46 See Chapter 11, pp. 121–122.

47 Robert Spencer, "CAIR's Hooper: US Muslims' 'Mental Health Issues' Cause Them to Fake Hate Crimes," Frontpagemag.com, December 27, 2016. http://www.frontpagemag.com/fpm/265279/cairs-hooper-us-muslims-mental-health-issues-cause-robert-spencer.

48 Ibid.

Chapter 13

1 Serge Trifkovic, "The Golden Age of Islam is a Myth," Frontpagemag.com, November 15, 2002. http://archive.frontpagemag.com/readArticle.aspx?ARTID=21117; Richard Butrick, "The Golden Age of Islam—A Second Look," GatestoneInstitute.org, January 17, 2012. https://www.gatestoneinstitute.org/2757/golden-age-of-islam; Raymond Ibrahim, "The Muslim World's Inferiority Complex," RaymondIbrahim.com, May 11, 2011. http://raymondibrahim.com/2011/05/11/the-muslim-worlds-inferiority-complex/.

2 Trifkovic, "The Golden Age of Islam Is a Myth."

3 Robert Spencer, "Platitudes and Naivete: Obama's Cairo Speech," JihadWatch.org, June 4, 2009. https://www.jihadwatch.org/2009/06/platitudes-and-naivete-obamas-cairo-speech.

4 J. Christian Adams, "Fact or Fiction?: 1001 Muslim Inventions Comes to Washington D.C.," Frontpagemag.com, August 23, 2012. http://www.frontpagemag.com/fpm/141447/fact-or-fiction-1001-muslim-inventions-comes-j-christian-adams.

5 Interview with Robert Spencer, October 26, 2017.

6 Robert Spencer, "Platitudes and Naivete: Obama's Cairo Speech."

7 Ibid.

8 Daniel Greenfield, "A Fake Museum for a Fake Palestine," The Point in Frontpagemag.com, May 20, 2016. http://www.frontpagemag.com/fpm/262899/fake-museum-fake-palestine-daniel-greenfield.

9 See Chapter 8, "The Control Factor—and the Con."

10 Robert Spencer, "Obama at Muslim Brotherhood-linked Mosque: 'Muslim Americans Keep Us Safe'," Frontpagemag.com, February 4, 2016. http://www.frontpagemag.com/fpm/261703/obama-muslim-brotherhood-linked-mosque-muslim-robert-spencer; Robert Spencer, "Obama's Muslim Founding Fathers," Frontpagemag.com, July 29, 2014. http://www.frontpagemag.com/fpm/237427/obamas-muslim-founding-fathers-robert-spencer.

11 Joseph Klein, "Islam: Has It 'Always Been Part of America'?," Frontpagemag.com, February 9, 2016. http://www.frontpagemag.com/fpm/261764/islam-has-it-always-been-part-america-joseph-klein.

12 The rigid rules that Christians under the Islamic State have to abide by if they take dhimmi status ("protected" non-Muslim people living in inferior status) is a clear example of this cruel loophole non-Muslims can choose to survive under Islam, and it is rooted in Islamic teachings. See Robert Spencer, "11 Dhimma Rules That Christians Must Obey in the Islamic State," JihadWatch. org, September 7, 2015. https://www.jihadwatch.org/2015/09/11-dhimma-rules-that-christians-must-obey-in-the-islamic-state. See also Bat Ye'or, Islam and Dhimmitude: Where Civilizations Collide (Cranbury, NJ: Fairleigh Dickinson University Press/Associated University Presses and Lancaster, UK: Gazelle Book Services Ltd., 2002, 2nd printing, 2003) and Bat Ye'or, Eurabia: The Euro-Arab Axis (Cranbury, NJ: Fairleigh Dickinson University Press/Associated University Presses, 2005).

13 Chapters 4, 5, and 8 demonstrate how and why many dhimmis in the West need to keep their identity, community and psychological stability intact by utilizing their narcissism and willful blindness to deny the truth about jihad.

14 Pamela Geller, "UK Islamic Preacher Urges Muslims to Go on Welfare (Jizya) and Plot Jihad," PamelaGeller.com, February 17, 2013. http://pamelageller.com/2013/02/uk-islamic-preacher-urges-muslims-to-go-on-welfae-jizya-and-plot-jihad.html/#sthash.JLA2e9Ih.dpuf.

15 See Dinesh D'Souza's summary of his interview with Stanley Fish, one of the world's leading John Milton scholars. Fish elaborates on how Lucifer is portrayed in Paradise Lost and in the Western tradition, explaining Lucifer's strategy against God as well as his tactics and motives with Eve in the Garden. Dinesh D'Souza, America: Imagine a World Without Her (Washington, DC: Regnery Publishing, 2014), pp. 83–84. For our own discussion on Lucifer's deception of Eve, see Chapter 3, "The Utopian Virus."

16 D'Souza, America. Imagine a World Without Her, pp. 82–87.

17 Ibid., p. 85.

18 The Muslim Brotherhood document the Explanatory Memorandum is a perfect example of this Islamist strategy. An internal document of the Muslim Brotherhood that captured by the FBI in 2005, the memorandum outlines the Brotherhood's design to destroy America by America's own hands as part of its overall goal of "eliminating and destroying Western civilization from within, and sabotaging its miserable house." See Discover the Network's profile, "The Muslim Brotherhood's General Strategic Goal' for North America." http://www.discoverthenetworks.org/viewSubCategory.asp?id=1235.

19 Palestinian "activist" Linda Sarsour's deceptive games of the meaning of Jihad are a blatant example of this deception strategy. See Chapter 11, pp. 125–127.

20 Dr. Stephen M. Kirby, "Do We All Believe in the Same God?" Frontpagemag.com, December 22, 2014. http://www.frontpagemag.com/fpm/247921/do-we-all-believe-same-god-dr-stephen-m-kirby.

ENDNOTES

21 See Chapter 10. See also William Kilpatrick, "One Nation Under Allah?" Frontpagemag.com, September 21, 2015. http://www.frontpagemag.com/ fpm/260192/one-nation-under-allah-william-kilpatrick.

22 This whole deception is founded on the Muslim Brotherhood playbook, a strategy that is outlined in Muslim Brotherhood documents such as the *Explanatory Memorandum*. http://www.discoverthenetworks.org/viewSubCategory.asp?id=1235.

23 Ibid.

24 Chapter 9, "Psychopath," p. 93.

25 See Chapter 12, "The Cry-Bully and the Victims Who Weren't."

26 See Chapter 9, p. 148.

27 See Chapter 9, pp. 148–149.

28 For a documentation of the severe child abuse and neglect in Islamic cultures, see Jamie Glazov, *United in Hate: The Left's Romance with Tyranny and Terror* (Los Angeles: WND Books, 2009), Chapter 11: "The Seeds of Death," pp. 131–145. For an analysis of the severe maternal attachment disorder prevailing in jihadist cultures, see Nancy Hartevelt Kobrin, *Maternal Drama of the Chechen Jihadi* (New Rochelle, New York: MultiEducator Inc., 1994).

29 Robert Spencer, *The Truth About Muhammad* (Washington, DC: Regnery, 2006), p. 36.

30 See Glazov, *United in Hate*, Chapter 11: "The Seeds of Death," pp.131–145.

31 Chapter 9, "Psychopath," pp. 97–98.

32 Sayyid Abul A'la Maududi, *Towards Understanding the Qur'an*, trans. and ed. Zafar Ishaq Ansari, rev. ed. (Leicester, UK: The Islamic Foundation, 1999), vol. 3, p. 202.

33 M. H. Abrams, *The Mirror and the Lamp: Romantic Theory and the Critical Tradition* (New York: W. W. Norton, 1958), p. 42.

34 For a profound analysis of the differences between Islam and the Judeo-Christian tradition on the concept of the individual and his relationship with his creator, see Nonie Darwish, *Wholly Different: Why I Chose Biblical Values Over Islamic Values* (Washington, DC: Regnery, 2017).

35 See Chapter 10, "Jihadist Psychopath," pp. 100–101.

36 For a documentation of the hatred for individuality, creativity, music, joy, and laughter in Islam, see Glazov, *United in Hate*, Chapter 11: "The Seeds of Death," pp. 131–145.

37 David Pryce-Jones, *The Closed Circle: An Interpretation of the Arabs* (Chicago: Irvin R. Dee, 2002), p. 134.

38 Nicole Rojas, "Pharmacist 'Showed Child Beheading Video and Said Isis Were Not Bad People'", Ibtimes.co.uk, September 26, 2017. http://www.ibtimes. co.uk/leicester-man-showed-child-beheading-video-said-isis-were-not-bad -people-1640795.

39 JPost Staff, "WATCH: Child Dressed As Jihadi Beheads His Teddy Bear," JPost. com, August 24, 2015. http://www.jpost.com/Middle-East/ISIS-Threat/ WATCH-Islamic-Jihad-video-shows-child-beheading-his-teddy-bear-413079.

40 Ellie Cambridge, "Cubs of the Caliphate," TheSun.co.uk, January 8, 2017.
https://www.thesun.co.uk/news/2564492/harrowing-isis-video-shows
-children-as-young-as-10-beheading-and-shooting-kurdish-prisoners-in-syria/.

Chapter 14

1 The dhimmi is the non-Muslim who accepts his subordinate legal status/
inferiority to receive "protection" from harm from the Jihadist Psychopath. We
describe him in Chapter 13, p. 145.
2 Kenneth Levin, *The Oslo Syndrome: Delusions of a People Under Siege* (Smith
& Kraus Inc., 2005).
3 Ibid., pp. xvii.
4 Ibid., pp. xvii.
5 Ibid., pp. xvii.
6 Ibid., p. xvi.
7 Ibid., p. xvi.
8 Stockholm syndrome is the psychological condition in which captives feel and
express empathy and sympathy toward their captors and abusers, often to the
point of defending and identifying with them. We discuss how this syndrome
works in the context of Jihad Denial in Chapter 8.
9 Bill Siegel, *The Control Factor: Our Struggle to See the True Threat* (New York:
Hamilton Books, 2102), Chapter 9, pp. 135–157.
10 Ibid., p. 135.
11 Ibid., p. 136.
12 Ibid.
13 Ibid., p. 139.
14 Ibid., p. 141.
15 Chapter 8, "The Control Factor—and the Con," pp. 84–85.
16 Siegel, p. 150.
17 Ibid., p. 152.
18 Martha Stout, *The Sociopath Next Door* (New York: Three Rivers Press, 2005),
p. 87.
19 See Introduction, pp. xxxv–xxxvi. See also Chapter 18, "Jihadist Psychopath
Blocks Trump."

Chapter 15

1 The dhimmi unbeliever is the non-Muslim who accepts his subordinate legal
status/inferiority to receive "protection" from harm from the Jihadist
Psychopath. We describe him in Chapter 13, p. 145.
2 For the Jihad Denial agenda, see Chapters 4–6.
3 Stephen Coughlin, *Catastrophic Failure: Blindfolding America in the Face of
Jihad* (Washington DC: Center for Security Policy Press, 2015), pp. 507–510.
4 The specious argument of jihadists being a small group of extremists who
misunderstand Islam is dissected and discredited in Chapter 5.
5 Coughlin, p. 508.

6   Frank Gaffney, "The Coughlin Affair," Townhall.com, February 25, 2008. http://townhall.com/columnists/frankgaffney/2008/02/25/the_coughlin_affair/page/full.

7   The Obama administration's enabling of Islamic supremacism is documented throughout this entire text, and especially in Chapter 1, this chapter, and the upcoming Chapters 16 and 17.

8   See Chapter 1, "The Case," p. 4.

9   Jonah Bennett, "Gates: Obama Ignored NSC's Unanimous Advice On Egypt to Be On the 'Right Side of History,'" DailyCaller.com, March 17, 2016. http://dailycaller.com/2016/03/17/former-secdef-obama-ignored-unanimous-national-security-team-because-he-wanted-to-be-on-the-right-side-of-history/.

10 The *Explanatory Memorandum* is a perfect reflection of the Brotherhood's goals vis-à-vis the United States. An internal document of the Muslim Brotherhood captured by the FBI in 2005, it outlines the Brotherhood's design to destroy America by America's own hands as part of its overall goal of "eliminating and destroying Western civilization from within, and sabotaging its miserable house." See Discover the Network's profile, "The Muslim Brotherhood's General Strategic Goal" for North America." http://www.discoverthenetworks.org/viewSubCategory.asp?id=1235. For a powerful expose on the Brotherhood, see Erick Stackelbeck, *The Brotherhood: America's Next Great Enemy* (Washington, DC: Regnery, 2013).

11 Josh Gerstein, "DNI Clapper Retreats from 'Secular' Claim On Muslim Brotherhood," Politico.com, February 10, 2011. http://www.politico.com/blogs/joshgerstein/0211/DNI_Clapper_Egypts_Muslim_Brotherhood_largely_secular.html?showall.

12 Daniel Greenfield, "Muslim Brotherhood Tyrants Show Their True Faces," Frontpagemag.com, December 3, 2012. http://www.frontpagemag.com/fpm/167740/muslim-brotherhood-tyrants-show-their-true-faces-daniel-greenfield.

13 Ibid.

14 Kirsten Powers, "The Muslim Brotherhood's War on Coptic Christians," TheDailyBeast.com, August 22, 2013. https://www.thedailybeast.com/the-muslim-brotherhoods-war-on-coptic-christians; Raymond Ibrahim, "Exposed: Egypt's Institutionalized; Persecution of Coptic Christians," Frontpagemag.com, May 5, 2015. http://www.frontpagemag.com/fpm/256430/exposed-egypts-institutionalized-persecution-raymond-ibrahim. See also Raymond Ibrahim, *Crucified Again: Exposing Islam's New War on Christians* (Washington, DC: Regnery, 2013).

15 Ibid.

16 See Chapter 1, "The Case," pp. 5–7.

17 Mohamed Elibiary profile, DiscoverTheNetworks.org, http://www.discoverthenetworks.org/individualProfile.asp?indid=2560.

18 Robert Spencer, "Mohamed Elibiary Declares Victory Over the Constitution," Frontpagemag.com, October 31, 2013. http://www.frontpagemag.com/ fpm/209242/mohamed-elibiary-declares-victory-over-robert-spencer.

19 Coughlin, p. 358.

20 Mohamed Elibiary profile, DiscoverTheNetworks.org.

21 The *Unholy Alliance* is the term this work uses to label the Left-Islamic supremacist alliance, a phenomenon documented by David Horowitz in his work, *Unholy Alliance: Radical Islam and the American Left* (Washington, DC: Regnery, 2004), and on his website/database, DiscovertheNetworks.org. See the description of the alliance in our Introduction, pp. xxxiii–xxxiv. For more discussion and analysis on the Left's romance with Islamic supremacism and how this romance is an extension of the Left's alliance with communism during the Cold War, see Jamie Glazov, *United in Hate: The Left's Romance with Tyranny and Terror* (Los Angeles: WND, 2009).

22 John Brennan profile, DiscoverTheNetworks.org, http://www.discoverthenetworks.org/individualProfile.asp?indid=2577.

23 Patrick S. Poole, "FBI Escorts Known Hamas Operative Through Top-Secret National Counterterrorism Center as 'Outreach to Muslim Community,'" Breitbart.com, September 27, 2010, http://cdn.breitbart.com/Big-Peace/2010 /09/27/FBI-Escorts-Known-Hamas-Operative-Through-Top-Secret-National -Counterterrorism-Center-as--Outreach--to-Muslim-Community.

24 "National Security Hawks Call for Brennan's Resignation," FoxNews.com, September 29, 2010, http://www.foxnews.com/politics/2010/09/29/ national-security-hawks-brennans-resignation/.

25 John Brennan profile, DiscoverTheNetworks.org, http://www.discoverthe networks.org/individualProfile.asp?indid=2577.

26 John Brennan profile, DiscoverTheNetworks.org, http://www.discoverthenetworks.org/individualProfile.asp?indid=2577; see also Patrick Poole, "Meet John Brennan, Obama's Assassination Czar," PJMedia.com, June 6, 2012, http://pjmedia.com/blog/meet-john-brennan-obamas-assassination-czar/2/. For the Benghazi betrayal, see Colonel Phil Handley, "Betrayal in Benghazi," Frontpagemag.com, May 29, 2013. http://www.frontpagemag.com/ fpm/191373/betrayal-benghazi-colonel-phil-handley

27 Drew Zahn, "Shock Claim: Obama Picks Muslim for CIA Chief," WND.com, February 10, 2013, http://www.wnd.com/2013/02/shock-claim-obama -picks-muslim-for-cia-chief/.

28 Ibid.

29 Huma Abedin profile, DiscoverTheNetworks.org, http://www.discoverthenetworks.org/individualProfile.asp?indid=2556; see also Lee Stranahan, "Hillary Clinton's Top Aide Huma Abedin Published Articles that Blamed USA for 911, Blamed Women for Violence," Breitbart.com, August 21, 2016. http://www. breitbart.com/big-government/2016/08/21/hillarys-top-aide-huma-abedin -articles-blaming-usa-911/.

ENDNOTES

30 Frank Gaffney, *The Muslim Brotherhood in the Obama Administration*, David Horowitz Freedom Center pamphlet, 2012. http://horowitzfreedomcenter-store.org/collections/pamplets/products/the-muslim-brotherhood-in-the-obama-administration.

31 Nancy Cordes, "Michele Bachmann Refuses to Back Down on Claims about Huma Abedin," CBSNews.com, July 19, 2012. http://www.cbsnews.com/news/michele-bachmann-refuses-to-back-down-on-claims-about-huma-abedin/.

32 Robert Spencer, "Vindicated Bachmann Under Attack," Frontpagemag.com, January 14, 2013. http://www.frontpagemag.com/fpm/173462/vindicated-bachmann-under-attack-robert-spencer.

33 Ibid.

34 Coughlin, p. 344.

35 Ibid., p. 340.

36 Ibid., p. 499.

37 Mohamed Elibiary profile, DiscoverTheNetworks.org.

Chapter 16

1 Coughlin, p. 182.

2 Ibid., p. 344.

3 See Chapter 1, "The Case," pp.21-22; Robert Spencer, "Hillary Lets the Jihadist Cat Out of the Bag," Frontpagemag.com, January 24, 2013. http://www.frontpagemag.com/2013/robert-spencer/hillary-lets-the-jihadist-cat-out-of-bag/print/.

4 See Chapter 1, "The Case," pp. 7–9.

5 Coughlin, p. 347.

6 Ibid., p. 348.

7 Ibid., p. 344.

8 Ibid., p. 337.

9 John Guandolo, "Islam's Message to 'Islamophobes'—Shut Up or Else," UnderstandingTheThreat.com, April 16, 2015. https://www.understandingthe-threat.com/islams-message-to-islamophobes-shut-up-or-else/.

10 Chapter 1, pp. 7–9.

11 Coughlin, p. 509.

12 Ibid., p. 344.

13 Ibid., p. 333.

14 Ibid., p. 341.

15 Ibid., p. 509.

16 Ibid., p. 508.

17 Ibid., p. 182.

Chapter 17

1 Bill Siegel, *The Control Factor: Our Struggle to See the True Threat* (New York: Hamilton Books, 2102), pp. 6–9.

2 The *Explanatory Memorandum* is an internal document of the Muslim Brotherhood captured by the FBI in 2005 that outlines the Brotherhood's design to destroy America by America's own hands as part of its overall goal of "eliminating and destroying Western civilization from within, and sabotaging its miserable house." See Discover the Network's profile, "The Muslim Brotherhood's General Strategic Goal' for North America." http://www. discoverthenetworks.org/viewSubCategory.asp?id=1235.

3 Ibid.

4 Robert Spencer, "The Hijrah Into Europe," Frontpagemag.com, September 4, 2015. http://www.frontpagemag.com/fpm/260019/ hijrah-europe-robert-spencer.

5 See Chapter 1, "The Case," pp. 11–12.

6 See Chapter 5, "Not All Muslims Do That!", pp. 50–51.

7 See Chapter 1, "The Case," pp. 11–12.

8 Deborah Weiss, "Democrats Castigate 'Anti-Muslim' Speech in Proposed Legislation," Frontpagemag.com, January 26, 2016. http://www.frontpagemag. com/fpm/261550/democrats-castigate-anti-muslim-speech-proposed-debo-rah-weiss; Robert Spencer, "Secretary of State Clinton Says State Department Will Coordinate with OIC on Legal Ways to Implement UN's Resolution Criminalizing 'Defamation Of Religion,'" JihadWatch.org, August 3, 2011. http://www.jihadwatch.org/2011/08/secretary-of-state-clinton-says-state -department-will-coordinate-with-oic-on-legal-ways-to-implement.

9 Deborah Weiss, *The Organization of Islamic Cooperation's Jihad on Free Speech* (Washington, DC: Center for Security Policy Press, 2015).

10 Stephen Coughlin, *Catastrophic Failure. Blindfolding America in the Face of Jihad* (Washington DC: Center for Security Policy Press, 2015), pp. 308–314.

11 Ibid., p. 22.

12 Brian Hayes, "Obama: 'The Future Must Not Belong to Those Who Would Slander the Prophet of Islam," TopRightNews.com, January 7, 2015. http:// toprightnews.com/obama-the-future-must-not-belong-to-those-who-would -slander-the-prophet-of-islam/.

13 Matthew Vadum, "A New Global Police to Fight 'Violent Extremism' in the U.S.?" Frontpagemag.com, October 6, 2015. http://www.frontpagemag.com/ fpm/260363/new-global-police-fight-violent-extremism-us-matthew-vadum.

14 Siegel, p. 7.

15 Sun Tzu, *The Art of War* (Filiquarian Publishing, LLC, 2006), p. x.

16 Ibid.

17 Ibid., p. 7.

18 See Chapter 1, "The Case," pp. 4–5.

19 Chapter 1, "The Case," pp. 15–16.

20 Chapter 6, "See No Islam, Hear No Islam," pp. 68–69.

21 Robert Spencer, "Obama DHS Secretly Scrubbed 1,000 Names from U.S. Terror Watch Lists," JihadWatch.org, March 1, 2016. https://www.jihadwatch.

ENDNOTES

org/2016/03/obama-dhs-secretly-scruubed-1000-names-from-u-s-terror
-watch-lists.

22 For the best work on how the Muslim Brotherhood is now shaping U.S. policy,
see Stephen Coughlin, *Catastrophic Failure. Blindfolding America in the Face of
Jihad* (Washington DC: Center for Security Policy Press, 2015), p. 22. The
Soviet/Cold War analogy is raised in two episodes of *The Glazov Gang* with
guest Stephen Coughlin, in which Coughlin discusses the analogy of denying
the existence of the KGB, yet asking the KGB for advice. See Jamie Glazov,
"Stephen Coughlin on 'Muslim Brotherhood: Above the Law in America'— on
The Glazov Gang," JamieGlazov.com, November 10, 2015. http://jamieglazov.
com/2015/11/10/stephen-coughlin-on-muslim-brotherhood-above-the-law-in-
america-on-the-glazov-gang/; and Jamie Glazov, "Stephen Coughlin on
'Catastrophic Failure'—on The Glazov Gang," JamieGlazov.com, November 3,
2015. http://jamieglazov.com/2015/11/03/
stephen-coughlin-on-catastrophic-failure-on-the-glazov-gang/.

23 Chapter 16, "Mind Control Under the Jihadist Psychopath."

24 Coughlin, p. 171.

25 Jeffrey T. Kuhner, "The Betrayal of the Navy's SEAL Team 6," *Washington
Times*, June 7, 2013. http://www.washingtontimes.com/news/2013/jun/7/
the-betrayal-of-the-navys-seal-team-6/#ixzz2aJSEDod0.

26 Coughlin, p. 411.

27 Ibid., p. 411.

28 Ibid., p. 412.

29 Ibid., p. 414.

30 Sun Tzu, *The Art of War* (Filiquarian Publishing, LLC, 2006), p. 7 and p. 15.

31 The *Unholy Alliance* is the term this work uses to label the Left-Islamic
supremacist alliance, a phenomenon documented by David Horowitz in his
work, *Unholy Alliance: Radical Islam and the American Left* (Washington, DC:
Regnery, 2004), and on his website/database, DiscovertheNetworks.org. See
the description of the alliance in our Introduction, pp. xxxiii–xxxiv. For more
discussion and analysis on the Left's romance with Islamic supremacism and
how this romance is an extension of the Left's alliance with communism
during the Cold War, see Jamie Glazov, *United in Hate: The Left's Romance
with Tyranny and Terror* (Los Angeles: WND, 2009).

32 Lukas Mikelionis, "US Relaxes Rules of Engagement to Help Troops in
Afghanistan Defeat Taliban," FoxNews.com, October 4, 2017. http://www.
foxnews.com/us/2017/10/04/us-relaxes-rules-engagement-troops-in
-afghanistan-to-defeat-taliban.html.

33 Glazov Gang Video, "Daniel Greenfield on the Real Meaning of 'Allahu Akbar'",
JamieGlazov.com, March 27, 2015. http://jamieglazov.com/2015/03/27/
daniel-greenfield-on-the-real-meaning-of-allahu-akbar-on-the-glazov-gang/.

34 Ingeborg Olsson, "Swedish Archbishop Prefers Allah," *Dispatch International*,
October 15, 2013, http://www.d-intl.com/2013/10/15/swedish-archbishop
-prefers-allah/?lang=en.

35 Raymond Ibrahim, "Pope Francis: A Fool or Liar for Islam?", Frontpagemag.
    com, August 2, 2016. http://www.frontpagemag.com/fpm/263709/
    pope-francis-fool-or-liar-islam-raymond-ibrahim.
36 Robert Spencer, "'Robert Spencer and Pamela Geller Are Still Fighting Back
    against Their Ban' from the UK," JihadWatch.org, January 22, 2014. http://
    www.jihadwatch.org/2014/01/robert-spencer-and-pamela-geller-are-still
    -fighting-back-against-their-ban-from-the-uk.
37 Robert Spencer, "Britain Embraces Jihad Terror," Frontpagemag.com, June 26,
    2013. http://www.frontpagemag.com/fpm/194663/britain-embraces-jihad
    -terror-robert-spencer.

Chapter 18

1 Peter Holley, "'Radical Islamic Terrorism': Three Words That Separate Trump
   from Most of Washington," WashingtonPost.com, March 1, 2017. https://
   www.washingtonpost.com/news/the-fix/wp/2017/02/28/radical-islamic
   -terrorism-three-words-that-separate-trump-from-most-of-washington
   /?utm_term=.02616b063472.
2 See Introduction, p. 17.
3 Gabby Morrongiello, "Trump Will Ask Congress to End Diversity Visa Lottery
   After New York Attack," WashingtonExaminer.com, November 1, 2017. http://
   www.washingtonexaminer.com/trump-will-ask-congress-to-end-diversity
   -visa-lottery-after-new-york-attack/article/2639262.
4 Flynn is the coauthor with Michael Ledeen of a book that provides a road map
   to defeating the enemy and urges the importance of labeling that threat: *The
   Global War Against Radical Islam and Its Allies* (New York: St. Martin's Press,
   2016); Gorka's book, *Defeating Jihad: The Winnable War* (Washington, DC:
   Regnery, 2016), does the same thing in its own unique and powerful way.
   Bannon, meanwhile, was executive chairman of the mega political website,
   Breitbart News.
5 Mohamed Elibiary profile, DiscoverTheNetworks.org. http://www.discoverthe
   networks.org/individualProfile.asp?indid=2560.
6 Daniel Greenfield, "Did Susan Rice Spy on Trump Officials for Muslim
   Brotherhood?", Frontpagemag.com, September 15, 2017. http://www.
   frontpagemag.com/fpm/267873/did-susan-rice-spy-trump-officials-muslim-
   daniel-greenfield; Daniel Greenfield, "Why Obama Really Spied on Trump,"
   Frontpagemag.com, September 20, 2017. http://www.frontpagemag.com/
   fpm/267923/why-obama-really-spied-trump-daniel-greenfield.
7 Max Greenwood, "Kushner, Flynn Met with Russian Ambassador During
   Transition," TheHill.com, March 2, 2017. http://thehill.com/homenews/
   administration/322093-michael-flynn-and-jared-kushner-met-with-russian
   -ambassador-before.
8 Greenfield, "Did Susan Rice Spy on Trump Officials for Muslim Brotherhood?"
   and Greenfield, "Why Obama Really Spied on Trump."

9 Robert Spencer, "McMaster Drags Trump Into the Swamp," JihadWatch.org, May 15, 2017. https://www.jihadwatch.org/2017/05/robert-spencer-mcmaster -drags-trump-into-the-swamp.

10 Michael Wilner, "Gorka says McMaster has 'Obama Lens' on Threat of Radical Islam," JPost.com, August 27, 2017. http://www.jpost.com/American-Politics/ Ex-White-House-staff%C3%A9r-Gorka-comes-to-General-McMcasters -defense-503557.

11 Greenfield, "Did Susan Rice Spy on Trump Officials for Muslim Brotherhood?" and Greenfield, "Why Obama Really Spied on Trump."

12 Defined in our Introduction, the *Unholy Alliance* is the term this work uses to label the Left-Islamic supremacist alliance, a phenomenon documented by David Horowitz in his work, *Unholy Alliance: Radical Islam and the American Left* (Washington, DC: Regnery, 2004), and on his website/database, DiscovertheNetworks.org. For more discussion and analysis on the Left's romance with Islamic supremacism, and how this romance is an extension of the Left's alliance with communism during the Cold War, see Glazov, *United in Hate*.

13 Greenfield, "Did Susan Rice Spy on Trump Officials for Muslim Brotherhood?" and Greenfield, "Why Obama Really Spied on Trump."

14 Ibid.

15 Ibid.

16 U.S. officials' reliance on fifth column Muslim Brotherhood advisers is discussed in Chapter 15, pp. 165–171.

17 Pamela Geller, "McMaster FIRES Another Top Counter Jihad Official at National Security Council," PamelaGeller.com, August 3, 2017. https:// pamelageller.com/2017/08/mcmaster-fires-top-counter-jihad.html/.

18 Ibid. See also Jordan Schachtel, "McMaster Brings Top Obama Admin Officials Into NSC," ConservativeReview.com, August 31, 2017. https://www.conservati-vereview.com/articles/mcmaster-brings-top-obama-administration-officials -into-nsc-sources-say.

19 Bannon ended up leaving Breitbart in January 2018 after feuding with President Trump over his negative remarks about the president's family in the new book *Fire and Fury* by Michael Wolff. Breitbart News, "'Populist Hero' Stephen K. Bannon Returns Home to Breitbart," Breitbart.com, August 18, 2017. http://www.breitbart.com/big-journalism/2017/08/18/populist-he-ro-stephen-k-bannon-returns-home-breitbart/; Margaret Talev, Joshua Green, and Gerry Smith, "Bannon Leaves Breitbart After Trump Feud," *Bloomberg Politics*, January 9, 2018. https://www.bloomberg.com/news/articles/2018 -01-09/bannon-exits-breitbart-after-feud-with-trump-over-book-remarks.

20 Gorka, *Defeating Jihad: The Winnable War*.

21 Robert Spencer, "Sebastian Gorka and Another Broken Trump Promise," PJMedia.com, August 29, 2017. https://pjmedia.com/homeland-secu-rity/2017/08/29/sebastian-gorka-another-broken-trump-promise/; Robert Spencer, "Gorka out of Trump administration over President's failure to

identify Islamic terrorism as Islamic," JihadWatch.org, August 26, 2017. https://www.jihadwatch.org/2017/08/gorka-out-of-trump-administration -over-presidents-failure-to-identify-islamic-terrorism-as-islamic.

22 Daniel Greenfield, "Secretary of State Rex Tillerson Stated, to Chris Wallace on Fox News Sunday, that Sebastian Gorka was 'Completely Wrong,'" The Point at Frontpagemag.com, August 27, 2017. http://www.frontpagemag.com/ point/267703/secretary-state-tillerson-attacks-gorka-radical-daniel-green-field; Robert Spencer, "Tillerson: Gorka 'Completely Wrong' to Hit Trump for Not Saying 'Radical Islam,'" JihadWatch.org, August 27, 2017. https:// www.jihadwatch.org/2017/08/tillerson-gorka-completely-wrong-to-hit -trump-for-not-saying-radical-islam.

23 Robert Spencer, "Mattis Says al-Qaeda Terrorists 'Defame Islam,'" JihadWatch. org, March 26, 2017. https://www.jihadwatch.org/2017/03/mattis-says-al -qaeda-terrorists-defame-islam.

24 Daniel Greenfield, "Mattis Says US Took Out Al Qaeda Terrorist for Defaming Islam," Frontpagemag.com, March 26, 2017. http://www.frontpagemag.com/ point/266241/mattis-says-us-took-out-al-qaeda-terrorist-daniel-greenfield.

25 Raheem Kassam, "Hamas-Linked Council on American-Islamic Relations Welcomes Resignation of Dr. Seb Gorka," Breitbart.com, August 28, 2017. http://www.breitbart.com/london/2017/08/28/hamas-linked-council -american-islamic-relations/.

26 CAIR profile, DiscoverTheNetworks.org. http://www.discoverthenetworks. org/Articles/cairprofilestand.html.

27 Dan Riehl, "Brigitte Gabriel: 'Something Has Happened in the Trump Presidency' Regarding Radical Islam," Breitbart.com, September 12, 2017. http://www.breitbart.com/radio/2017/09/12/brigitte-gabriel-something -has-happened-in-the-trump-presidency-regarding-radical-islam/.

28 John Hayward, "Reports: White House Considers Branding Muslim Brother-hood a Terrorist Organization," Breitbart.com, February 8, 2017. http:// www.breitbart.com/national-security/2017/02/08/white-house-debates -terrorist-designation-muslim-brotherhood/.

29 Holy Land Foundation for Relief and Development profile, DiscoverThe Networks.org. http://www.discoverthenetworks.org/printgroupProfile. asp?grpid=6181.

30 Ryan Mauro, "Obama Justice Department Saves Brotherhood Fronts Prosecu-tion of 'Unindicted Co-Conspirators' Dropped," Frontpagemag.com, April 20, 2011. http://www.frontpagemag.com/fpm/90930/obama-justice-department-saves-brotherhood-fronts-ryan-mauro; Patrick Poole, "Did Obama and Holder Scuttle Terror Finance Prosecutions?" PJMedia.com, April 14, 2011. http:// pjmedia.com/blog/did-obama-and-holder-scuttle-terror-finance -prosecutions/.

31 Maxwell Tani, "Trump Used the Most Controversial Phrase Inside His Administration During His Major Address to the UN," BusinessInsider.com,

September 19, 2017. http://www.businessinsider.com/trump-mcmaster
-radical-islamic-terrorism-2017-9.

32 Robert Spencer, "Trump State Department: Tillerson Out, Pompeo In,"
JihadWatch.org, March 13, 2018. https://www.jihadwatch.org/2018/03/
trump-state-department-tillerson-out-pompeo-in.

33 Ibid. See also: Joseph Klein, "Tillerson Ousted from State Department,"
Frontpagemag.com, March 14, 2018. https://www.frontpagemag.com/
fpm/269590/tillerson-ousted-state-department-joseph-klein.

34 Robert Spencer, "McMaster Out, Bolton In," JihadWatch.org, March 22, 2018.
https://www.jihadwatch.org/2018/03/mcmaster-out-bolton-in.

35 Daniel Greenfield, "Trump's Choice of Bolton Reflects American Greatness,"
Frontpagemag.com, March 23, 2018. https://www.frontpagemag.com/fpm
/269687/trumps-choice-bolton-reflects-american-greatness-daniel-greenfield.

36 Ibid.

37 Alexander Maistrovoy, "The Hypnotic Dance of Death," JihadWatch.org,
January 28, 2016. http://www.frontpagemag.com/fpm/261637/hypnotic-dance
-death-alexander-maistrovoy.

38 See Chapter 1, "The Case," pp. 13–15.

Conclusion

1 Shelby Steele, *The Content of Our Character* (New York: HarperPerennial,
1991), p. 109.

2 Alexander Maistrovoy, *Agony of Hercules or a Farewell to Democracy (Notes of
a Stranger)* (Xlbiris, 2016), p. 153.

3 Thomas Sheridan, *Puzzling People: The Labyrinth of the Psychopath* (Vellumi-
nous Press, 2011), p. 60.

4 Ibid., p. 64.

ACKNOWLEDGMENTS

I am most grateful and indebted to Robert Spencer, John Perazzo, Daniel Greenfield, and Nichole Hungerford, all of whom read the rough drafts of this book and provided numerous constructive criticisms, comments, and recommendations that greatly enhanced the work.

I owe deep thanks to David Horowitz. Thank you, David, for all that you have made possible for me.

I am profoundly grateful to Michael Finch, president of the Freedom Center, for his friendship, support, and generosity of spirit. It will always be treasured.

Thank you, Aynaz Anni Cyrus for being a guardian angel and a providential godsend in my life.

Much appreciation goes to Stephen Brown, Emmanuel, Dorion, Vern, Sonny, Dan, Ricky, Stephanie Knudson, Anna Atell, and Ali for their friendship and support throughout the entire endeavor. You greatly enabled my perseverance.

I am indebted to Professor J. L. Granatstein, my academic mentor, who helped build the foundation that allowed me to take on this project.

To Grace, who fertilized the soil in which my idea for this work grew. I am deeply appreciative.

I thank Lynne Rabinoff, my agent, for all her masterful help in making the publication of this work possible. You are wonderful.

To Shaiya, I cherish all your love and earnest devotion.

250

ACKNOWLEDGMENTS

Finally, to Papochka. Few words can express my appreciation for everything you are and have given me. Thank you for bringing me to the Free World. Thank you for the example you set, the upbringing and guidance you gave me, and the love you showered me with. Thank you for the priceless spiritual and intellectual nourishment—and for the role model of courage and nobility you set by standing up against totalitarianism, risking everything. Thank you for teaching and showing me what is important in life and what it takes to be a man and a human being.

Thank you for introducing me to Jesus Christ.

This book is for you.